## *DEVELOPMENTS IN POLITICS* TITLES AVAILABLE FROM BLOOMSBURY ACADEMIC

Helen Drake, Alistair Cole, Sophie Meunier and Vincent Tiberj (eds)
DEVELOPMENTS IN FRENCH POLITICS 6

Maria Green Cowles and Desmond Dinan (eds)
DEVELOPMENTS IN THE EUROPEAN UNION 2

Richard Heffernan, Colin Hay, Meg Russell and Philip Cowley (eds)
DEVELOPMENTS IN BRITISH POLITICS 10

Erik Jones, Paul M. Heywood, Martin Rhodes and Ulrich Sedelmeier (eds)
DEVELOPMENTS IN EUROPEAN POLITICS 2

Stephen Padgett, William E. Paterson and Reimut Zohlnhöfer (eds)
DEVELOPMENTS IN GERMAN POLITICS 4*

Gillian Peele, Christopher J. Bailey, Jon N. Herbert, Bruce E. Cain and B. Guy
Peters (eds)
DEVELOPMENTS IN AMERICAN POLITICS 8

Stephen White, Paul Lewis, and Judy Batt (eds)
DEVELOPMENTS IN CENTRAL AND EAST EUROPEAN POLITICS 5*

Stephen White, Richard Sakwa and Henry E. Hale (eds)
DEVELOPMENTS IN RUSSIAN POLITICS 9*

\* Rights world excluding North America

# Developments in European Politics

## 3rd Edition

### Edited by
### Veronica Anghel &
### Erik Jones

*Eduard*
*Dragusin 2022*

BLOOMSBURY ACADEMIC
LONDON • NEW YORK • OXFORD • NEW DELHI • SYDNEY

BLOOMSBURY ACADEMIC
Bloomsbury Publishing Plc
50 Bedford Square, London, WC1B 3DP, UK
1385 Broadway, New York, NY 10018, USA
29 Earlsfort Terrace, Dublin 2, Ireland

BLOOMSBURY, BLOOMSBURY ACADEMIC and the Diana logo
are trademarks of Bloomsbury Publishing Plc

First published in Great Britain, 2006
This edition published 2022

Editorial selection and matter © Veronica Anghel & Erik Jones, 2022
Individual chapters © their individual authors 2022

A catalogue record for this book is available from the British Library.

Library of Congress Cataloging-in-Publication Data
Names: Anghel, Veronica, editor. | Jones, Erik, editor.
Title: Developments in European politics / Edited by Veronica Anghel & Erik Jones.
Description: Third edition. | London ; New York : Bloomsbury Academic, 2022. |
Series: Developments in politics | Includes bibliographical references and index. |
Identifiers: LCCN 2022011475 (print) | LCCN 2022011476 (ebook) |
ISBN 9781350336346 (hardback) | ISBN 9781350336339 (paperback) |
ISBN 9781350336353 (pdf) | ISBN 9781350336360 (epub) | ISBN 9781350336377
Subjects: LCSH: European federation–Congresses. | Europe–Economic
integration–Congresses. | Europe–Politics and government–1989—Congresses.
Classification: LCC JN15 .D455 2022 (print) | LCC JN15 (ebook) |
DDC 341.242/2–dc23
LC record available at https://lccn.loc.gov/2022011475
LC ebook record available at https://lccn.loc.gov/2022011476

ISBN:     HB:     978-1-3503-3634-6
          PB:     978-1-3503-3633-9
          ePDF:   978-1-3503-3635-3
          eBook:  978-1-3503-3636-0

Series: Developments in Politics

Typeset by Integra Software Services Private Limited
Printed and bound in Great Britain

To find out more about our authors and books visit www.bloomsbury.com
and sign up for our newsletters.

# Contents

# List of Figures and Tables

## Figures

## Tables

# Contributors

**Veronica Anghel** is a Lecturer at the Johns Hopkins University – School of Advanced International Studies and Max Weber Fellow at the European University Institute.

**Lisa A. Baglione** is Professor of Political Science at Saint Joseph's University.

**Erik Jones** is the Director of the Robert Schuman Centre for Advanced Studies at the European University Institute.

**Léonie de Jonge** is Assistant Professor in European Politics at the University of Groningen.

**Jennifer Fitzgerald** is Professor of Political Science at the University of Colorado, Boulder.

**Nicole Lindstrom** is a Senior Lecturer in Politics at the University of York.

**Sonia Lucarelli** is Professor of International Relations at the University of Bologna.

**Rosa Maryon** is a doctoral candidate in international relations at Cardiff University.

**Alice Mattoni** is Associate Professor at the University of Bologna.

**Kimberly J. Morgan** is Professor of Political Science and International Affairs at George Washington University.

**Regine Paul** is Professor of Political Science at the University of Bergen.

**Simona Piattoni** is Professor of Political Science at the University of Trento.

**Julia Rone** is a postdoctoral researcher at the Minderoo Centre for Technology and Democracy at CRASSH, Cambridge.

**Clare Saunders** is Professor of Politics at the University of Exeter.

**Vera Scepanovic** is a Lecturer in International Relations and European Studies at Leiden University.

**Julia Schulte-Cloos** is a Research Fellow at the Robert Schuman Centre for Advanced Studies at the European University Institute.

**Simone Tholens** is Senior Lecturer in International Relations at Cardiff University.

# Preface and Acknowledgements

This volume has been a long time in development, both because of a rapidly changing political landscape in Europe, and because of recent transformations in academic publishing. Ultimately, a great team of contributors moved it forward. The scholars who agreed to participate in this project did so before the Covid-19 pandemic took hold of our lives and schedules. They remained committed to our collective effort throughout a very demanding time.

The pandemic and subsequent lockdowns disproportionately affected women scholars by placing more demands on their time and more obstacles on their career paths. We are therefore even more grateful to an all-female list of contributors for making the *Developments in European Politics* volume the beneficiary of their scholarship and resilience. The original *Developments in West European Politics* included just two women – Ute Collier and Joni Lovenduski. Redressing that historical imbalance takes a much longer commitment than the editors' choice to reach out only to women academics this time round. We are particularly honoured to have witnessed the commitment of those early career scholars who worked with us while trying to overcome the obstacles of a contracted job market.

Many thanks also go to Steven Kennedy, Paul Heywood, Martin Rhodes, Vincent Wright and Uli Sedelmeier. Steven was the driving force behind the *Developments in…* series when it began at Macmillan. Vincent, Paul and Martin were the original editorial team behind *Developments in West European Politics*. Paul and Martin brought Erik Jones in when Vincent stepped back for the second edition of that book. This new group moved from *West European Politics* to *European Politics* when Uli joined the editorial team. Together they published two volumes as *Developments in European Politics*. When Martin, Paul and Uli stepped back, Veronica Anghel took on the responsibility for ensuring that the volume remained true to the ideal of Europe writ large.

Veronica and Erik changed the way the volume is structured, shortened the length of the individual contributions, and changed the focus of analysis in key areas. Some of the physical changes were necessary because of the way publishing has evolved in the digital age. Physical books are not how most students engage with the literature. Instead, they rely on digital access. This gives greater flexibility in choosing what students will read, but it tends to shift greater responsibility onto course instructors to provide a sense of coherence.

We did not design this book to be a one-stop shop for European politics. Instead, we invited our contributors to use their short chapters to open debates that course instructors can deepen by going to other resources that are electronically available. We have also encouraged our contributors to cite a wide-ranging literature, to highlight what contributes to the arguments they make, and to set out what is at stake in the debate.

We had to make difficult choices in selecting areas for coverage. Some topics such as the increasing role of technology and digital technology, and digital platforms in our lives have been left out for a future edition. Although we discuss human rights such as gender equality and refugee and migrant rights, we did not carve out a single chapter that deals with minority rights, postcolonial challenges and the systemic racism that Europe faces. We acknowledge these shortcomings and look forward to all other suggestions of improvement.

We believe this volume is a worthy successor to the excellent work that came before it. Europe is different from a decade ago and so is the *Developments in…* series. But the study of Europe remains at least as important as it was when Steven Kennedy commissioned *Developments in West European Politics* twenty-five years ago and the strength of the scholarly community willing to engage in that work is if anything even greater.

*Bologna and Florence*
*June 2022*

# Abbreviations

| | |
|---|---|
| AfD | Alternative for Germany (political party) |
| CEAS | Common European Asylum System |
| CEE | Central and Eastern Europe |
| CEO | chief executive officer |
| CETA | Comprehensive Economic and Trade Agreement |
| CFSP | Common Foreign and Security Policy |
| COP15 | Conference of the Parties, 15th Meeting |
| Covid-19 | Covid-19 coronavirus |
| CSDP | Common Security and Defence Policy |
| CVM | Cooperation and Verification Mechanism |
| E3+3 | Germany, France, and UK + China, Russia, and US (see P5+1) |
| EAW | European Arrest Warrant |
| EBRD | European Bank for Reconstruction and Development |
| ECJ | European Court of Justice |
| EFP | European Foreign Policy |
| EIGE | European Institute for Gender Equality |
| ENF | Europe of Freedom and Nations (political group) |
| EP | European Parliament |
| EPF | European Peace Facility |
| EPP | European Peoples' Party (political party) |
| EPPO | European Public Prosecutor's Office |
| ETA | Basque Homeland and Liberty (political party) |
| ETS | emissions trading system |
| EU | European Union |
| EUBAM | EU Border Assistance Mission |
| EUCAP | EU Capacity Building Mission |
| EUTM | EU Training Mission |
| EVS | European Values Survey |
| GDP | gross domestic product |
| ICG | International Crisis Group |
| ICT | information and communications technology |
| IDEA | Institute for Democracy and Electoral Assistance |

| | |
|---|---|
| IEA | International Energy Agency |
| IPU | Interparliamentary Union |
| IRA | Irish Republican Army |
| ISDS | investor-state dispute settlement |
| JCPOA | Joint Comprehensive Plan of Action |
| JHA | Justice and Home Affairs |
| LAI | local autonomy indicator |
| LGBTQIA+ | lesbian, gay, bisexual, transgender, queer, intersex, asexual and more |
| MEP | Member of European Parliament |
| MLG | multi-level governance |
| MP | Member of Parliament |
| NATO | North Atlantic Treaty Organization |
| NGO | non-governmental organization |
| OC | organized crime |
| OCG | organized crime group |
| OECD | Organization for Economic Cooperation and Development |
| OLAF | European Anti-Fraud Office |
| P5+1 | five permanent members of the UN security council plus Germany |
| PESCO | Permanent Structured Cooperation |
| PEGIDA | Patriotic Europeans Against the Islamicisation of the Occident (political movement) |
| PR | proportional representation |
| PRM | political recruitment model |
| PVE | preventing violent extremism |
| SNP | Scottish National Party (political party) |
| SYRIZA | Coalition of the Radical Left – Progressive Alliance (political party) |
| TCA | Trade and Cooperation Agreement (between the UK and the EU) |
| TTIP | Transatlantic Trade and Investment Partnership |
| UK | United Kingdom |
| UKIP | United Kingdom Independence Party (political party) |
| UN | United Nations |
| UNFCCC | United Nations Framework Convention on Climate Change |
| UNODC | United Nations Office on Drugs and Crime |
| UNSMIL | United Nations Support Mission in Libya |
| US | United States |

| V4 | Visegrad 4 – Czech Republic, Hungary, Slovakia and Poland |
| VoC | Varieties of Capitalism |
| WWF | World Wildlife Federation |
| XR | Extinction Rebellion (environmentalism movement) |

# Introduction

## Veronica Anghel and Erik Jones

This manuscript went into production as Russia invaded Ukraine. The Russian war against Ukraine will have transformative effects on European politics and the world order. It is difficult to foresee the full extent of the transformations. But it is possible to take stock of the developments against which future events will take place. To understand the importance of such benchmarking, it is useful to reflect on the history of this publication.

More than a decade has passed since we published the last edition of *Developments in European Politics*. The changes that have taken place are immense. The scale of change is not unprecedented. But the culmination of factors that influenced the course of European politics was transformative. Few looking ahead from 2011 would have anticipated what Europe would look like today; even fewer looking back can claim to have foreseen what would ultimately come to pass.

The purpose of this introduction is to set the stage for the contributions that explain such changes. In doing so, we aim to take those slow-moving developments that rose to the surface over the past decade and show how they became woven together. In anticipation of each author's contribution, we aim to highlight why the different threads they follow are so hard to disentangle. We also suggest that studying certain trends in recent developments in European politics can provide a solid foundation for gazing into the future. We pick up that forward-looking analysis in the conclusion.

The stage-setting focuses on four themes: the rise of authoritarian politics, the mismanagement of globalization, the perception of collective insecurity, and the disintegration of Europe. These phenomena not only shape contemporary debates about Europe but also condition the function of European institutions at all levels of government and the aspirations of European citizens.

Each of these themes played a part in the last edition of *Developments in European Politics*. Their traces go back to the very first volume in the *Developments in...* series. Nevertheless, we argue that these themes have become increasingly important in the European context over recent years.

Compared to previous volumes, we aimed to focus more on the attitudes of European citizens as the motor of European politics, in addition to discussing the role of structures and institutions. We also focus more readily on Europe's role in the world. Ultimately, the contribution of this volume is to identify what Europe is, where it came from, what its most significant structural challenges are, and what Europeans can make of it.

# The rise of authoritarian politics

The end of the Cold War set the stage for the triumph of liberal democracy over its ideological alternatives. However, the spread of authoritarian attitudes in Europe and beyond provided the most unsatisfying and ambiguous denouement of the last decades. The victory of liberal democracy was never going to bring an end to political disagreement or violent conflict. But it should have allowed like-minded societies to resolve their differences in more consensual and predictable ways. It should also have made it possible for people everywhere to aspire to similarly participatory forms of government, productive patterns of economic activity, far-reaching human rights agendas and inclusive institutions for social welfare.

This turned out to be more difficult than initially anticipated. Many in Europe place prosperity and security over individual freedom. While they often paid lip service to the importance of liberty, they lent their support to political leaders who showed scant regard for minority rights or for institutionalized checks and balances (Luce 2017). This is by no means a uniquely European or transatlantic phenomenon (Lührmann and Lindberg 2019). Many people outside Europe and the United States aspired to achieve prosperity and security even at the expense of personal liberty (Zakaria 2007). Often those aspirations crystallized in the most dynamic emerging market economies – with China being only the most prominent example.

The point to underline is that this preference for perceived prosperity and security over liberty underscored a wave of autocratization. Authoritarian innovations were often delivered through democratic means (Curato and Fossati 2020; Enyedi 2020). Those (would-be) political leaders who embraced this trade-off used democratic institutions to gain the power necessary to re-engineer how economics and politics works.

These leaders were often unsuccessful the first time around. Viktor Orbán and Jaroslaw Kaczynski are two prominent examples; Silvio Berlusconi is another. But that initial set-back did not stop them from returning to power or from paving the way for others to promote much of the same agenda. In other European member states such as Austria, Bulgaria, Croatia or Romania, politicians inimical to liberal agendas have been ruling or influencing these countries' politics for decades.

The preference for prosperity and security may be democratic, but it is also illiberal. And the harsh reality of the post-Cold War period is that illiberal political preferences were present across the globe, including in Europe. In that sense, there is nothing new about European populism either in the West or in the East (Jones 2007, 2017). Indeed, much of what gets characterized as democratic backsliding is actually the rise to power and co-option of democratic institutions by groups that never embraced liberalism to begin with (Anghel 2020; Anghel and Jones 2021). Those who benefited most from the transition used their new resources to cement their hold over political and economic power (Ganev 2001), showing that there can be no democracy without democrats.

What is new is the prominence of authoritarian attitudes during the first two decades of the twenty-first century. When they returned to power, Orbán and Kaczynski made no secret of their illiberal political views. Berlusconi may have continued to use liberal rhetoric, but his successor as leader of the Italian centre right, Matteo Salvini, was less circumspect. Meanwhile, governments across Europe began to rely on or include political movements that would previously have been considered unacceptable for high office. That prominence was not just a result of the attractiveness of illiberal ideas; it was also a reaction to the failure of liberal political leadership to deliver prosperity and stability more equitably among widely diverse social groups. It did not help either that many in Europe assumed they could take the resilience of liberal democracy for granted.

# The mismanagement of interdependence

The failure to deliver prosperity more fairly and equitably among Europeans is perhaps the greatest source of disappointment. The great strength of liberalism as a political ideology is its emphasis on individual choice and its presumption of the harmony of the interests. Both elements can be exaggerated. But it is possible to make an argument based on the liberal classics that connects individual choices in politics and economics to the mediation of interests in local and international markets that leads to a complex division of labour resulting from a mix of equality of opportunity and revealed comparative advantage. The outcome should make everyone better off. Prosperity measured in terms of economic growth is progress in this respect (Lepenies 2016).

Unfortunately, two elements complicate this picture. One is the way that the institutions we refer to collectively as markets interact both within and across national boundaries (Myrdal 1956); the other is the high costs associated with coordinating decision-making across countries to stabilize how those markets perform across the business cycle (Cooper 1968). These complicating factors are well known both in Europe and across the Atlantic. That is why Europeans have invested so much effort in building the European Union; it is also why successive US administrations have focused so much attention on sustaining multilateral institutions and maintaining the transatlantic relationship.

The problem decision-makers faced on both sides of the Atlantic is that the costs of bringing national economies together and managing their interdependence tend to grow disproportionately over time and as national economies become more closely knit together. This cost may be worth paying if the countries share many institutions and values in common. That is why regional integration was so successful among the countries of Western Europe, for example. But those costs tend to rise as (and if) the differences across countries widen. The impact may not be immediately obvious. Economic actors can often find incentives to trade from one place to the next. But the high cost does show up when political coordination becomes necessary – as during trade negotiations or crisis management.

A good example on the trade front would be the Doha Round of liberalization talks within the World Trade Organization. Those talks were meant to extend the advantages of market integration from Europe across the Atlantic, and from the Atlantic economy to the world writ large. That proved too ambitious, and the talks failed (Jones 2006). The problem was not entirely due to the scope of the effort, however. The same fate befell the negotiations for the Transatlantic Trade and Investment Partnership (TTIP) a decade later (Young 2017). Even a much simpler agreement between the European Union and Canada almost collapsed because of coordination problems. The failure to conclude those arrangements placed significant constraints on growth and employment.

On the crisis management front, there is no better example than the events that unfolded after the collapse of US subprime mortgage markets in 2007. Few members of the liberal elite on either side of the Atlantic covered themselves with glory, even if, ultimately, the system worked and the world narrowly averted disaster (Drezner 2014). As Adam Tooze (2018) made clear, the crisis damaged the appeal of liberalism across the globe, but particularly within Europe. It also damaged the appeal of multilateral policy coordination, which seemed not only expensive but also relatively ineffective to protect vulnerable groups.

Here too, critics of liberalism pushed a different line of argument. They advocated the importance of national sovereignty and they promised to put the interests of their constituents first. These critics emerged on the left as well as on the right. As their appeal increased, they pulled increasing numbers of voters away from the mainstream political parties (movements or currents) of the centre. The mismanagement of interdependence – whether real or perceived – added momentum to the shift toward illiberal preferences in this respect.

# The perception of collective insecurity

Liberalism also lost ground in terms of security. The rise of Islamic Terrorism in the aftermath of 9/11, the waves of migration that followed the Arab Spring and the direct and hybrid Russian attacks against Europe and the United States highlighted different weaknesses of liberalism. These simultaneous challenges also served to focus the attention of different parts of Europe on different security needs, proportionally to the level of perceived danger, increasing the fragmentation of decision-making. In turn, the perception of increased threat functioned as an amplifier of outgroup hostility, making it easier for ingroups to accept limitations on individual freedoms, and to agree to redirect funds from public services towards defence spending.

These consequences were hardly limited to the United States. The attack on the Twin Towers and the Pentagon was followed by attacks in Istanbul in 2003, Madrid in 2004, London in 2005. The violence continued across the early years of the twenty-first century, culminating in a series of attacks in Paris, Nice, Brussels and Berlin in 2015 and 2016. This act of terrorism across Europe caused national convulsions and resulted in a series of measures to restrict civil liberties and freedom of movement. The most visible outcome was the erection of heavy barriers to shield pedestrian areas in many European cities.

Europeans also had to contend with the direct and indirect effects of the instability created when the United States invaded Afghanistan and Iraq. The direct effects came in the form of terrorist reprisals against those governments that allied with American military forces. For many years after 9/11 both American and Jewish facilities in Europe garnered special protection.

The indirect effects came via the destabilization of authoritarian regimes across the Middle East and the region of North Africa, which came to a head in 2011 with the Arab Spring. This was initially celebrated as a new victory of democratic liberalism – and with good reason. European governments had propped up those regimes too long and the people in that part of the world are as deserving of individual liberty as any other. Unfortunately, early expectations were quickly disappointed. Rather than a rebirth of liberalism, the region entered a period of prolonged instability.

Many European governments – led by Britain and France – advocated a more proactive role in these developments, toppling Muammar Gaddafi in Libya and working to undermine Bashar al-Assad in Syria. But many others – notably Italy and Spain – worried about what the consequences of further instability would be for the flow of migrants across the Mediterranean. That flow started almost immediately as regimes in North Africa fell and then continued to gain momentum through the migration crisis of 2015 and 2016.

The combination of terrorism and migration created a sense of insecurity across much of Southern and Western Europe. It also led to outgroup hostility among Europeans throughout the continent. At much the same time, the growing assertiveness of Russia and the resistance of organized crime created tensions across Central and Eastern Europe. Russian lead cyber-attacks on critical infrastructure in the transatlantic space, together with hybrid and traditional war the Kremlin waged in the immediate European neighbourhood rekindled fears of Russian aggression mainly in the Baltic states and parts of Eastern Europe. Those fears would come to be justified.

The annexation of Crimea confirmed a new era of renewed Russian aggression. This forced the North Atlantic Treaty Organisation (NATO) to ask member states to increase their defence spending. Member states formally agreed to it, but not all implemented the necessary budgetary changes. Not every alliance member pushed back equally against Russia either. The EU and United States reacted sluggishly to Russian aggression, while some European leaders in France, Italy, Germany, Austria, Hungary and not least in Donald Trump's administration were more inspired than repelled by Vladimir Putin's increased authoritarianism. Leaders such as France's National Rally Marine Le Pen, Italy's League Matteo Salvini, Hungary's Fidesz Viktor Orbán and Austria's Freedom Party Heinz-Christian Strache curated personal relations to representatives of the Kremlin.

Before the invasion of Ukraine, the major success of Russian foreign policy in Europe was the division it created among member states to stand up to the Kremlin's alternative interpretation of democracy and rule of law. The invasion of Ukraine motivated member states into collective defensive action, but attitudinal changes take a longer time. Divisions over the handling of Russia will continue to inform decision-making. This feeds back into the story of elite political competition over resources and uninterrupted rule in the countries of Central and Eastern Europe. While few leaders overtly support Vladimir Putin's model, many borrow from the Kremlin's playbook. In part, this reflects the inequities and ineffectiveness of the 'dual transition' from communism to capitalism; in part, it also reflects the struggle for power between different groups within the region (Hellman 1998). This approach to informal governance through groups of interests and the overlap of business and political interests is important insofar as it tends to spill across national boundaries through personal connections, business relationships, religious affiliations, ethnic ties and historic grievances. Not least, an ineffective stance of European countries against Russia leads to a loss of influence of European foreign policy in aspiring members states in the Western Balkans, and those included in the European Neighbourhood Policy.

Taken together, terrorism, migration and Russian aggression have created a widespread sense of collective insecurity. Moreover, this was an insecurity for which the United States can provide little reassurance. From a European perspective, US foreign policy destabilized the Middle East and then successive US administrations refused to accept responsibility for the implications of that instability. The United States antagonized and then failed to contain or ameliorate the situation with Russia as well. Then the Trump Administration openly challenged the importance of NATO, the transatlantic relationship and the practice of multilateralism. European security depends on its partnership with the United States. For a long time, Europeans had reasons to feel a sense of isolation and abandonment. The invasion of Ukraine has galvanized both sides of the Atlantic into collective action. It remains to be seen whether changes will be more profound than ad hoc decision-making.

# The disintegration of Europe

With the benefit of hindsight, it is relatively easy to see how the failure of large multilateral trade talks, the spread of the global economic and financial crisis, the subsequent European sovereign debt crisis, the threat of terrorism, the perceived threat of migration and Europe's weak stance toward Russia might be used by political entrepreneurs to discredit both the British government and Britain's membership in the European Union. But such hindsight is misleading both about the chain of events that led to the referendum on British membership and about the motivation of those who voted to leave. In turn, a too easy reading of Britain's exit from the European Union creates a false model for interpreting developments in other countries.

When British Prime Minister David Cameron called for an in-or-out vote on British membership in January 2013, he did so because there was already a large part of the British population that was determined to express their opinion. His argument in calling for the vote was that there is no way to avoid having a public debate about British membership, and so the only responsible choice is to do so openly and in a way that would encourage everyone in Britain to participate. This move allowed him to postpone that debate until after the 2015 parliamentary elections. It also made it possible for Cameron to hold his Conservative Party together and claim an unexpectedly decisive victory. Cameron assumed he would win the referendum easily. When he started to lose ground in the campaign, he tried to scare the electorate with the economic consequences of leaving. Right up until the votes were counted, his team believed they were winning the argument. They miscalculated.

This kind of miscalculation is hardly unique to Britain. The Danish political class miscalculated prior to the June 1992 referendum on the Maastricht Treaty. French President François Mitterrand miscalculated when he called his own referendum after the Danish votes were counted. The French and Dutch governments both miscalculated when they held referendums on the European Constitutional Treaty in 2005.

These other referendums did not result in those countries leaving the European Union, but they did slow the process of European integration in the 1990s and they prevented a more significant evolution of the European Union in the 2000s. In each case, moreover, the motivations voters expressed after the fact told a different story. The Danes said they were willing to pay a high economic price to maintain their political independence; the French said they feared Europe would transfer too much power from the state to the market; and the Dutch said they did not want a Europe that large countries might be able to dominate.

What these rationales have in common is a sense of collective destiny apparently defined by national boundaries. The British have that as well. The question is whether other countries might make choices that will have being in or out of the European Union as a consequence. Such a choice does not have to be a referendum on membership. There are other choices with similar effects.

The importance of choice is what we learned when the Greeks voted to reject the bailout package offered by the European Council in July 2015. The Greek government suddenly faced the reality that it would have to accept something even worse or effectively lose its EU membership. The Cypriot government faced a similar choice around bank bailouts in 2013. Indeed, on both occasions the government initially miscalculated and only later recovered from its mistake. Recovering from its mistake is not something that David Cameron's government could do.

The threat of European disintegration comes from a principled choice made at the national level that is inconsistent with the European project. That is the real lesson from Brexit. The British chose to withdraw from the European Union's legal framework; no British government could reconcile that choice with continued membership.

The problem for the European Union is that taking back control is not the only possible irreconcilable choice. Governments (and peoples) could choose something that is principled and yet illiberal. The debate over abortion rights in Poland is one illustration; the debate over LGBTQIA+ rights in Hungary is another. But the choice does not have to be related to infringements of human rights. Here it is worth recalling the Italian debate over fiscal policy in 2018 and 2019. The issues in that debate were highly technical. But from the perspective of the German government and the European Central Bank they went to the heart of whether Italy could stay in the euro area or in the European Union. Fortunately, the Italian government did not miscalculate the strength of its bargaining position. If it had done so, the debate over Europe's future would look very different today.

Such miscalculations are more likely when governments do not share a commitment to core values. That is why the rise of authoritarian preferences among some groups and elites is so important. Governments who do not have confidence in one another are more likely to make suboptimal choices. The mismanagement of interdependence towards less cooperation carries additional costs. And miscalculation is more likely when governments misjudge the real threats they face or feel insecure of their position in negotiations.

The more such perceptions of insecurity spread, the more likely governments are to act without due consideration for the consequences. Such miscalculations are important in a European context because they tend to slow, change or even reverse the pattern of European integration. In an extreme case, they may even result in disintegration. The point to underscore is that 'extreme' is not the same as 'unlikely'.

# Hidden fragility and strength

Much as there is no democracy without democrats, the future of Europe is limited without Europeans. By the end of this decade Europeans appear less committed to Europe's core values of liberal democracy, free markets, solidarity and tolerance. They also appear less able to deliver the kind of prosperity and stability for which the project of the European Union was created. Indeed, only one country left Europe physically, but perhaps more importantly, others such as Poland and Hungary left Europe in terms of commitment to European values they had previously agreed to uphold. An accepting disposition from other member states legitimizes a pluralist understanding of democracy even further, departing from initial standards.

The Covid-19 pandemic showed that Europe has hidden strength as well as fragility. European leaders chose to come through the pandemic together. The political and economic body of Europe emerged stronger as a consequence. What we do not know is whether this is a decisive turn in European politics and whether European leaders are ready to build on the momentum of their success, or a temporary deviation from a longer trajectory.

The only way to answer that question is to take stock of recent developments. That is what the contributions that follow have to offer. The conclusion looks forward using that analysis as a foundation.

# 1

# Democracy and Accountability in Twenty-First Century Europe

*Simona Piattoni*

The last two decades have witnessed a veritable decline in popular confidence in democracy as a system of rule. After the third wave of democratization at the end of the 1980s, democracy appeared to be the only legitimating discourse for any political regime that cared to be sustained by one. A decade later, confidence in the capacity of democratic procedures to secure legitimate and effective governments dramatically declined. This is most apparent in the surge of populist ideas that devalue the complex multilateral arrangements and the institutional safeguards typical of twentieth-century liberal democracies and rather hark back to nativist understandings of communities (and often distinct ethnic groups within them) entitled to place their fate above those of all others. Slogans such as 'gaining back control' or 'my community first' have peppered the discourses of the political leaders of some of the oldest liberal democracies and more extreme appeals to 'illiberal democracy' – that is, electoral democracy shorn of the complications deriving from the rule of law and the protection of individual rights – have been propounded as the new democratic normal. The postwar period characterized by open markets, multilateralism and individual rights thus appears to have given way to an understanding of democracy as simply gaining consensus for policies that favour a narrowly defined community.

I trace the roots of this phenomenon in two developments, one empirical and the other theoretical. The empirical development is the apparent loss of control experienced by the national citizenries as a consequence of European integration and globalization, with European integration increasingly perceived as the handmaiden of globalization. The theoretical development is identified with a streamlined notion of democracy as 'delegation with accountability' characterized by the existence of a chain of delegation that runs from the sovereign national citizenries through elected politicians to decision-makers ideally paired by a matching chain of accountability flowing in the opposite direction.

My contention is that this notion of democracy promises a degree of direct correspondence between the needs and preferences of the national citizenries and the decisions of their legislators that cannot be delivered in a world of increased interconnectedness. The economic and social circumstances that determine the life chances of European citizens and the mechanisms that preside over the translation of national communities' needs and preferences into relevant decisions escape the narrow control of any national community. An apparent loss of control grips many European political systems, torn between responsiveness towards their national community and responsibility towards other EU member states (Mair 2013). This feeling is amplified when global interconnectedness and financial crises are factored in (Alonso and Ruiz-Rufino 2020). The temptation to eschew accountability altogether by blaming external constraints grows stronger, and this may lead to embracing populist and illiberal versions of democracy.

To be fair, a certain amount of democratic discontent also characterized the postwar period, but it was only at the end of the century that this phenomenon started to dominate the political science literature. In the 1990s, virtually every book on the subject began by recording the weakening of democracy throughout the world. The opening statements of the books on democracy since then are even gloomier and record the unravelling of liberal-democratic values in Europe, where it had won its most significant battles. Although the manifestations of this democratic malaise are different in different countries, in this contribution I will highlight the common ailments, discuss the possible causes and review the current analyses and recommendations with a focus on Europe.

In this chapter, I first provide a brief overview of the (relatively) distant causes of this democratic malaise, dating back to the second half of the twentieth century, and dwell in particular on the last three decades. Starting from the conventional notion of democracy as 'delegation with accountability',

I then review the principal empirical, analytical and normative challenges to democracy brought by recent developments. I argue that by clinging to this perhaps outdated notion we are unable to describe the current problems of democracy, propose effective remedies and craft legitimating discourses for new solutions. I conclude by pointing to some of the current developments in the debate on democracy.

# The origins of contemporary democratic discontent

With the collapse of communism and the fall of the Berlin wall, the main contender with liberal democracy – Soviet communism – imploded. Democracy remained the sole legitimating discourse for any political regime that did not want to openly subscribe to brutality as a governmental tool. Yet, at the turn of the century, citizens appeared increasingly disenchanted with the practical functioning of their democracies. Works like those of Susan Pharr and Robert Putnam (2000) asked what was troubling the 'trilateral' democracies, referring to the democracies of Europe, North America and Asia. The book openly referred to a previous work that had been tasked to investigate the 'crisis of democracy' in the 1970s by the Trilateral Commission. This organization, founded by David Rockefeller in 1973, had commissioned a study into the causes of the apparent 'ungovernability' of Western democracies (of North America, Europe and Japan) which resulted in a famous study (Crozier et al. 1975). While the concerns that informed that study appeared to be the same as those of Pharr and Putnam, the diagnosis had changed.

In the 1970s the main cause of discontent had been identified with 'democratic overload'. This phrase captured two distinct yet correlated sources of discontent. The first was materialistic in nature: after having recovered from the war and having satisfied their primary needs, people had started to ask for more, and governments had obliged by setting up (particularly in Europe) generous welfare provisions such as universal education, free public health and extensive social security. This had improved living standards but also overstretched state capacities and induced an excessive intrusion of government into people's lives, not to mention excessive bureaucracy and tax pressure.

The second was a cultural shift among citizens who now cultivated 'post-materialistic' values, which included demands for greater involvement in decision-making and more freedoms. The two sources of discontent were interestingly intertwined: as greater material security prompted more participation in public affairs and demands for a better quality of life, these in turn placed heavier burdens onto government and caused the intensification of some of those phenomena against which people had started to rebel. The upshot was that people were, simultaneously, more demanding and more dissatisfied: this was what the Trilateral Commission picked on, eventually recommending scaling down governmental action. After two decades of collective mobilization in the 1960s and 1970s, people began to understand political participation in more individualistic and selective terms.

The liberal turn of the 1980s, paradoxically, had both progressive and conservative aspects. It was progressive insofar as the demands for greater involvement and better quality of life led to requests for people's freedom to decide ones' religious, sexual and lifestyle orientations – not to mention of course full civil rights. It was conservative in that it identified in the state, which had to a large extent made the material progress possible, the cause of the current problems and suggested a retrenchment from it. With the devaluation of all that was public and the extolment of all that was private came an increasing suspicion towards political intermediation, which was now perceived as the cause of democracy's ailments. The 'excessive' mobilization which had characterized the 1960s and early 1970s gave way to a different type of mobilization characterized by a relative disengagement from broad political revendications and in favour of more limited issues such as the environment, peace and sexual freedom (for the original statement, see Inglehart 1977). This decline in political participation was now negatively assessed and argued to lead to a poorer quality of democracy. According to this view, the social capital that had been accumulated in the previous decades of social engagement was now being superficially squandered by retrenching towards more narrowly conceived rights (Putnam 2004), much in line with the mounting neoliberal mood.

The market now was hailed as the real bastion of democracy, allowing everyone to record their own preferences and have them satisfied through a (supposedly) invisible mechanism that impersonally matched demand and supply without the cumbersome intervention of the state. Inspired by such works as Milton Friedman's *Capitalism and Freedom* (1962), the marketplace now replaced the *agora* and the city hall as the locus in which people could exercise their freedoms. The overarching principle governing the market – the maximization of individual utility – appeared as the sole, authentic driver of human behaviour, shorn of the confusing and misleading garb of the general interest or the public utility.

Social disengagement, increasing trust in private institutions and, most of all, extolment of the virtues of the market became the theoretical justifications for an age of political retrenchment and disintermediation which weakened traditional collective actors (political parties, trade unions, other associations) and replaced them with social movements often dedicated to the pursuit of single causes and identity issues. Political parties, in particular, had troubles keeping up with such a change (cf. Schulte-Cloos, this volume) and those that did found themselves before a difficult choice: whether to support identity causes and integrate single issues into their party platforms (thus losing their traditional social referents and fragmenting their programmes; Lilla 2017) or embrace market values and base on the system's performance their legitimacy (thus making themselves captive of economic ups and downs). In a nutshell, the choice was between input and output legitimacy (Scharpf 1999), but while the 'input side' was becoming ever more fragmented, the 'output side' was becoming ever more elusive.

Democracy won its battle against communism right when its capacity to deliver satisfactory outputs became increasingly problematic. Lured by the successes of capitalism, the former communist regimes of Eastern Europe fell under the pressure of the crushing comparison between the two regimes' social and economic performances and opted for liberal democracy. This shift did not only entail greater freedom and rising prosperity in Eastern Europe but also unexpected hardship in the guise of increased uncertainty and heavier individual responsibility. The seeds of disenchantment, after the first inebriation, were sown then (cf. de Jonge, this volume).

Meanwhile, the drive for ever-growing productivity gains led mature industrial economies to decentralize their production and extend their value chains in the rural economies of Southeast Asia and other emerging economies thus contributing to the progressive industrialization of the latter. The communist regime of China also opted for open trade and capitalist development. While the fallout in terms of democratization was uneven, one thing became clear: the world had become enveloped in global networks of production and trade, and all economies and societies had become interconnected.

In Europe, economic interdependence had been willingly pursued since the 1950s and increasingly so since the 1970s. Its consequence in terms of democratic performance appeared here sooner than in other parts of the world. In his rich production, Fritz Scharpf (see, e.g., Scharpf 2000) singled out interdependence as the main cause of democratic ailment. Interdependence meant that democratic decisions made in one country affected the choices available in other countries, particularly the members the European Union (EU) and the neighbouring countries: no EU member state was properly 'sovereign' anymore. Whichever promises representatives and represented exchanged domestically on election day, their fulfilment was in fact dependent upon the decisions made together by European member states at EU level.

The source of the increasing disconnect between national citizenries and political elites was now identified with this growing interdependence, which constrained the room of manoeuvre of national executives. If the fragmentation of representation inherited from the previous period dulled the possibility of fashioning coherent and convincing political programmes (input), the increased interdependence of an integrated Europe and a globalized world hampered the possibility of delivering desired outcomes (output).

The growing dissatisfaction with democracy and the growing distance between citizens and elites, that had been labelled as 'anti-politics' two decades earlier (Berger 1979), was called 'post-democracy' (Crouch 2004) or, more simply, 'void' (Mair 2013) in the first decade of the twenty-first century. The latter capture a new difficulty with European democracies: whether because the technological, economic and social transformations of the 1980s and 1990s had fragmented the conventional social referents of political parties and shifted the attention of politicians towards big companies and financial players (Crouch 2004) or because EU interdependence had limited member states' sovereignty and created a distance between what citizens demanded and what their representatives could deliver (on Mair's responsiveness–responsibility dilemma, see also Bardi et al. 2014), what ensued was scepticism in democracy's capacity to respond to people's needs throughout Europe.

More recently, a new, but in many ways old, phenomenon emerged: national populism (or nativism). The hiatus that opened between cosmopolitan elites that could profit from globalization and register their preferences through market choices (the 'anywheres') and the masses that felt the displacement caused by globalization and had no way of registering their own preferences as members of national and local communities (the 'somewheres') bred a populist discourse that hypostatized a fundamental difference between the two (Goodhart 2017; de Jonge, this volume).

Populism in fact reproduces all the problems highlighted above even as it appears to respond to them. In is *anti-political* in that it distrusts representative political institutions and opts for a radical version of democracy deprived of its liberal traits (Zakaria 2007; Mounk 2018). It is *post-democratic* in that it draws its justification from the increasing inequality between the haves and the have-nots brought about by globalization and validates the apparent contraposition between elites and masses, forfeiting the attempt to craft collective answers to societal problems (Rodrik 2001; Piketty 2014). It is *hollow* in that it presumes to provide simple answers to complex problems and turns back the clock to a foregone past (if it ever existed) in which national communities could presume to be fully in control of their own destinies. In Europe, a new cleavage – the 'transnational' one – appears to obliterate all traditional cleavages pitting those who embrace transnational governance against those who want to 'gain back control' (Hooghe and Marks 2017).

In the second decade of the twenty-first century, growing policy interdependence particularly among euro members further strained the already difficult balance between responsiveness to national constituencies and responsibility vis-à-vis EU partners. As a consequence of the euro crisis, a cycle that had already run its course in the Thirties under similar circumstances (i.e. a constraining monetary regime) repeated itself, and outward responsibility had to trump inward responsiveness. In the 2010s, like in the 1930s, the outcome was a sudden awareness of stringent international constraints and a surge in populism and a questioning of liberal representative democracy in some younger democracies were the consequences (see the articles in the special issue edited by Bardi, Bartolini and Trechsel 2014 for an overview of the causes and consequences of this predicament).

Yet in a way populism and nativism rekindled mass interest in politics. In Europe, in addition to the euro crisis and the measures that had to be implemented in order to counter it, the other issue that was associated with such a change was mass migration, also a consequence of globalization and heightened interconnectedness (Hobolt and de Vries 2016; Kokkonen and Linde 2021). This spurt in EU-level politicization – in theory a good thing as it allegedly compensated for the decline in political involvement of the previous decades – however, came at a cost: the declining legitimacy of liberal democracy.

According to De Wilde and Zürn (2012), the depoliticization that had been actively sought by European elites after the Treaty Establishing a

Constitution for Europe debacle in 2005 could eventually not prevent a re-politicization of EU politics, given the ever more contentious extension of EU authority over an increasing number of policy areas. According to these authors, however, this politicization does not necessarily represent a negative development, but is rather a Janus-faced phenomenon – it manifests itself both as stronger criticism of EU authority and as greater attention to and use of EU institutions for the manifestation of discontent – and has therefore both a de-legitimizing and a legitimizing effect.

In what follows, I elaborate on the latest manifestation of democratic discontent and underline how heightened interdependence challenges empirically, analytically and normatively the mainstream notion of liberal democracy. This notion increasingly appears incapable of describing the reality of today's democratic governance, directing our attention to the real axes of political mobilization, and providing a legitimating discourse for contemporary democratic governance structures.

# The limits of democracy as 'delegation with accountability'

Particularly in European parliamentary systems, the conventional notion of democracy as 'delegation with accountability' posits the existence of a chain of delegation that departs from the sovereign people (the demos) and, through its democratically elected representatives, authorizes the executive to make and implement decisions on its behalf (Strøm et al. 2003). It further posits the existence of a matching chain of accountability that from the executive, through the monitoring activity of parliament and thanks to its sanctioning powers, makes sure that the decisions and actions taken on behalf of the demos do in fact seek to enact the 'will of the people' as expressed at election time.

## Empirical challenges

This apparently simple notion of democracy presupposes many non-obvious conditions that have become more problematic in recent times, particularly in the European interconnected context. Three stand out: 1) the existence of a *demos* that recognizes itself as such and on whose behalf political decisions can be made (the principal); 2) sufficiently clear decision-making procedures that allow to identify who did what, when and how (the agents); 3) unbroken chains of delegation and accountability connecting principals and agents.

To begin with, principals are becoming increasingly fragmented and may fail to recognize themselves as one *demos* due to rampant phenomena such as the rediscovery of sub-national identities, the pursuit of many disparate walks-of-life identities and the multiculturalism induced by successive waves of migrations. In these circumstances, the political preferences of the principal and the criteria according to which the activity of the agents is assessed diverge. On their side, agents may have a hard time translating such divergent preferences into coherent actions and may be tempted to pursue many disparate requests failing to craft a coherent vision for society. In the EU, this problem is even more acute as the principals are indeed many and have not yet developed a 'we-feeling' (Weiler 1995). There is no EU *demos* yet: many disparate *demoi* co-exist even within societies once considered as homogeneous and even more so within the EU as a whole. This situation is often referred to as the problem of 'many eyes' that will assess differently decisions that affect everyone (Papadopoulos 2007).

The second problem has to do with the difficulty of clearly identifying who exactly is responsible for what, so that holding agents to account becomes very difficult. The complexity of decision-making and the involvement of many levels of government and civil society actors, all claiming a say in the process, blur individual and institutional responsibilities (Hobolt and Tilley 2014). Self-serving credit-claiming and blame-shifting on the part of the agents frustrates the citizens' attempt to hold agents to account and breeds a sense of impotence and manipulation. This phenomenon is, once again, particularly acute at EU level, whose institutional architecture differs from that of any of its member states and cannot be classified according to existing categories (whether parliamentarism or presidentialism, international organization or federal system) and where most policies involve the simultaneous activation of many levels of government (Piattoni 2010). In the literature on the EU, this problem is sometimes referred to as the problem of 'many hands' (Papadopoulos 2007).

Puzzlement as to who decides what, when and how and who should be held to account for what – the broken chains of delegation and accountability – engenders a breakdown in legitimacy flows between represented and representatives. Once more, this phenomenon is most apparent at EU level (Scharpf 2009), but it can be observed also within national democracies. All the phenomena recalled above – the fragmentation of national citizenries in multiple *demoi* having different identities and sometimes radically different policy preferences; the fraying of the linkages between voters and politicians due to the social fragmentation of social classes and the social displacements induced by globalization; the involvement of different levels of government and societal groups in policy delivery along multi-level governance schemes – affect the flows of authority and legitimacy also at the national level. For EU member states, having to accept yet another level of decision-making which often trumps national preferences adds complexity, confounds responsibilities and induces a sense of powerlessness in national citizenries. Democracy as 'delegation with accountability' fails to capture the working of contemporary democracies and empties of meaning the conventional claims made in their defence.

# Analytical challenges

Political science models that start from a notion of democracy as 'delegation with accountability' may misguide both analysts and legislators and may lead to the implementation of the 'wrong' remedies. Once more, several analyses compete in explaining current democratic ailments.

The conventional delegation theory assumes that principals are interested in minimizing the agents' tendency to interject their own interests in the discharge of their duty, which should be to act in the principal's interest. These are thus assumed to be interested in monitoring the agents, avoiding their shirking and skirting, and holding their agents to account (Kiewiet and McCubbins 1991). Recent analyses cast doubts on this supposedly universal tendency and observe that often principals wilfully fail to monitor their agents.

The phenomenon is more acute when the chain of delegation involves multiple actors, acting as principals or agents at each turn. In this case, principals placed at intermediate links of the chain of delegation may neglect to strictly monitor their agents so as to be able to shift the blame downward for the eventual failure. For example, parliamentary parties may neglect to monitor the executive's activity so as to be able to blame it for failing to resolve societal problems, or members of the executive may fail to monitor public officials that depend on them for the same reason. Under these circumstances, citizens cannot hold their agents to account and eventually impose the necessary sanctions (Bovens 2007) because they simply do not know who to blame. Placed before long chains of delegation and accountability, citizens may be unable to effectively sanction their agents not for want of interest in doing so, but because the model failed to anticipate these 'perverse' behaviours.

Alternatively, one could argue that liberal democracy is challenged not so much by the citizens' lack of interest in being informed about politics and monitoring their representatives, but by incremental institutional changes that upset the existing checks and balances but remain rather somewhat hidden from the public view. A major such shift was brought about by the creation of independent administrative agencies that are sometimes only partially independent from political power but that, when they are fully so, may constitute another kind of democratic threat. In recent times, because of the diffusion of the monetarist creed in making the stability of the currency into an absolute priority, central banks have become increasingly independent from national executives (and the European Central Bank more so than any other bank), thus injecting a powerful dose of technocratic non-majoritarianism in representative democracies that otherwise function along majoritarian principles (Stone-Sweet and Thatcher 2002).

If citizens feel alienated from politics, it is also because politics has willingly accepted to be displaced by non-majoritarian institutions which deprive citizens of their say over important policy areas (Mair 2013). The justification for the diffusion of non-majoritarian institutions assumes that shielding certain policy areas from political influences would yield collectively better policies, an assumption that rests on strong ideological premises (Majone 2014). The conventional notion of democracy as 'delegation with accountability' thus has a hard time theorizing these phenomena and may suggest remedies that fall short of addressing the actual problems.

## Normative challenges

A normative debate has addressed the disconnect between democratic theory and practice during the last three decades, advancing two main arguments. First, liberal representative democracies have been corrupted by political classes unable to interpret and govern global transformations and are therefore destined to go through a prolonged period of crisis hopefully followed by their renewal. Second, liberal representative democracies inevitably disappoint even their most fervent supporters because they are based on false premises, so correctives must be introduced. These theories focus on current contemporary liberal representative democracies, but to some extent also include a criticism of the conventional notion of democracy as 'delegation with accountability'.

The first criticism – that corrupt political classes have been unable to govern epochal transformations – is at the basis of the populist critique of liberal democracy. In Europe, political elites have allegedly been willing to favour foreign (financial) interests and to sacrifice the welfare of their citizens in order to retain their roles as mediators between international financial elites and national institutions for personal gain. More radically, populists posit that elites are inherently corrupt, and that institutional paraphernalia must be ditched in favour of a more direct connection between the people and the leaders who, belonging to the people and speaking on behalf of the people, can truly pursue the people's interests (de Jonge, this volume). Direct democracy or, at most, electoral democracy are extolled as the sole genuine mechanisms for letting the people speak while liberal institutions, that tend to place majoritarian outcomes in a protective shell of liberal rights, are downgraded. Egregious examples of this trend are provided by some of the Central and Eastern European democracies such as Hungary and Poland (Csehi and Zgut 2021).This celebration of direct democracy leads to a dangerous dichotomization of the two components of liberal democracy, potentially yielding 'undemocratic liberalism' and 'illiberal democracies' (Mounk 2018). As we have seen, growing inequality and hegemonic neoliberal discourses lend some credibility to this criticism and fan the growth of populist parties such as PiS in Poland, Fidesz in Hungary, True Finns in Finland, Front National in France, Fratelli d'Italia in Italy and many other such people's parties. Newly democratic countries, such as Hungary, Poland, Romania and Bulgaria, are particularly prone to such dichotomization, but fairly stable (though not unproblematic) democracies such as Austria, Finland, France and Italy are also vulnerable (Schulte-Cloos, this volume).

The second criticism is premised on a fundamental scepticism about democracy's assumption that citizens are interested in being informed about and participating in political affairs – a 'realist' view of democracy as it were (Achen and Bartels 2017). According to this view, most citizens cannot understand the socio-economic causes behind current problems and therefore cannot really assess their representatives' actions since they are fundamentally uninterested in politics. Should they be enticed to participate in politics, they would become intensely partisan, so that their views would be clouded by irrational fanaticism (Brennan 2018). The deliberative mantra that more political participation improves the quality of democracy because it exposes people to contrasting views and trains them to be convinced by the better arguments (Bohman 1996) is supposedly contradicted by the fact that people tend to expose themselves only to arguments that reinforce their original views and interact only with like-minded individuals thus locking themselves in increasingly more impermeable echo chambers (Brennan 2018: Ch. 2). Democracy thus needs to be limited and corrected by epistocratic (from *episteme*, truth, and *kratos*, power – the rule of the wise) devices that grant greater decision-making powers to people who prove to 'know more', such as giving more votes to knowledgeable people or setting up highly selective bodies that can halt or revise popularly made decisions (Brennan 2018: Ch. 8).

# Conclusion

This chapter explored the challenges to liberal democracy that come from decades of powerful socio-economic changes and from the political reactions to these changes. Both have created a highly interconnected context in which traditional democracies appear to perform poorly. The reaction to these challenges has gone in the direction of denying politics of its deeper meaning and replacing it with unbridled market mechanisms thus ultimately creating a void between represented and representatives. Alternatively, they promoted a retrenchment behind outdated notions of national sovereignty in an effort, on the part of narrowly defined national citizenries, to 'gain back control' thus pushing liberal democracies down a spiral of illiberalism that may lead to dictatorship. An alternative route would lead to crafting a new notion of democracy and new decision-making mechanisms for highly interconnected contexts like the European one.

In concluding, my contention is that political theory should indeed go beyond the mere criticism of current liberal democracies and the conventional notion of democracy, and craft democratic standards better apt for highly interconnected contexts such as Europe (Piattoni 2017). One such theory proposes to replace the notion of democracy with that of *demoicracy* to mark the fact that, within the EU as well as within our national democracies, we must get used to govern with other *demoi*, 'though not as one' (Nicolaidis 2013). Differences must be acknowledged, and mechanisms must be introduced that allow for the coexistence of different standards.

Wherever possible, common standards on which all can agree should be adopted. In a national context, this is not so different from a consociational view of democracy (Bogaards and Helms 2019); in an international context it may be equivalent to crafting some sort of federal solution (Fabbrini 2015).

A second line of theorizing proposes higher standards of democracy and requests that the interests and ideas of all affected people (and not just those of the sovereign citizens formally entitled to decide) must be fully tracked for non-dominance to be avoided (Pettit 1997). How this can be done is of course the object of some debate. Some point to the possibility of implementing deliberative solutions at the level of single policy provisions, to then upload and generalize the procedures thus devised once representative institutions have certified their utility (the directly deliberative polyarchy of Sabel and Zeitlin 2007). Others aim at giving back to parliaments their rightful centrality by making so-called interparliamentary dialogues into a 'third virtual chamber' (Crum and Fossum 2009) or by turning them into a sort of joint constitutional assembly that stands guard over the proportionality of European legislation in defense of the preferences and values of the respective national citizenries, albeit in a more political and deliberative notion of subsidiarity (Cooper 2012; Bellamy and Kröger 2014).

A third argument considers as legitimate only those international arrangements that facilitate and improve the quality of democratic decision-making at the level of nation-state, implying that more articulate institutional architectures and discourses must be crafted to legitimate multi-level governance systems (Lord 2006, 2015; Bellamy 2019). In the decades to come we will see which of these options will have prevailed and which other democratic ailments will appear, in the awareness that democracy is a complex and delicate architecture that needs continuous institutional and normative upkeep.

# Questions for discussion

1  Democracy is inherently imperfect, hence subject to continuous criticism. Which phases of democratic discontent have been witnessed in Europe in the last century? How did they manifest?
2  The 'discovery of interconnectedness' has caused both a disconnect between masses and elites and a rekindling of political mobilization. What were the main drivers for political engagement in the early twenty-first century?

3  What are the analytical, empirical and normative assumptions of liberal representative democracy in Europe? What is their role in driving the current democratic discontent?
4  What democratic innovations could be mobilized to make sense of the heightened interconnectedness among Europeans and ease perceived difficulties of governing together?

# Recommended for Further Reading

Barber, B. (2003) *Stronger Democracy: Participatory Politics for a New Age.* Berkeley, CA: The University of California Press.
Caramani, D. (2015) *The Europeanization of Politics: The Formation of a European Electorate and Party System in Historical Perspective.* Cambridge: Cambridge University Press.
Ferrin, M. and Kriesi, H. (2016) *How Europeans View and Evaluate Democracy.* Oxford: Oxford University Press.
Goodin, R. (2008) *Innovating Democracy: Democratic Theory and Practice After the Deliberative Turn.* Oxford: Oxford University Press.
Innerarity, D. (2018) *Democracy in Europe. A Political Philosophy of the EU.* London: Palgrave Macmillan.

# 2

# Representation and Accountability

## *Julia Schulte-Cloos*

Representative democracy in Europe depends on the capacity of parties to offer political alternatives, integrate the demands of voters into their platforms and responsibly translate them into policies when elected to office. Elections, thus, are the key element in the representative model. Elections offer voters the chance to both articulate by whom they would like to be represented and to hold elected officials accountable via the threat to revoke this authorization (Pitkin 1967). In recent decades, this model of representative democracy has come under substantial pressure. Long-term processes of social change related to cultural liberalism and globalization have transformed the policy concerns of the electorate (Kriesi 2016).

The established parties previously engaged in representing the interests of a majority of citizens along the traditional left-right dimension of political conflict had difficulties in responding to voters' changing demands. Since the 2000s, established parties found themselves increasingly challenged by new political actors including populist radical right and radical left parties, Green parties and 'valence populist' parties (Zulianello 2020) in Eastern Europe. The rise of these new challenger parties is not only an expression of the declining representative capacity of mainstream parties, it is also intrinsically connected to the different economic and political crises that Europe has been witnessing over the last twenty years (Kriesi and Pappas 2015; Hutter and Kriesi 2019).

What the new political actors across Europe have in common is that they call into question the sustained capability of mainstream parties to represent the interests and preferences of European citizens. While mainstream parties mostly emphasize issues related to the economic dimension of political conflict, challenger parties tend to run on political platforms that emphasize issues related to the policy challenges arising from an increasingly globalized world and interconnected European Union. In doing so, some of the challenger parties also adopt a decisively anti-system or populist strategy of appealing to voters (Hopkin 2020).

This chapter examines how political representation and accountability across Europe have been affected by the changes that European party systems have been witnessing over the last decades. It sheds light on the drivers of these changes and the resulting implications for the representation of citizens' political preferences.

The chapter has six sections. The first discusses the most important long-term processes of social change that have shaped European societies and politics over the past decades. The next four sections show how these processes found their reflection in transforming political space in Europe. Not only did they contribute to the electoral decline of mainstream parties who previously used to represent the interests of a large majority of the electorate along the traditional left-right dimension of political conflict, coupled with the consequences of multi-level competition in the European Union, they also gave rise to the success of new challenger parties.

These challenger parties represent the new substantive demands of citizens that map on a new, cultural cleavage of political competition. Many of them also articulate voters' political distrust towards the mainstream political elite. Finally, this chapter shows that challenger parties across Europe have increasingly participated in government, allowing them to represent voters' new demands in cabinet.

# Long-term processes of social change and the transformative impact of recent crises

According to Seymour Martin Lipset and Stein Rokkan (1967), party systems are the expression of deep-seated conflicts that exist in society, which are commonly referred to as 'cleavages'. Cleavages can be understood as persistent disagreements of interest between social or political groups that may give rise to open conflict (Rae and Taylor 1970: 1–21). Such cleavages reflect not only the socio-structural divides within a society but also related sets of conscious beliefs about these divides as much as their articulation and mobilization by political actors and organizations (Bartolini and Mair 1990: 213–20).

One cleavage has proven to be particularly resilient in Western European societies and has lent the party systems a remarkable stability from the 1920s onward, making some scholars even speculate the party systems had been 'frozen' (Lipset and Rokkan 1967: 50; Mair 1997: 82). This resilient cleavage revolves around questions of economic redistribution, commonly referred to as 'class cleavage' or 'left-right cleavage'. It has been most pronounced in Northwestern Europe while it has been less manifest in Southern Europe and the countries of Central Eastern Europe (CEE) for reasons related to their regime legacies and their belated democratization (Deegan-Krause 2007; March 2012), which took place only in the second half of the 1970s in Southern European countries (with the exception of Italy) and in the 1990s in the CEE countries.

Owing to an ongoing process of social transformation that most societies have witnessed starting in the late 1960s, however, this traditional cleavage has been complemented by another critical divide within societies. Scholars have chosen different names to refer to this cleavage: e.g. 'GAL-TAN' cleavage (Hooghe et al. 2002), which is short for 'Green, Alternative, Libertarian' and 'Traditional, Authoritarian, Nationalist', or 'integration-demarcation' cleavage (Kriesi et al. 2008). As this cleavage internally divides the respective social groups pitted against each other by the class cleavage (i.e. the cleavage cuts across – or is 'cross-cutting' – the class cleavage), most scholars argue that European party competition has become two-dimensional. Central to the formation of this cultural cleavage are processes of social transformation brought about, first, by ongoing value changes among European societies and, second, by continuously accelerating levels of globalization.

In his famous account on value change, Ronald Inglehart (1977) argues that a 'silent revolution' took place in many Northwestern European countries. At the heart of this silent revolution lie the high levels of material security that shaped Western societies in the postwar period, socializing an entire generation into the absence of any existential threat to their physical and material survival, thereby naturally fuelling their interest and curiosity for so-called 'post-materialist' values like self-autonomy, the expression of preferences related to lifestyle and emancipative values, and to common goods like climate and the environment.

This silent revolution was facilitated by the occupational changes within post-industrial societies, most notably with the rise of higher education, the feminization of the labour force, increasing levels of employment in the service sector and a growing number of highly skilled, non-routine professional workers (Oesch 2006). These processes were conducive to an intergenerational value change. As the dominant mainstream parties did not take on the new demands of the postwar generation, parties from the so-called 'New Left' started to form and gain traction. This wave of the New Left lies at the heart of the formation of many Green parties across Northwestern Europe.

Closely related to the changes that gave rise to the 'silent revolution', European societies have also increasingly been subject to transformations resulting from processes of 'de-nationalization' (Zürn 1998) and globalization, more generally. Levels of exposure to globalization have greatly varied not only across European countries and the different European regions, but, importantly, also within the different countries. These varying levels of exposure to globalization have impacted individuals and their lives to different degrees, triggering different attitudinal consequences. While some individuals feel that the various aspects of globalization mostly contribute to enhance their lives, others perceive negatively of the economic and cultural changes that are responsible for rapidly transforming their environment and everyday lives.

Not only have these socio-economic benefits and risks of global and European economic integration become increasingly salient since the 1990s, with growing levels of intra-European migration and growing numbers of migrants arriving to the EU coming from third countries, the public became aware of the cultural implications of the opening-up of national boundaries, inciting political demands for a protection against the perceived perils and threats resulting from the inflow of non-native persons, ideas or traditions (Mudde 2007; Arzheimer 2018). As mainstream parties neglected these political concerns, starting from the 1980s, European party systems experienced a so-called wave of the 'New Right'. Populist radical right parties like Front National in France or the Freedom Party of Austria took on the culturally conservative policy demands of voters.

The Great Recession, the ensuing European financial crisis and the European migration crisis have put the social ramifications of European integration and globalization further in the spotlight of public attention, contributing to the politicization of related conflicts. When the governments of crisis-ridden Southern European countries were forced to implement strict austerity measures imposed by international and European donors during the sovereign debt crisis, Eurosceptic radical left challengers attracted considerable electoral support by articulating their opposition to further European market integration (Holmes and Lightfoot 2016; Kriesi 2016; March 2016; Hopkin 2020).

In Northwestern European countries, in contrast, the European financial crisis gave rise to Euroscepticism from the New Right. Its success was further fuelled by the ensuing migration crisis, which started to unfold from late 2014/early 2015 onwards and offered radical right actors ample opportunities for instrumentalizing the European project in nativist terms (Pytlas 2021). It remains unclear in what ways the experience of the Covid-19 crisis, the most recent related trends of democratic backsliding observed during the pandemic in some of the CEE countries and the expected large-scale decline of European economies resulting from the policy measures to contain the pandemic will impact party competition. The pandemic could boost the success of populist radical challengers of different types across the continent.

# The electoral decline of mainstream parties

The electoral success of mainstream parties across Europe has been on the decline, pointing to a decreasing capacity of these parties to represent voters' policy demands. This development can be traced both to the long-term structural changes and the sequential crises experienced by European countries during the 2010s (as discussed above). While the long-term changes contributed to a shrinking electoral core constituency of mainstream parties, after being part of the government during the various crises, in addition, several of these mainstream parties have also been punished by voters for their lack of sufficient accountability.

Figure 2.1 shows the vote share that mainstream parties achieved in all national elections that have been held between 1980 and 2020 across Northwestern European countries. As the figure clearly shows, the vote share of mainstream parties has been steadily decreasing across all countries in Northwestern Europe. In the majority of countries, mainstream parties achieved the highest vote share (marked points with country labels) in the decades prior to the 2000s, while their electoral performance was at an all-time low (marked points with country labels) in the national elections held since 2015.

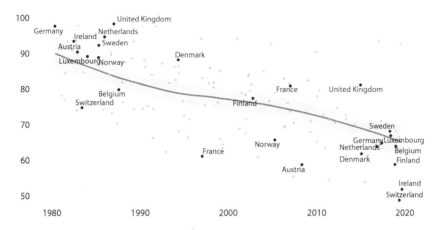

**Figure 2.1** Mainstream parties' vote share in Northwestern Europe.
Compiled from ParlGov database (Döring and Manow 2021).

The electoral fate of social democratic parties has been particularly affected by the challenges posed by social transformation across Europe. As post-industrial societies are characterized by the rise of highly skilled, non-routine workers, the traditional core clientele of social democratic parties is declining. Today, social democratic parties draw their electoral support mostly from a highly educated, new middle-class support base (Kitschelt 1994; Gingrich and Häusermann 2015). From the mid-1990s, social democratic parties emphasized supply-side economic management, balanced budget while also attaching greater salience to social liberalism and environmentalism, a strategy that has been called 'third way' or 'new middle' and is associated with the decline of social democratic parties.

While this decision on the part of social democratic parties to turn their attention to more left-libertarian issues and to endorse market integration in Europe had been motivated by an attempt to meet the demands of their new electoral support base, this approach entailed the risk, however, to further lose some of their former core electoral clientele, i.e. manual and routine workers who demanded protection from the exposure to global market competition. Feeling alienated by some of these progressive values and looking to preserve their social status against the risks of globalization and labour market competition resulting from international integration, the off-shoring of production sites in foreign countries and the influx of low-skilled production workers from third countries, these low-skilled voters increasingly opt for parties from the New Right who promote a different type of egalitarian social policy, defined exclusively in terms of citizenship

(Houtman and Derks 2008; Oesch and Rennwald 2018). As a consequence, between 2000 and 2017 most social democratic parties secured their lowest levels of support since the period of democratization in their respective countries (Benedetto et al. 2020).

# Multi-level competition in the EU and its effects on national party politics

Next to the socio-structural transformations and crises that have shaped European societies in the past decades, the multi-level structure of political competition within the European Union has also contributed to party system change across Europe. The expanding scope and breadth of European integration has contributed to an increased salience of the new cultural cleavage, thereby further decreasing the appeal of mainstream parties who mostly continue to represent voters' interests on the traditional left-right dimension of political conflict. The institution of direct elections to the European Parliament (EP) has also contributed to a process of increasing fragmentation of national party systems (Dinas and Riera 2018; Schulte-Cloos 2018). Readily coined 'second-order' national elections by scholars in response to the results of the first EP elections in 1979 (Reif and Schmitt 1980; Eijk et al. 1996), even after nine legislative rounds and a total of 175 European electoral campaigns held in the different member states, the supranational contest is still marked by lower levels of popular participation, lower campaign efforts by mainstream political parties and a related lower barrier-to-entry into the European legislature for small and newcomer parties.

Figure 2.2 shows that since the first direct elections to the European Parliament in 1979, across all three European regions, turnout has consistently been lower in the European elections than in the respective preceding national election within a given country. There are less than ten observations that reported a higher level of popular participation in the supranational elections than in the previous domestic contest. In the last European elections in 2019, the negative differential of electoral turnout in the European and national elections appears very similar across all three regions – and less pronounced than in previous European elections among

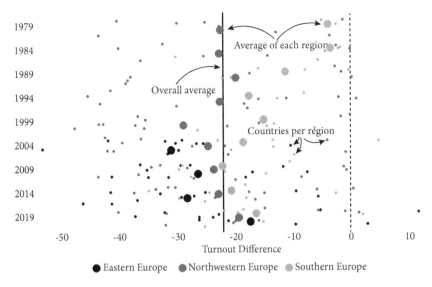

**Figure 2.2** Turnout difference between EP Elections and National Elections.
Compiled from ParlGov database (Döring and Manow 2021).

Northwestern and Eastern European countries. While turnout levels in national elections tend to greatly vary across European regions and public participation rates are much lower in CEE countries than in the rest of Europe, there is a converging trend across European regions regarding the negative differential levels of turnout in the supranational and the preceding national contests.

The lacklustre public interest in the European elections suggests that this institution, to date, has not met the objective to instil a European political identity among citizens (Tindemans 1975). While attracting little public attention and excitement, research shows that the European elections, and party politics at the European level increasingly contribute to shaping national politics and party competition at the national level (Kriesi 2016). Following their success in the EP elections, for instance, populist right parties enjoy greater visibility within national politics and manage to succeed also in domestic contests (Schulte-Cloos 2018).

The permissive electoral formula applied in the EP elections (proportional representation) also facilitated the rise of the United Kingdom Independence Party (UKIP) in the European elections, which critically added to the salience of the membership question in British domestic politics and ultimately increased a related intra-party conflict among the Conservatives to the extent that then Prime Minister Cameron promised a public referendum on this issue (Bremer and Schulte-Cloos 2019). Partisan politics at the European level also played an important role in domestic politics in Hungary. Facing the threat of electoral decline at the European level, for years, the Conservative mainstream European party group (European People's Party, EPP) had been reluctant to sharply criticize the 'democratic backsliding' and authoritarian attacks by the ruling party Fidesz of Hungarian Prime Minister Orbán, thereby contributing to stabilizing his government (Kelemen 2017).

Thus, while public interest in the EP elections remains very limited, the multi-level structure of the EU increasingly contributes to shape party competition at the national level. Notably, this works in favour of such party actors who aim to represent voters' scepticism towards European integration and their demands for a greater protection of national sovereignty.

# New challenger parties and party system fragmentation

The decline of mainstream parties and the growing demand of voters for representation of issues related to the 'new' cleavage is also evident in the trend of new parties that have formed across all three regions of Europe. As seen in Figure 2.3, the number of newly founded political parties has been steadily rising since the early 2000s. While the level of new party entry has been highest in Eastern Europe, reflecting the prevalent lower level of party system institutionalization (Kitschelt 1992; Mair 1997), Southern and Northwestern Europe also saw a notable increase in party formations in the course of the Great Recession and the subsequent European financial crisis (Hernández and Kriesi 2016). These newly formed parties include populist left parties like Podemos in Spain or Levica in Slovenia, Green parties like ORaH in Croatia or the Portuguese party 'People Animals Nature', populist right parties like the German AfD and some noteworthy anti-establishment and anti-corruption newcomers taking a liberal-centrist and somewhat populist position, like the Lithuanian National Resurrection Party or the Czech party 'Action of Dissatisfied Citizens', most frequently found in the CEE countries (Sikk 2012: 467; Engler et al. 2019).

Many Green parties across Northwestern Europe have their origins in the 1970s and early 1980s when the changing electoral demands of

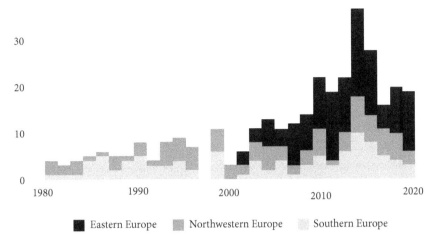

**Figure 2.3** New party formations.
Compiled from ParlGov database (Döring and Manow 2021).

voters triggered the formation of left-libertarian, so-called new social movements. Above all, these formations were concerned with 'new' issues like the protection of the environment, nuclear disarmament and a pacifistic outlook on international politics – all of which continue to represent the culturally liberal pole of party competition along the 'new' cleavage in contemporary European politics. Advancing a vision of 'new politics' and an unconventional political style, which emphasizes participatory elements in policymaking, after a period of organizational institutionalization, these Green formation mostly aligned to the left-libertarian political side of conflict (Poguntke 1987), favouring a strong social welfare state and redistribution (see also the discussion in Kitschelt (2019: 81f.) that draws attention to the initial heterogeneous activists among some of the Green formations, e.g. the German Greens).

Green formations have been less successful in the Southern European countries with a strong 'old' left and, in absence of strong post-materialistic values (Jordan 1991; Deegan-Krause 2007), they were also mostly less influential in the CEE countries with the exception of a short period of legislative representation after the end of the Communist regime (Frankland 2016). Recently, environmental concerns and environmental activism has received renewed public attention when new climate movements (e.g. the youth-led group 'Fridays for Future') mobilized several millions of young activists across different parts of Europe. This revival of environmental activism might further increase the salience of policy issues advanced by Green parties, thereby possibly fuelling their electoral success across Europe in the future.

Several authors argue that the expansion of progressive values and ideas and their institutional and legislative representation through Green and left-libertarian parties has nurtured its own backlash and provoked a cultural counter-reaction among parts of the electorate (Ignazi 1992; Bornschier 2010; Norris and Inglehart 2019). This counter-reaction is directed against the growing cultural diversity in modern European societies, rising numbers of immigrants and asylum seekers, an erosion of national identities and oftentimes also against membership in the European Union. Such culturally conservative sentiments resonate among individuals who feel threatened and alienated by the rapid progression of cultural change and demand the return to a less diverse, ethnically and ideationally more homogeneous and traditionalist society (Rydgren 2008).

In recent scholarly accounts, the rise of the radical right across Europe has also been attributed to the unevenly distributed economic benefits and risks resulting from globalization and automation. Studying variation in support for the withdrawal from the EU during the 'Brexit' referendum in the UK, Colantone and Stanig (2018) finds that support for 'Leave', indicative of support for the prevalence of populist right sentiments across the British population, is a function of import shocks from China experienced by certain regions. The experience of local economic deprivation, thus, appears also critical to understand voters' populist right sentiments (see also Jackman and Volpert 1996 for a comparative account studying cross-country variation in radical right support and economic conditions at the macro-level). The picture seems to be somewhat more mixed in settings of multi-party competition and electoral choice in proportionally representative (PR) systems, where recent analyses suggest that support for populist right parties is not only a function of exposure to economic aspects of globalization (import shocks and disruption of the local economy) but also of exposure to the cultural aspects of globalization (immigration inflows) (Caselli et al. 2020).

# Crisis of representation and challenger parties in government

The rise of challenger parties across Europe is an expression of the changing socio-structural cleavages in society. Yet, in addition to these socio-structural transformations, voters' political grievances also contribute decisively to the electoral success of challenger parties. These political grievances are inherently linked to the declining representative capacity of party systems in Western Europe (Mudde 2004; Kriesi 2014). Mainstream parties have mostly neglected the substantive 'new' demands of voters or started to integrate these demands into their policy profiles belatedly. This usually happened in response to the evident electoral success of a challenger party or under a non-negligible public pressure (Abou-Chadi and Krause 2018).

The unresponsiveness of mainstream parties has nurtured anti-elitist sentiments and political disaffection among voters that contribute decisively to the success of populist challenger parties (Lubbers et al. 2002; Akkerman et al. 2014; Caramani 2017). These sentiments lie at the heart of a 'crisis of representation' across Europe that has increasingly been subject to scholarly attention, focusing on the success of populist parties and the implications for party choice and party competition across Europe (see the contributions by Piattoni and de Jonge in this volume).

Recent research studies the conditions under which parties from the radical left and the radical right can benefit from such populist sentiments (Kriesi and Schulte-Cloos 2020). For example, Hanspeter Kriesi and I looked at the relationship between political disaffection and voting for a radical left or radical right party in fifteen European countries, located mostly in the north-west. We find that political distrust only drives a vote for these parties when they are excluded from government. In contrast, when the parties are represented in cabinet their supporters are no less distrustful than supporters of mainstream parties. Thus, voters' political disaffection appears to partly originate in the failure of mainstream parties to integrate their substantive demands into policymaking.

The representation of new challenger parties in government might contribute to mitigate voters' political disaffection. Figure 2.4 shows the representation of Green, populist left, populist right and populist centrist parties in government from 1980 to 2020 across countries. The graph highlights two complementary observations. It shows that government participation of these challenger parties still remains the exception. Yet, Figure 2.4 also suggests that challenger parties have been represented in political office more frequently in recent decades. In addition, their relative size in the cabinet has increased, which can be seen by the strength of the shading in Figure 2.4. Scholars still have to understand the long-term effects that the government participation of challenger parties have for the political satisfaction of their voters and their populist and anti-elitist sentiments.

But even when government participation is still an unlikely outcome, voters might be motivated to electorally participate when a challenger party

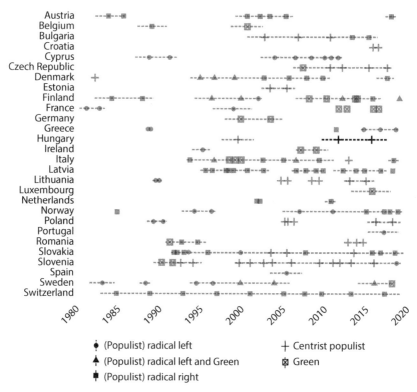

**Figure 2.4** Challenger parties' government participation.

Compiled from ParlGov database (Döring and Manow 2021); Wikipedia.

that claims to represent their substantive demands runs in an election. Schulte-Cloos and Leininger (2022) show that the German populist radical right AfD significantly benefits from the electoral mobilization of those parts of the electorate who display high levels of political disaffection at a time prior to the existence of the party.

# Conclusion

How did European party systems transform over the past decades, what has been driving these changes and what are the resulting consequences of these transformations for patterns of electoral competition and the representation of citizens' interests? This chapter began from the notion that in the representative model of democracy, parties are central to articulating and representing voters' political demands. Mainstream parties who previously used to represent the interests of a majority of citizens across Europe have lost much of their electoral appeal in response to both ongoing processes of socio-structural transformation of societies and to the integration of member states into the European multi-level structure. These two developments have been coupled with the sequential experience of the European sovereign debt crisis, the migration crisis and the Covid-19 crisis.

During these various crises, voters in some European states have perceived governing mainstream parties as unresponsive to their demands. This put the representative model of democracy further under pressure and increased the salience of issues related to the 'new' cultural dimension of political conflict. Such new electoral demands have been articulated most successfully by challenger parties, resulting in legislative and executive representation of these parties in all parts of Europe. Many challenger parties adopt a populist and anti-system discourse to appeal to voters. In doing so, they capitalize on the political dissatisfaction of parts of the electorate and the political grievances that some citizens harbour while feeling unrepresented by the established political mainstream parties. Future trends of party competition and political representation across Europe also depend on challenger parties' capacities to sustain lasting electoral ties to the voters.

# Questions for discussion

1 Which processes contributed to mainstream parties losing some of their representative capacity?
2 What characterizes voters' apparent 'new' demands for political representatives?
3 What consequences can we expect Europe's multi-level governing system to have for party competition?
4 Under which conditions are challenger parties likely to build lasting ties with the electorate?

# Recommended for Further Reading

Betz, H. G. (1994) *Radical Right-Wing Populism in Western Europe*. Basingstoke and London: Macmillan.

Hooghe, L. and Marks, G. (2018) 'Cleavage Theory Meets Europe's Crises: Lipset, Rokkan, and the Transnational Cleavage', *Journal of European Public Policy* 25(1): 109–35.

Inglehart, R. (2007) 'Postmaterialist Values and the Shift from Survival to Self-Expression Values', in J. Dalton and H.-D. Klingemann (eds), *The Oxford Handbook of Political Behavior*, 223–39. Oxford: Oxford University Press.

Kriesi, H., Grande, E., Lachat, R., Dolezal, M., Bornschier, S. and Frey, T. (2006) 'Globalization and the Transformation of the National Political Space: Six European Countries Compared', *European Journal of Political Research* 45(6): 921–56.

Lipset, S. M. and Rokkan, S. (1967) 'Cleavage Structures, Party Systems, and Voter Alignments: An Introduction'. In S. M. Lipset and S. Rokkan (eds), *Party Systems and Voter Alignments: Cross-National Perspectives*, 1–64. New York: Free Press.

# 3

# Local Governance and Local Communities in Europe

*Jennifer Fitzgerald*

Some European localities are world-famous and connote dramatic historical images: Budapest, Hungary, Dublin, Ireland, Paris, France, Prague, Czech Republic,.... In contrast, most local communities in these same countries are significantly less conspicuous: Iborfia, Ventry, Saint Chrisoly-de-Blaye, Vysoká Lhota.... Whether big or small, bustling or sleepy, or somewhere in between, the diverse collection of Europe's local communities serve as the foundational building blocks of society across the continent.

Local governments constitute the lowest level of legally empowered political administration; they are the part of the state that sits closest to the people. Their responsibilities typically include service delivery in the areas of health care, education, housing, policing and infrastructure. These policy spheres have major implications for people on a day-to-day basis, and policy design and administration at the local level can even make the difference between life and death. Therefore, learning about local governance is essential for understanding European politics and the functioning of democracy more broadly.

Accordingly, in a shift from the typical media attention on national political figures, leaders of Europe's local communities featured prominently in the news in 2020 when the Covid-19 pandemic first swept the continent. The virus put many town mayors in the international spotlight for their various efforts to keep their citizens healthy.

Italy was particularly hard hit by the virus from the beginning, and Italian mayors' tirades against residents who were defying local quarantine orders drew journalistic attention and turned into an internet sensation. *The New York Times* summarized these mayoral efforts: 'They have launched insult-armed drones. They have personally confronted scofflaws on the streets. They have mocked women for getting their hair done because no one would see them in their closed caskets. They have asked all their dog-walking citizens if their pets had prostate problems' (Horowitz 2020). Local government leaders have played an outsized role during the pandemic, providing a poignant example of the ways small-scale governance can have global implications.

Localities may not usually make worldwide headlines, but their effect on people's lives make them essential to study and understand. Furthermore, recent studies trace the connections between local contexts and dramatic political outcomes such as the rise of populism (Rodríguez-Pose 2020; Patana 2021) and challenges to the EU's integrity via the Brexit referendum (Fitzgerald 2018; Olivas Osuna et al. 2021). These considerations of the importance of local politics motivates this chapter. It explores the contours of local governance across European countries, identifying variations on key dimensions, highlighting common trends and paying attention to the ways individuals relate to their local communities. Notably, this chapter considers the ways that local structures and local feelings shape the living conditions of Romani people in Europe.

By integrating knowledge about local politics, we gain insight into current challenges of bringing different groups together in society. Recognizing the importance and diversity of local governance in Europe yields an important corrective to what has been called 'methodological nationalism' – or the taken-for-granted notion that the national level represents the natural arena for the study of politics (Chou 2020). By taking the local seriously, this chapter puts a continental spin on former American Speaker of the House Tip O'Neil's famous adage: 'all politics is local'.

# Designing local institutions: the great debate

As with all things political, questions of how local governance should be structured evoke a lively set of debates. The main lines of controversy centre on the optimal number, size and autonomy level for local units. Consider two stylized combinations of these features. System A is a country divided into many small local units, each with minimal political authority. System B represents a country with the opposite traits: relatively few, large localities with significant political autonomy. These features entail stark trade-offs with weighty implications.

In favour of a type-A system with a greater number of small local units is the 'small is beautiful' argument. It hinges on the concept of closeness: small-scale community in which governing authority resides in close proximity to the people – some argue – is essential for democracy to function (Dahl 1967; Dahl and Tufte 1973). In contrast to the ways citizens may relate remotely to their national parliamentarians or heads of state, many village, town and city-dwellers are personally acquainted with their local mayors or council members and are directly engaged in community life (Bhatti and Hansen 2019). When people have access to their leaders and when those leaders have specific knowledge of what their communities need, services can be tailored and flexible.

Smaller-scale governance is also quite popular, enhancing citizens' trust in institutions, feelings of representation and support for democracy (Matsubayashi 2007). Moreover, people tend to feel very connected to and proud of their local communities, a concept known as localism. Positive externalities of localism include better mental health, mutual economic aid among neighbours, low crime rates and environmental sustainability (Putnam 1993; Hirschfield and Bowers 1997; Bess et al. 2002; Uzzell et al. 2002; Callois and Aubert 2007).

The competing argument advocates for type-B systems. It is known as the 'bigger is better' argument; fewer, larger governing units – some argue – come with significant advantages. Notably, public service delivery is more efficient where the scale of governance is greater (see Alesina and Spolaore 2003; Blom-Hansen et al. 2014). The logic is that by pursuing economies of scale, local governments can better provide key public services. Larger governing units also have a greater pool of skilled, specialized personnel as well as more funds to do the business of governing.

There is also evidence that larger local units draw higher levels of democratic turnout in elections because there is 'more at stake' (Gendzwill 2019). Furthermore, larger local units tend to have weaker levels of localism. Though some benefits of localism are detailed above, other research reveals drawbacks: when people are too fervently connected to their local communities, society at large suffers from social fragmentation, distrust in national authorities, market inefficiencies, anti-minority attitudes and far-right extremism (Winter 2003; DuPuis and Goodman 2005; Green and White 2007; Fitzgerald 2018).

Over time in Europe, most countries have redesigned their state structures, progressively enlarging and empowering local administrative units to look more like type-B than type-A systems. They have done this through two key processes:

1 amalgamation creates new, larger local governing units out of smaller, pre-existing ones; and,
2 devolution is the shift in formal authority from higher units of governance (typically the national level) to lower units, empowering local authorities.

These changes have major implications for citizens, and so continually reflecting on the relative merits of different systems of local power is important.

# Local institutions in Europe

The study of local governance typically focuses on *municipalities*, which are in most countries the lowest administrative units within the hierarchies of state authority structures. Municipal units in Europe are grouped into a diverse set of intermediary administrative units known as counties, provinces, departments or regions. So while municipal governments are not the only authorities operating beneath national governments, they tend to offer the most direct opportunities for democratic self-rule. One way to compare across countries is to consider the number of municipal units. At the high end, France is made up of over 36,000 municipalities. On the other side of the spectrum is Lithuania with sixty municipal units. A survey of European countries reveals no simple cross-national pattern; the number of localities does not seem to correlate with geographic location, wealth, population or territorial size of a country.

Dividing national populations (United Nations 2019) by their number of municipal entities (vom Hove et al. 2019) can expand our understanding of just how close local governments are to the governed in numeric terms. There is enormous variation across European countries on this factor, as well. Czech Republic has the lowest average number of residents per municipality with approximately 1,700. Denmark, in contrast, has nearly 60,000 residents per municipality. (The Czech population in 2019 was 10,689,209; the country has 6,258 municipal units. Denmark's 2019 population was 5,771,876; they have 98 municipalities.)

A third angle on variation across countries is the level of authority held by individual local governments. This, too, varies greatly from one European country to another and in certain cases within countries as well. As noted in this chapter's introductory section, local governments typically take the lead on policy arenas such as health care, primary education, policing and housing as well as local transportation, environment, recreation and culture. Furthermore, countries differ on the extent to which localities are empowered to tax, spend and make policy as well as elect their own community leaders.

Levels of local autonomy can be measured in a number of ways. For instance, the Organization for Economic Cooperation and Development (OECD) reports tax authority levels as the percentage of total government expenditure that is spent by localities. This measurement strategy has the advantage of being quite straightforward and thus readily comparable across countries. High levels of local expenditures denote the weight and volume of local service responsibilities relative to those of other government levels.

Another metric is the Local Autonomy Index (LAI), designed by Ladner and Keuffer (2021). The LAI combines a broad range of factors that signify independence of local communities. These include: policy scope (number of different service areas for which local governments have responsibility), organizational freedoms (localities can design their own political systems), political discretion (ability to make decisions about the services localities provide), as well as fiscal authority.

Table 3.1 displays the levels of local autonomy for twenty-six European countries on the basis of these two measures. Looking closely at the comparative patterns of local fiscal autonomy on the left side of the table: Greek local governments have the least spending autonomy at 7.5 per cent, meaning that only 7.5 per cent of total government expenditures are spent by the local governments. In contrast, Danish municipalities have the highest amount of spending power, with control over more than 60 per cent of government expenditures (OECD 2018). The gap between Denmark and its Scandinavian neighbours – all of which rank high on this scale – is striking. It represents the intentional reforms of the Danish government to make local units chiefly responsible for the well-being of their citizens.

Turning to the LAI index, displayed on the right half of Table 3.1, we see a very similar ranking of local autonomy levels across countries. Yet some countries move several positions from the left side to the right side of the

**Table 3.1** Local autonomy measures and rankings (highest to lowest)

| Fiscal spending authority level | | Local authority index | |
|---|---|---|---|
| Denmark | 63.6 | Switzerland | 78.9 |
| Sweden | 50.4 | Finland | 78.5 |
| Finland | 40.1 | Iceland | 78.0 |
| Norway | 33.9 | Sweden | 77.7 |
| Poland | 33.9 | Germany | 73.3 |
| Iceland | 31.4 | Denmark | 72.5 |
| Netherlands | 30.6 | Poland | 72.3 |
| Czech Republic | 28.8 | France | 69.6 |
| Italy | 27.5 | Norway | 69.0 |
| Latvia | 27.1 | Austria | 67.8 |
| Estonia | 24.1 | Estonia | 65.9 |
| Lithuania | 23.8 | Spain | 65.8 |
| United Kingdom | 23.0 | Czech Republic | 65.2 |
| Switzerland | 20.5 | Luxembourg | 63.1 |
| France | 19.4 | Hungary | 62.7 |
| Slovenia | 19.3 | Portugal | 62.5 |
| Germany | 17.4 | Italy | 59.4 |
| Slovak Republic | 16.9 | Lithuania | 57.8 |
| Austria | 15.4 | Belgium | 57.2 |
| Belgium | 13.3 | Slovak Republic | 56.1 |
| Hungary | 13.2 | Netherlands | 54.6 |
| Portugal | 13.2 | Latvia | 53.7 |
| Spain | 11.5 | Greece | 52.8 |
| Luxembourg | 11.1 | United Kingdom | 47.4 |
| Ireland | 8.9 | Slovenia | 46.2 |
| Greece | 7.5 | Ireland | 36.2 |

Note: Fiscal spending is a percentage of government spending at the local level (source: OECD 2018). Local authority index is an eleven-item measure including policy, political and financial autonomy (source: Ladner and Keuffer 2021).

figure. In Switzerland, for instance, the amount of government expenditures spent by municipalities ranks in the middle of the scale, but it has the greatest level of authority in terms of decisions over how to spend those funds across a wide range of policy areas. This second metric aligns with conventional understandings of Switzerland as one of the most decentralized political systems in the world.

Still, these two measures provide a relatively consistent measure of local autonomy levels; they are correlated with one another at.88 (a perfect correlation would be 1.0). The table's grouping – with the most empowered localities near the top – is quite consistent from the left to the right side of the table. Yet this similarity across measures of local autonomy does not address changes over time, to which we now turn.

# Trends in local governance: devolution and amalgamation

With a sense of the number, size and strength of European countries' local governments as they stand today, it is also important to consider some major municipal trends that have been unfolding over time. Devolution of authority to local levels of governance has been ongoing in many European countries. In the UK, for instance, the Localism Act of 2011 devolved new roles to local governments and empowered local communities in expanded areas of policymaking. In Scandinavia, too, progressive downward shifts in fiscal authority have empowered local governments in recent decades. In Finland and Sweden, the percentage of government spending controlled by local authorities has increased markedly in recent years. Some Eastern European countries, such as Latvia, have engaged in fiscal decentralization to local units, while others such as Hungary have taken the opposite approach and curtailed fiscal powers of localities in recent decades. From 1995 to 2018, the fiscal autonomy of Latvian localities grew from 19 to 27 per cent while the trend in Hungary was a decline from 23 to 13 per cent (OECD 2018).

Municipal amalgamation – also known as municipal merging – is a process through which local governing units are combined to create new, larger municipal units. For the constitutive localities, this means a loss of formal authority which is transferred to the novel, combined municipal units (Steiner 2003).

Switzerland is a country that has engaged in municipal amalgamation over time. In 1848 Switzerland was composed of 3,208 municipalities (called communes), and as of 2019 there were 2,740. Some of these mergers were voluntary; others were mandated. Notably, unpopular mergers can spur sharp public resentment and provoke far-right extremist backlashes (Fitzgerald 2018).

In contrast to Switzerland's incremental approach, Denmark engaged in amalgamation at a rapid pace. Per the 2007 governmental reforms, the number of Danish municipalities went from 275 to 98. Denmark represents a case where amalgamation and devolution have gone hand in hand. If we consider the debates over how local governance should be organized, we can see that Denmark has applied a strategy aimed at maximizing economies of scale through the creation of relatively large municipal units that are also highly empowered. As such, the Danish government is moving along the continuum between a type-A small is beautiful system to a type-B bigger is better model with all the pros and cons that can accompany such a shift.

# Citizens and their local communities

Armed with knowledge of some key dimensions of local governance in Europe, we can move on to examine the ways people relate to their local communities. A central concept to explore is the extent to which people feel a sense of belonging to their localities. Studying people's connections to their local areas can help to shed light on the perspective of regular people when it comes to small-scale politics.

There is not a great deal of research on local attachments in European countries. Political scientists have instead devoted significant attention to differing levels of *national* ties in different countries, and so we use this phenomenon as a comparative baseline to gauge local sentiments. The most recent European Values Survey (EVS 2017) illuminates patterns of national and local ties across countries. The survey asks: 'People have different views about themselves and how they relate to the world... would you tell me how close do you feel to...[Your village, town or city]?' It then replicates this root question, offering instead [Your country] in place of the local option. The response options for both survey items are: 'very close', 'close', 'not very close' and 'not close at all'.

Figure 3.1 plots closeness to localities (on the horizontal axis) and closeness to national communities (on the vertical axis). Each dot on the figure represents the combination of two percentages (percentage of survey participants in each country who answered either 'very close' or 'close' to the local attachment question and percentage of survey participants in each country who answered either 'very close' or 'close' to the national attachment question) for a single country. The dashed trend line represents the average relationship between these two measures across countries; countries below the line have particularly high levels of local attachment relative to national attachments. Countries above the line have especially high affinities for their country relative to their local communities. Note that most of the countries sit in the upper-right quadrant of the grid; local attachments are generally stronger than national affinities in Europe.

Comparing local attachments to national attachments, some countries have higher levels of national closeness while others have higher levels of local closeness. Notably, France, Iceland, Denmark and Finland host more national than local attachment on average. The opposite patterns of greater local ties as compared to national ones can be seen in Albania, Italy, Bosnia and Herzgovina (B&H) and Spain. Albanians stand out at as having the widest gap between feeling close to the localities over the nation, leaning strongly toward their local communities. Per the same World Values Survey,

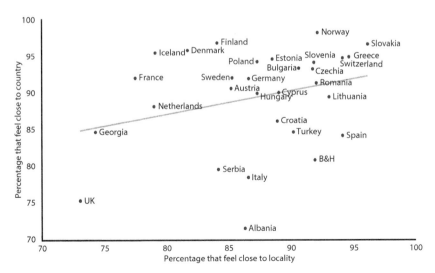

**Figure 3.1** Feeling close to local and national communities.

Compiled from European Values Survey, Wave 7, 2017–2020.

Albanians are the most likely among all of these European populations to say that they 'always' vote in local elections (a whopping 77.4 per cent of Albanian respondents declared this).

Looking more carefully at citizens' affinities for their local communities, some relevant studies point to a gendered dimension. European women have greater confidence in local governments than men do, and women also view local governments more favourably than national governments (Fitzgerald and Wolak 2016). Similarly, women tend to know more about local politics while men tend to know more about national politics (Verba et al. 1997). Women are also increasingly elected to local leadership roles in Europe; the percentage of mayors who are women increased in almost every country from 2008 to 2018. Among EU countries, Slovakia had the highest proportion of female mayors (over 35 per cent) as of 2018 (Tskhelishvili et al. 2019).

# Cooperation and conflict in localities

Local communities are the places where different kinds of groups in a society come into direct contact with each other. This means that such spaces can offer great opportunities for inter-group cooperation, but some localities host significant levels of social discord. This is particularly the case when members of defined local groups perceive that they are in competition with one another for jobs, public services, housing or amorphous dimensions of social status. Localized conflicts are made more or less likely based on their institutional arrangements and the ways residents feel about their communities.

A survey of research into the likelihood of friction between social groups in a local arena points to the importance of institutional factors and structures on one hand and public feelings on the other. Perhaps no single minority group in Europe is more affected by local-level institutions and localized sentiments than the Roma. Also known as Romani or Romany, Roma are an ethnic group that migrated from Southeast Asia to Europe from the sixth to the eleventh centuries. They are Europe's largest minority ethnic group, numbering approximately twelve million. They are also known for their collective experience of social exclusion, stigmatization, poverty and discrimination. Historically they have made Central and Eastern Europe home, but millions also live in Eastern and Northern Europe.

Local governance and local sentiments play a profound role in shaping the treatment and destinies of Roma across Europe. This is in part the case because the strains faced by Roma communities require the kinds of services that are at the heart of local governments' responsibilities. For instance, Roma are disproportionately affected by poor-quality water, sanitation and hygiene services. Roma are also often characterized by 'low socioeconomic status, low level of formal education and schooling… and a seminomadic lifestyle' (Anthonj et al. 2020: 11).

While the European Union has mandated that its member states develop policies to aid and integrate their Roma populations, some of the most critical decisions related to basic infrastructure, housing, education and health fall to local governments. Research on a Roma community in Slovakia highlights some of these local policy challenges and their serious implications:

> Vrakovce is a small village located along the main highway connecting two regional towns. A Roma neighbourhood is located in a small valley on the outskirts and overlooking the village. Similar to other cases, no house is connected to a water supply and the main water source is a single water conduit serving the community of 500 people… There [are] no sewage services and wooded pit latrines are dug and erected near the houses on the hilltop. Sewage and human excrements [mix] here with mud and the situation is appalling, especially during the rainy autumn period.
>
> (Filčák et al. 2018: 6)

Basic decisions for action or inaction on the part of local governments can have life and death consequences for Roma and other vulnerable local residents. Notably, Roma residents are rarely represented on local councils, exacerbating the shortfall between their communities' physical, social and economic needs and local governments' success in addressing them (Škobla and Filčák 2016).

This lack of representation for ethnic minorities like the Roma is the case even in some of the world's wealthiest countries. Amnesty International summarizes the situation for Roma in Sweden:

> Thousands of Roma face a constant struggle for food, sanitation and health care. In winter, when temperatures plummet, this becomes a struggle for survival… Harassment, discriminatory treatment by the police and the failure of Swedish authorities to recognize the rights of these EU migrants and address their basic needs echoes a wider anti-Roma prejudice, discrimination and racism that persists across Europe.
>
> (Amnesty International 2018)

Conflicts over local space, local resources and Romas' very presence in many local communities have fuelled far-right parties from Timişoara, Romania (Creţan and O'Brien 2019) to Chatham, UK (Smith 2018) through localist mechanisms. In more extreme instances, physical attacks on Roma have occurred across Europe. For instance, a rash of physical aggressions against Roma in outlying areas of metropolitan Paris in 2019 (Vitale 2019) and in Waterford, Ireland in 2014 (Costello 2014) made headlines for their ferocity.

These societal rifts fall upon local governments to address, as do the strains faced by many Roma groups. The Covid-19 pandemic has brought anti-Roma sentiment to a fever pitch in some parts of Europe, as they are disproportionately blamed for spreading the virus. Media reports detail the particularly harsh treatment Roma have suffered as Covid-19 scapegoats, while also being especially hard-hit by the virus (see, for instance, Walker 2020).

The lives of Roma in Europe are in many ways shaped by local governance and local communities. Moreover, because local spaces serve as the backdrop for inter-group relations, public sentiments among non-Roma also shape the ways groups are able to either cooperate or engage in conflict with each other.

Looking backward in this chapter, each of the highlighted dimensions of variation across countries is relevant for Roma. The number of municipalities signifies the number of possible different approaches and policies implemented by local authorities in relation to Roma. A greater number of municipalities tasked with Roma welfare, for instance, can mean inefficiency, inequality and confusions about responsibility across localities (per type-A systems) (Lane and Smith 2021). Municipalities with few residents and small tax bases tend to also have local leadership that lacks the qualifications or experience necessary to oversee critical service delivery (Guga 2017).

Devolution of authority to municipalities (per type-B systems) renders municipal governments increasingly responsible for the welfare of residents, including Roma, but oftentimes these shifts in power are not accompanied by the fiscal resources necessary to govern effectively (Sellers and Lidström 2012). Municipal amalgamation may serve as a corrective to some of these challenges by creating larger local units, but it can also inflame and politicize localism and sharpen friction between social groups (Fitzgerald 2018).

# Conclusion

Local community governance represents a complex but vital topic in studies of European politics. When we overturn the typical top-down, nationally based view of political institutions and consider the local first, novel understandings and viewpoints emerge. This chapter has provided comparative data on a range of institutional and behavioural dimensions of local politics, weighing some of the pros and cons of each. It also invites readers to consider the ways in which these formal structures and informal sentiments shape life at the local level, particularly for a highly vulnerable population: Roma.

The Covid-19 crisis posed a series of significant challenges for Europe's local communities as they struggled to support residents' well-being. Accompanying the direct threat of the virus itself came unemployment, insufficient food access and diminished public service provision in many corners of Europe. Yet the crisis also created new opportunities for comparative analysis of local politics. Since the virus was an exogenous factor that affected all cities, towns and villages, the local-level reactions of political leaders and citizens can teach us a great deal about the functioning of local politics.

Returning to the theme of Italian mayors that opened this chapter, some were more successful than others in addressing residents' needs for food access in the midst of the pandemic (Cattivelli and Rusciano 2020). Similarly, journalistic accounts suggest that where elected leaders in Italy and other countries fell short on this measure, action came from citizens' groups and even in some cases Mafioso organizations (Bettiza 2020). This diversity of Covid-19 responses provides researchers an opportunity to examine how well different local structures and societies function in the face of a common threat like a pandemic. Such an inquiry stands to bring more locally oriented facts and phenomena to light, in search of better policies, enhanced well-being, and ultimately stronger democracies.

# Questions for discussion

1   Why do some people feel more attached to their communities than others? Are there individual-level, community-level and/or national-level factors that you think might shape people's feelings in this regard?

2  Under what conditions could a local mayor bring different groups in their community together? What could justify the accumulation of more formal authority in the hands of local elites?
3  Should local communities be responsible for addressing urgent public issues such as the Covid-19 pandemic? Consider arguments in favour and against this policy.
4  A different level of community in Europe not covered in this chapter is the sub-national region, situated between the national state and the local municipality. In many cases, these regions seek additional autonomy – if not outright independence – from their central governments. Examples are Scotland in the UK and Catalonia in Spain. How might the themes in this chapter relate to such independence movements and to the residents of such regions?

# Recommended for Further Reading

Chou, M., Moffitt, B. and Bunsbridge, R.(2021) 'The Localist Turn in Populism Studies', *Swiss Political Science Review*, 6 November. https://doi.org/10.1111/spsr.12490.

Gagnon, A. (2021) 'Constructed Attitudes toward the Roma: A French Case', *Canadian Journal of Political Science* 53 (4) (24 February). https://doi.org/10.1017/S0008423920001110.

Strebel, M. and Kübler, D. (2021) 'Citizen Attitudes toward Local Autonomy', *Comparative European Politics* 19: 188–207.

Schulte-Cloos, J. and Bauer, P. (2021) 'Local Candidates, Place-Based Identities, and Electoral Success', *Political Behavior* (31 May). https://doi.org/10.1007/s11109-021-09712-y.

Sunier, T. (2021) 'Islam, locality and Trust: Making Muslim Spaces in the Netherlands', *Ethnic and Racial Studies* 44(10): 1734–54.

# 4

# Informal Institutions: The World's Open Secrets

## Veronica Anghel

Informal institutions shape regimes, elite decision-making and citizen behaviour. Politics – in the formal sense – would not work if informal institutions did not exist. But what are informal institutions? Identifying them turns out to be a complicated task. Compared to formal institutions, such as parliaments, parties, elections or constitutions, informal institutions are not coded in writing. Nevertheless, constitutions, party charters, party manifestos and electoral rules are not alone in structuring people's behaviour. Individuals perpetuate unofficial widely known patterns that also organize behaviour. These collective norms and practices generate informal institutions. Because they are unofficial and unwritten, informal institutions have a less concrete and therefore less readily observable existence. That makes them harder to study.

The formal rules that generate political institutions tell us how politics is supposed to work, what is possible and what is not. The problem is that you cannot write a rule for every occasion. The realm of shared informality instructs what to do in such circumstances. Informal institutions are the world's open secrets. Examples of informal rules that also govern politicians and citizens' behaviour may be the peaceful transition of power, civil disobedience, charity or corruption. People know them and use them. They are useful to organize societies, but they have also been linked to slower rates of development. For this reason, informal institutions may be a problem and a solution. Think about the network of favours politicians do for their constituents and the loyalty they expect at the ballot box. Imagine the relationships politicians have with the people who finance their campaigns. Consider the incentives expected by bureaucrats in some systems to overcome the red tape.

The world of informal institutions is vast. It is also vitally important. By acknowledging their largely overlooked influence, we can reframe many expectations associated with the creation and adoption of formal rules. In the context of European politics, this endeavour may also explain the failure of universal packages aimed at improving the quality of governance (Petrova 2021) or democracy (Agh 1999). We can also systemically analyse certain patterned behaviours of political elites at the local level (Kelemen 2017), national level (Klima 2020) and supranational level (Christiansen and Neuhold 2013) that parallel formalized institutions.

Increasing concern with informal aspects of politics is timely. In the past decade, Europe witnessed a decline in the authority of traditional formal institutions and an increase in anti-establishment sentiments (Hobolt 2016). Political parties, parliaments and the confines of the liberal-legal order more widely experienced a dilution of authority and saw their legitimacy called into question by different groups of people (Schulte-Cloos, this volume). Some European politicians and members of the public found the offers of far-right groups appealing (de Jonge, this volume). Others withdrew from participation because of the inadequacy of the existing political offer (Cammaerts et al. 2014).

With the advent of the Covid-19 pandemic, interactions between the legal framework, political players and the public grew even more in complexity and changed in unknown directions (Jones 2020). Governments responded to new challenges with democratic or authoritarian innovations. And yet some organizational features of societies persist even as the efficiency of formal institutions is either called into question or their democratizing role is deliberately subverted by certain groups. What lies beneath the surface is the territory of informal institutions. Informal institutions regularly step up to compliment, substitute or challenge formally organized structures (Lauth 2000). This makes them extremely influential and resilient actors that current research does not systematically account for.

This chapter discusses the benefits and the risks of informal institutions from the perspective of their inherent tensions with formal institutions, their efficiency and their role for democracy. I continue with an overview of how formal and informal institutions interact. The second part looks at the informal institutions from the perspective of efficiency. The third investigates their nuanced role for democracy. The conclusion follows.

# The limitations of formal institutions

How do informal institutions interact with formal institutions? A recent example of differentiated outcomes under the pressure of similar formal institutions can be seen in the stalled democratization process of some Eastern European member states (Schimmelfennig and Winzen 2017; Anghel 2020). In the early 2000s, aspiring EU member states were considered to have made great advances in aligning national legislation to the *acquis communautaire* (Kelley 2004; Vachudova 2005). New members' post-accession compliance with EU law overshadowed that of older members (Sedelmeier 2011). Beyond adopting formal rules, we can nevertheless observe a discrepancy between the behavioural norms of formal institutions and the actual behaviour of individuals who accepted and populated these institutions.

In countries such as Poland, Hungary, Romania and Bulgaria the basic tenets of EU membership and national constitutions, such as the separation of powers and the independence of the judiciary are formally guaranteed, but are also subverted by informal institutions, such as corruption and clientelism. The challenges faced by states in the European Union's territory to the East when consolidating formal democratic institutions has fuelled a now decade-long debate on democratic backsliding (Cianetti et al. 2018; Vachudova 2020), with authors maintaining the EU works on a tacitly accepted rule of authoritarian equilibrium (Kelemen 2020). Recent research has underlined that, despite the formal commitment of some aspiring members to EU membership rules, the behaviour of decision-makers showed less devotion to fully embracing such demands (Anghel and Jones 2021).

Countries in the Western Balkans appear to embrace a similar approach to interpreting formal rules and show that multiple legislative changes are not implemented there either (Gordy and Efendic 2019). Building on its experience with the new members, the European Commission (2020) released a new methodology on EU enlargement and emphasized credibility in *acquis* implementation as one of the core principles by which to measure progress in the region's bid to join the EU.

Such context-driven observations substantiate criticism of initial institutionalist assumptions of concurrence between the expectations of behaviour inherent within institutions and actual individual behaviour.

March and Olsen (2010) summarized the need to bring back context into institutional analysis, as the transformation of institutions is uncontrollable, based on 'highly contextualized combinations of people, choice opportunities, problems, and solutions' (80). Neo-institutionalism, and in particular the rational choice institutionalist perspective, offers the possibility to structure an analysis of the tension between formal and informal institutions. The consequence is a better identification of missing ingredients – the behaviour of individual political actors and the patterns of collective action within political institutions. This helps us make better sense of real-life observations of how individual actors react to formal and informal institutional constraints relative to their interests. It also encourages us to step away from the assumption that formal institutions alone can guarantee efficiency.

In the context of a state, informal institutions have functional and dysfunctional roles. While unsanctioned by the state, they do have a differentiated relationship with the state and meet different functions, at times overlapping those of formal institutions. They may also have nuanced or different roles depending on the point in time of democratic consolidation. In developed democracies, where rule of law is consolidated, it has been argued these are complimentary, substitutive or conflicting (Lauth 2000). Austria's informal rule that the president will never dismiss the chancellor, despite a constitutional provision that allows for it, is a complementary informal institution. The Sicilian Mafia's offers of private protection conflict with weak law-enforcement institutions in Italy (Buonanno et al. 2015). A substitutive informal institution is functionally equivalent with a formal one, as it could be in the case of a religious charity doing the work of social services. Efforts to conceptualize such research have shown progress (Helmke and Levitsky 2006; Voigt 2018), and yet, empirical testing ($n \geq 1$) needs to catch up with formal theory ($n=0$). The Global Encyclopaedia of Informality is a starting point to archive and categorize informality on a grand scale (Ledeneva 2018).

# The efficiency of informal institutions

Once we observe the limitations of formal constraints to govern all political outcomes, the following question arises: how efficient are these informal institutions in improving the quality of citizens' lives? In the case of new democracies, informal institutions were expected to have an enhanced role during periods of transition, as temporary substitutes for functional formal institutions (Elster et al. 1998). An OECD working paper justifies their importance in poor countries because people 'are often ill-served by the limited formal institutions available' (Jutting 2003: 11).

In post-communist Eastern Europe, informal institutions were enabled by non-state networks and organizations. Charity was organized through religious-based social actions and worked as a substitute for social services. Entrepreneurial informal networks filled the gaps of a state bureaucracy in disarray, based on nepotism. Former communist political elites refashioned themselves as capitalist entrepreneurs, reinforcing clientelism. Political parties were an absolute necessity, but they came about as personalized networks built on loyalty to the leader rather than the formal, written rules of recruitment. In this context, forms of regulation such as party regulation have had an uneven impact in shaping party (system) development outcomes (Casal Bértoa and Van Bizen 2014). An implicit assumption of impermanence was associated with informal institutions.

However, informal institutions showed remarkable resilience in the long-run and allow us to make observations of their tense relations with state enforced behaviour. These tend to be more persistent than formal rules (North 1990), mostly explained by a lack of centre to direct and coordinate their actions (Lauth 2000: 25). Elster et al. (1998) forecast potential differentiated institutional outcomes using the examples of Bulgaria, Czechia, Hungary and Slovenia. Marinova (2011) used the case of ten post-socialist Central and East European countries to test the effectiveness of civil organizations in CEE countries as surrogates for the state in performing social welfare functions when the state is incapable of doing so. The field requires more research on the correlation between elite defections from formal rules and weakened democratic state building. Empirical investigations of the efficiency of informal institutions on the quality of governance are scarce. Comparisons between transforming Eastern European societies and other troubled democracies such as Latin America could also shed new light on the variation in effect.

Such observations of the long-running effects of informal institutions are not limited to new democracies. Writing in the wake of the *mani pulite* 1992–94 corruption scandal in Italy, Della Porta and Vannucci (1999) note that norms of corruption were 'more powerful than the laws of the state: the latter could be violated with impunity, while anyone who challenged the conventions of the illicit market would meet with certain punishment' (15).

By 2019, Italy (together with Greece) continued to score lower than traditional Western democracies in the Transparency International Corruption Index. The 2020 OLAF report of the EU also highlights Italy and France among the European countries with the most pending investigations of mismanaged EU funds (OLAF 2020).

The efficiency of informal institutions at the level of the European Union is another example that has occupied centre stage in recent years. The official EU rule that member states are equal before the Treaties has arguably been at odds with the informal rule of an overpowering EU core, made up of the select few founding members. The EU core is an example of an informal institution. Sticking to the example of Eastern Europe, we could argue that accepting this unspoken rule made further European integration possible. The decisional supremacy of old member states was accepted by post-communist states in exchange for membership (Anghel and Jones 2021).

In the wake of the euro crisis, Greece, Italy and new member states increasingly contested EU core supremacy. The informally organized Frankfurt Group (made up of European heavyweights Angela Merkel, Nicolas Sarkozy, Mario Draghi, José Manuel Barroso, Jean-Claude Juncker, Herman van Rompuy, Christine Lagarde and Olli Rehn) took control of the decision-making process over national budgets to make European governance work. How efficient this informal centralization of power was is not immediately obvious. On the one hand, the euro survived the crisis and the EU moved forward (Jones et al. 2016). On the other hand, the EU's management of the crisis alienated some members on its periphery and was connected to increased Euroscepticism (Nicoli 2017). Christiansen and Piattoni (2003) provide a range of examples of the way in which various institutional issues and policy processes in the EU work through informal administration.

It is important to note the difference between rule-breaking and rulemaking. Not every defection or alternative to formal rules establishes an informal institution. An informal institution sets a pattern of extensively accepted and expected structured behaviour. For example, informal payments in healthcare are widespread and expected in some European systems. States have continuously tried to introduce alternative formal rules, at times with minor effects (Baji et al. 2012). At this point in European history, there is an extensive representation of the informal institution of corruption, one that largely goes unsanctioned by authorities. By comparison, in no European state is embezzlement of hospital (or other public) funds a socially accepted rule. Through this example, we may notice that we operate with an organic concept that changes in time and rests on the evolving perception of ongoing social relationships. Consequently, while informal payments in healthcare are an accepted practice in, for example, contemporary Bulgaria, their status is not indefinite. For a comparison with an even more widely spread practice, consider how the institution of tipping, which creates the socially accepted rule of untaxed income, could evolve into being perceived as breaking tax laws.

Informal institutions may also enhance the performance of formal institutions (Weingast 1979; March and Olsen 2010). The electoral connection (Mayhew 1974) that makes politicians responsive to voters' preferences, lest they lose their next re-election bid, is one such example. Yet the shared understanding of accountability is loosening: party switching is a common European practice to avoid electoral costs (Klein 2019), non-partisan cabinet members were appointed in the aftermath of the eurozone debt crisis to evade government responsibility (Hopkin 2012) and cabinets have an increasingly short lifespan, blurring responsibility. Assessing the effect or function of other informal institutions is more difficult, but equally challenging for researchers. The replacement of corporatism with the primacy of politics in the Netherlands (Daalder 1996) is an example of one informal institution replacing another, the effects of which are still uncertain.

Some researchers consider that informal institutions can provide solutions to problems of social interaction and coordination (Ullman-Margalit 1978). Consequently, we can argue that the wilting of consociationalism under the shock of far-right politics in Austria or Switzerland (Hafez and Heinisch 2018; Helms et al. 2019) led to adverse effects on effective representation.

# Informal institutions and democracy

Informal institutions have primarily been conceptualized against the backdrop of failing governability, the lack of rule of law and the failure of effective representation in Latin America (see Helmke and Levitsky 2006) or Russia (see Ledeneva 1998, 2006). Given the weakening authority of traditional formal institutions in Europe, the study of informal institutions is now growing in importance in European studies. Although we do not look at the United States in this volume, it is worth noticing that the weakening of those informal norms that work to safeguard democracy has also become an American reality (Levitsky and Ziblatt 2018; Skowronek, Dearborn and King 2021).

The rise in power of far-right populists throughout Europe has raised some concerns about which informal rules governing democracies these politicians are willing to break. Take the case of Austria. The Constitution grants the president great powers – such as the dismissal of the Chancellor and the Federal government – but the informal rule is that Austrian presidents never use their veto power, and never have. Knowing this, the 2016 presidential election, which almost saw the FPO far-right populist candidate elected, was a source of great concern. National populists regularly display behaviours that challenge informal rules. FPO candidate Norbert Hofer had even made references to something he called neue Amtsverständnis (new understanding of the presidential office), announcing that we 'will be surprised about all the things that are possible' should he become president (Wolkenstein 2016).

The role of informal institutions in transitional settings has been more thoroughly analysed starting with work by Grzymala-Busse (2010). Grzymala-Busse noted that in new democracies informal institutions act to replace, undermine, support or compete with formal institutions. As we take this work further, we can also see how these institutions dilute these borders in time, changing categories from supporting, to competing, to undermining or weakening democratic rule. The case of Hungary's state capture under centralized political control opens many avenues of research (Fazekas and Tóth 2016). The central question that still guides the research agenda into the role of informal political institutions is whether their existence is coherent with democratic principles or whether the two collide (O'Donnell 1996; Lauth 2000). Further empirical investigations into their role in both established and transitional democracies are paramount.

The expected legal–liberal equilibrium between state institutions has been challenged by alternative behaviours, political strategies, norms and organizing rituals. The erosion of trust in the efficiency or value of traditional institutions (Holmberg et al. 2017; van der Meer 2010) was used by political elites to legitimize the manipulation of different aspects of the liberal-democratic design by reforming constitutions, laws and other formal rules on which liberal democracy was built (Fieschi and Heywood 2004; Rooduijn 2018; Grzymala-Busse 2019). A different avenue for defecting from the constraints of formal democratic institutions is through the use of informal institutions. The growing relevance of informal institutions is revealed by both democratizing Eastern European states (EU members and neighbours) and traditional Western democracies. Much like ideas, informal institutions know no boundaries.

The most commonly studied forms of informal institutions are corruption and clientelism; these impede democratization (Stockemer et al. 2013), slow growth and innovation (Rodríguez-Pose and Cataldo 2015) and sustain the concentration of power in the executive at the expense of the courts and the legislature (Magyar 2017). These informal institutions are pervasive in economically advanced and democratic states as well as new democracies (Wachs et al. 2020); they overshadow problems in the economies of transitional democracies (see e.g. Anderson and Tverdova 2003); and prevent the functioning of free markets in established ones (for Italy see Colazingari and Rose-Ackerman 1998; Della Porta and Vannucci 1999; for Greece see Trantidis and Tsagkroni 2017).

Other informal norms may positively reinforce democratic outcomes. Their weakening provides additional reasons for concern. Despite being the heartland of parliamentary democracy, Europe has witnessed an increase in the role of presidents and heads of state, thus weakening parliamentarianism and questioning democratic accountability (Neto and Strøm 2006). The conceptual disentangling of parliament as the formal institution and parliamentarianism as the informal institution is not immediately obvious. However, it carries a lot of weight in how we perceive the day-to-day activity of democracy. Weakening parliamentarianism in favour of the executive in the context of advancing informal politics correlates with the monopolistic concentration of real power (Hale 2011), despite the official continuation of parliamentary activity.

Civil disobedience is also an informal institution that is argued to sustain the progress of liberal-democratic institutions (Rawls 1971). A spike in the use of this tool in a wave of European mass protests from the UK, to France, to Ukraine (Wihl 2018; Edyvane 2020) led to controversial new formal constraints (e.g. the UK's 2015 legislation for civility, Injunctions to Prevent Nuisance and Annoyance; France's 2019 anti-riot bill, partially struck down by France's Constitutional Court; Spain's 2015 Law of Citizens' Security). Protesters challenged the unwritten rule of non-violent civil disobedience and national authorities began regulating behaviour. Distrust in government institutions creates a void that is filled by informal networks of association and civil organizations (Marinova 2011). By way of example, civil disobedience was organized through the informal networks for Fridays for Future that later became institutionalized as a transnational NGO.

Resistant informal norms, such as gender and racial bias practices, are also increasingly under scrutiny as they enter conflicts with formal national and international rules. These lie at the intersection between social and political informal institutions. In Europe, they are (slowly) being tackled through the enforcement of formal rules such as gender quotas (Krook 2006; Weeks and Baldez 2015) or antigypsyism legislation (Sayan 2019). Their effectiveness in shaping behaviour and overcoming informal rules requires further research and observations over the longer term.

Other informal institutions such as early marriages or elder councils as alternative systems of justice are still practised by communities in Europe despite national legislation and international treaties against them (Caffrey and Mundy 1997; Timmerman 2004; Bošnjak and Acton 2013 also refer to the rule of virginity at marriage for girls in a study on Chergashe Roma in Serbia and Bosnia). Similarly, church etiquette structures behaviour in a myriad of ways that conflicts with legislation; consider here the 2017 conflict between the legal recognition of gender dysphoria by the Greek authorities and orthodox monks who would still only accept birth-assigned males on Mount Athos.

The research into informal norms is also not restricted to the behaviour of states and supranational structures. The private sector is often the supply side of corruption and has a systemic role in state building. The study of informal corporate practices has been limited mostly to the normative field of business ethics. It can nevertheless be argued that corporate corruption is yet another face of an informal political institution. Consider the case of Siemens, which broke in 2006. The investigation revealed a stream of briberies to well-placed officials from Vietnam to Venezuela and from Italy to Israel. Many such cases are increasingly brought to light and are confirmed by progressively formalizing constraints on individual employee behaviour. Ethical training is also a means to achieve viable and resilient investment opportunities (Smimou 2020). A resistant informal corporate culture can circumvent them. As the spokesman for the association of federal criminal investigators in Germany declared, Siemens pursued institutionalized corruption and made bribery a business model (Schubert and Miller 2008).

# Conclusion

The chapter identifies four main ways in which recent European developments revealed the growing role of informal institutions. First, formal institutions are weakened by aggressive forms of populism and extremist discourse and actions. Second, informal institutions that reinforced the functionality of formal institutions are challenged by alternative societal and elite behaviours. Third, informal institutions that sustain discriminatory behaviour are under scrutiny as we increasingly hold democracy and civil rights implementation to a higher standard. Fourth, the evolution of democratization undergone by post-communist states demands a reassessment of our expectations of interactions between formal and informal rules. It also shows that the choice to implement democratic institutions of power sharing and checks and balances is not only a requirement of transition, but an ongoing struggle.

Mapping and measuring the effect of informal institutions is challenging. The opaque nature of most informal institutions requires intensive fieldwork. Consequently, case studies and small $n$ comparative analysis offer opportunities for advancement. Network analysis can increasingly make use of big data and large data sets to map grids of influence within and across states. Systems theory is also useful to reframe some of our initial expectations that states are unitary actors and would help disentangle different observational conditions within state systems (parties, religious institutions, NGOs, corporations, etc.).

The effect of most informal institutions will also be contingent on local specificities. From a normative point of view, research on informal institutions suggests that we cannot anticipate universal effects of institution building and policy implementation. The study of informal institutions is an argument in support of taking into account resilient local practices and norms when implementing changes, or when tracing outcome variation of formalized changes already made.

# Questions for discussion

1  How do formal and informal institutions differ? In what ways are they similar? Why does knowing the distinction between the two matter to understand political processes?
2  What factors drive the persistence of informal institutions? What factors can determine informal institutions to change?
3  What is the role of informal institutions in the democratization process of post-communist European Union states? Can you identify the main tensions for democratic consolidation between the legal framework and the informal institutions of corruption or clientelism?

**4** The Covid-19 pandemic altered social norms and practices extensively, with potential long-term repercussions. What political informal institutions could the health crisis modify?

# Recommended for Further Reading

Bicchieri, C. (2016) *Norms in the Wild: How to Diagnose, Measure, and Change Social Norms.* Oxford: Oxford University Press

Elster, J. et al. (1989) *Nuts and Bolts for the Social Science.* Cambridge: Cambridge University Press

Giordano, C. and Hayoz, N. (2013) *Informality in Eastern Europe.* Lausanne: Peter Lang Verlag.

Putnam, R. D. (1993) *Making Democracy Work.* New Haven, CT: Princeton University Press

Waylen, G. (2017) *Gender and Informal Institutions.* London: Rowman & Littlefield International.

# 5

# Two Decades of Transnational Social Movements in Europe

## Alice Mattoni and Julia Rone

In recent decades, several waves of protest hit Europe. These recent European political mobilizations and social movements have been part of global processes and transformations. For this reason, it is difficult to disentangle them from broader global mobilizations. Nevertheless, European movements show several unique features. To begin with, speaking of European social movements might refer to social movements within different states in the European continent more broadly. But it might also refer more specifically to the increasingly important transnationally coordinated movements that target EU institutions like the European Parliament or the European Commission. Mobilizing both within and outside the EU, at the level of the nation-state, the transnational level and the municipality level, European social movements in the last two decades have organized strategically at different scales depending on the issues they focus on as well as on specific political contexts.

Previous literature has presented the broad spectrum of social movements that developed in Europe in the past decades (Flesher Fominaya and Cox 2013; Fillieule and Acornero 2016; Flesher Fominaya and Feenstra 2019). In this chapter, we discuss several key trends in the making of contentious politics in Europe in the past two decades, especially at the European transnational level. We start with a brief discussion of the Global Justice Movement that proved to be one of the most relevant social movements of the early 2000s in Europe. The second part presents three different waves of protests linked to economic policies and inequalities, while the third section analyses the tension between the rise of progressive social movements on race, class and the environment, on the one hand, and the accompanying steady development of far-right movements in multiple European countries, on the other hand. We conclude by briefly discussing the potential effects of the Covid-19 pandemic on mobilizations in Europe.

# The Global Justice Movement in Europe

The Global Justice Movement has been particularly relevant in shaping transnational links and the many subsequent progressive social movements in Europe at the national level. The Global Justice Movement is also an example of the connections between movements that developed in other parts of the world, their transnationalization and how they became relevant in the European space.

The movement became visible worldwide with the anti-summit demonstrations in Seattle in 1999 which had great resonance in Europe. From that moment, activists in several European countries joined forces into a large social movement network that self-identified as a part of the Global Justice Movement. The movement organized many massive demonstrations, including counter-summit demonstrations that had their peak between 2000 and 2001. These protests occurred in several European cities and involved hundreds of thousands of activists from an extensive network of European social movement organizations that belonged to different traditions positioned within the broad progressive left-wing political area. For instance, in 2001, during the anti-G8 protests, the streets of Genoa, Italy saw, amongst others, the simultaneous presence of post-autonomous grassroots organizations linked to a network of squatted social centres and of the large pacifist network linked to Catholic grassroots organizations active on fair trade from a non-violent stance (della Porta et al. 2015).

The Global Justice Movement also organized the European Social Forum, inspired by the World Social Forum, initially organized in Porto Alegre, Brazil, in January 2001. The first European Social Forum occurred in Florence, Italy. There, about sixty thousand activists from all over the

European continent gathered to discuss practical alternatives to the neoliberal model and marched in the streets of Florence in November 2020 (della Porta et al. 2015). Activists organized other notable European Social Forums in Paris (2003), London (2004), Athens (2006), Malmo (2008) and Istanbul (2010). Since 2004, however, the European Social Forum has been met with criticism by the most radical activist organizations that participated in the first editions, which considered the organizational structure too hierarchical, exclusionary and not radical enough in its contents and objectives. For this reason, the most radical activist groups that participated in the first editions of the European Social Forum decided to organize parallel forums that occurred in the same city as the European Social Forum (Agrikoliansky and Sommier 2005).

Despite the decline of counter-summit demonstrations and the European Social Forum, the Global Justice Movement left an important legacy in at least two aspects. First, the Global Justice Movement was a powerful moment of socialization and grassroots politics for a whole generation. Second, and linked to this, many of the issues that the Global Justice Movement tackled, such as inequality, trade liberalization and debt, were also relevant in the social movements that followed it, such as mobilizations against precarity, the anti-austerity Indignados and Occupy movements as well as the transnational mobilizations against the Transatlantic Trade and Investment Partnership (TTIP) and the EU-Canada Comprehensive Economic and Trade Agreement (CETA) (Mattoni 2012; Gerbaudo 2017; Rone 2020). We discuss the impact of these protests in the following section.

# Contesting austerity and free trade in the aftermath of the economic crisis

Contentious politics related to the economic sector have been particularly vibrant in Europe in the past decade due to global transformations in the financial system, trade policy and the labour market. Additionally, important structural divergences between different countries within the European Union, such as Germany and the Netherlands, on the one hand, and Greece, Italy, Spain and Portugal, on the other hand, also became the trigger for social movement mobilization. In what follows, we discuss three waves of protest in Europe relevant for the understanding of two main tensions that characterize European social movements.

First, it is important to understand the tension between the national and the transnational level. Sometimes, European social movements can cross state borders and organize transnationally, as we saw in the mobilizations against precarity or TTIP and CETA. Other times they spread across different member states, remaining within the framework of domestic politics, without strong ties among social movement organizations belonging to different countries, as was the case with anti-austerity movements.

Second, we have to follow the tension between social movements and the European Union as a political actor. On some occasions, European social movements might consider the institutions of the European Union, especially the European Parliament, a potential ally, as in the case of the anti-TTIP and CETA mobilizations. Still, in protests such as those against austerity, the EU became a target for intervening in domestic politics. Crucially, this ambiguous attitude to EU institutions has been present also in social movements in non-EU countries such as Macedonia or Serbia, where the EU has been treated alternatively as an external ally for progressive movements or as an actor complicit in the failure of neoliberal interventions and state-building initiatives (Džuverović et al. 2021).

## Mobilizations against precarity

In the first half of the 2000s, activists in Italy began to mobilize to address the increased flexibilization of national labour markets. Instead of focusing only on temporary employment as a domestic issue, they framed this social problem as a European one. Consequently, they considered the European Union a relevant institutional actor to address their grievances. Consistently, activists quickly scaled up the Mayday Parade, a day of protest about temporary employment organized for the first time in Italy on the 1 May 2001. The day of protest quickly became a transnational event: it took the name of Euro Mayday Parade from 2004, and activists from all over Europe supported its organization through a transnational network of grassroots social movement organizations. They regularly met in European cities and worked together through a mailing list. In 2005, the Euro Mayday Parade took place in nineteen European cities, rising to twenty-two in 2006.

The Euro Mayday Parade against precarity is a telling example of social movement networks that can go beyond the domestic level to address a contentious issue from a European, rather than national, angle. This was possible thanks to the dense exchanges between activist groups that the Global Justice Movement protests in the previous years had already set in motion, and which continued to be relevant for the organization of the euro Mayday Parade (Mattoni 2012). Many activists who took part in the former were also involved in the latter. That said, the construction of a European political space around precarity was not always smooth. Activists spoke different languages, but they also had different experiences of what being a temporary worker meant in their respective countries.

Beyond the need for linguistic translation, what was relevant was creating a shared language on precarity able to go beyond the material and immaterial conditions of precarious workers in each European country (Doerr and Mattoni 2014). However, this political translation was always temporary, fragile and never fully constructed a shared space of contention on precarity at the European level. Hence, the Euro Mayday Parade is a telling example of the difficulties that activists experience when they shift their domestic mobilizations to the transnational European space.

# 'We are not goods in the hands of politicians and bankers': struggles against austerity

The Global Justice Movement in the early 2000s was the manifestation of a global, transnational movement in the European continent. The case of the Euro Mayday Parade is an example of domestic mobilizations that attempt to scale up and become a European social movement. Contrary to these preceding examples, anti-austerity protests that crossed many European countries at the beginning of the 2010s took the national level as a crucial locus for protest. While mobilizations spread across the European continent, they mainly remained oriented towards domestic politics and opposed the infringement of democratic national sovereignty by unelected institutions imposing austerity measures.

When it comes to who formed the social basis of protest, while the Global Justice Movement mobilized mainly the middle classes, movements against austerity also included full-time and part-time workers, as well as the unemployed (della Porta 2015: 23). Furthermore, if Global Justice Movement's mobilizations were dominated by people up to the age of twenty-nine, anti-austerity events were more diverse in terms of age participation, which was especially clear in the case of general strikes (della Porta 2015).

The remarkable cross-section of the population that took part in the May 2011 protests in Spain famously claimed 'We are not goods in the hands of politicians and bankers' and occupied the central square 'Puerta del Sol' in Madrid. This marked the beginning of a prolonged cycle of protest (Portos García 2016). Protests soon followed in countries such as Portugal and Greece, where citizens protested against their respective governments for imposing austerity under the pressure of the Troika: an informal body consisting of the European Commission, the European Central Bank and the International Monetary Fund.

There were also attempts to go beyond the domestic level of protest. Spanish activists involved in the Indignados mobilizations coordinated a Global Action Day against capitalism and austerity on 15 October 2011. On this occasion, about 951 cities in 82 countries organized a variety of demonstrations and other protest events across the globe, under the slogan 'United for Global Change' (Tejerina et al. 2013). During the Global Day of Protest that also occurred in Europe, in November 2012, traditional trade unions organized a European strike against austerity. Finally, in 2012, from 16 to 19 May, four Blockupy days of protests were organized in Frankfurt, Germany by a transnational network of activists already participating in their respective national movements. They wanted to disrupt the European Central Bank activities in Frankfurt to denounce the European financial policies and austerity measures implemented in many European countries (Pleyers 2016).

Nevertheless, these attempts at transnational collective action remained the exception rather than the rule in a wave of protest that was mainly revolving around the strong presence of national social movements. Although protests happened almost simultaneously in many European countries, social movement organizations did not create collective spaces for transnational meetings, like the European Social Forum and the Euro Mayday Parade preparatory meetings (della Porta and Mattoni 2014).

A possible explanation for this phenomenon can be that protests against austerity lacked a favourable political opportunity structure at the EU level. During the crisis, most important economic decisions were taken outside democratic scrutiny by the Troika. Anti-austerity movements thus could meaningfully protest mainly at the national level where national political institutions offered clear targets and politicians could be held responsible (della Porta and Parks 2018).

Another important development during the peak of anti-austerity movements was the rise of new municipalist movements scaling down from the national level and opposing austerity and neoliberalism in an attempt to reclaim their right to the city (Pirone 2020). The right to the city has become a key issue in both Eastern and Western Europe, within and outside the EU, with key mobilizations on urban issues rising in Spain, most notably Catalonia (Janoschka and Mota 2021), but also in Serbia (Džuverović et al. 2021) and Croatia (Dolenec et al. 2017), among others.

Such municipal movements, many of which are well connected transnationally, not only opposed initiatives aimed at privatizing the commons but also put forward novel ideas on organizing and governing public services such as healthcare and education, as well as utilities such as water and energy. Ultimately, they took the city as the most feasible and efficient entry point for democratic politics, where people can participate directly and meaningfully in policies that affect them.

Finally, while most research on anti-austerity protests – at the transnational, national and local level – has focused exclusively on social movements, it is important to note that trade unions have been a crucial yet often overlooked actor in these mobilizations. In the case of Portugal, unions reframed the democratic deepening demands of the Spanish Indignados in a way that focused more on precarity and the liberalization of labour (Carvalho 2019). In Italy and Greece, there was a difference between minority trade unions, ready to engage in more disruptive action, and majority trade unions that pursued more conventional protest activities (Rone 2020: 67).

Trade unions were also key actors in the French Nuit Debout movement, which opposed reforms designed to make the French labour market more flexible, making it easier for employers to fire people and reduce overtime work compensation. A late-comer to anti-austerity protests, the Nuit Debout mobilization started in March 2016 and gained wide-support among French intellectuals and left-wing parties. Nevertheless, the movement ultimately failed to prevent the liberalizing reforms from coming into force, with protesters gaining only a few concessions from the social democratic government of François Hollande.

As the politics of increasing inequality persisted in France during the Presidency of Emmanuel Macron, in 2018, a new street movement appeared – The Yellow Vests. This movement has been notoriously difficult to characterize as either far left or far right. Comprising of many protesters from different political backgrounds, the Yellow Vests took to the streets to protest against a newly introduced fuel tax. In the long term, the movement forced a reckoning with Macron's pro-business agenda and showed that it is impossible to think of policies that address climate change as divorced from policies of reducing inequality (Kinniburgh 2019: 115). Ultimately, in December 2018, President Macron pledged in a televised address several social measures that aimed more to appease protesters than bring a radical turn in French economic governance.

## TTIP-ing over democracy: struggles against free trade agreements

Some of the major protests in the aftermath of the crisis, especially the anti-austerity ones, marked a return to the national level. Nevertheless, the last decade also saw an increase in the 'Europeanisation' of social movements with not only purely European actors but also 'European targets, mobilizations and transnational movement networks' (Caiani and Graziano 2018). Even though both environmental and feminist movements, as well as municipalist ones, diffused successfully across the continent, probably the most prominent cases of Europeanization were movements against free trade agreements such as TTIP and CETA (Rone 2020). This was due to several reasons. First, trade policy has been an exclusive EU competence and has been the European Commission's responsibility as a par excellence European actor. Second, the European Union tried to democratize certain aspects of its external relations and empowered the European Parliament (Crespy and Parks 2017), making it both a clear target and a potential ally for activists. In turn, activists were further incentivized to connect and unite efforts at the Brussels level in order to increase their influence.

At the same time, Europeanization is a complex and differentiated process. Social movement players 'Europeanized' more and externalized protests, in terms of both targets and level of mobilization, when the political opportunity structure was more unfavourable at the national level (della Porta and Parks 2018: 19). Conversely, wherever movements faced a more favourable domestic opportunity structure, protesters tended to address their grievances at the national level (della Porta and Parks 2018: 19), even if trade policy is an EU competence.

The mobilization against TTIP and CETA was coordinated by a broad coalition of civil society organizations, trade unions and some radical Green and left parties that mobilized hundreds of thousands of citizens in Germany, Austria, Belgium and Spain. This coalition drew attention to the non-democratic and non-transparent ways in which free trade agreements were being negotiated, apart from the multiple threats they posed to labour, environmental and food standards in the European Union. Most importantly, activists opposed Investor-State Dispute Settlement (ISDS) mechanisms that constrain state sovereignty and the legitimate rights of governments and cities to regulate.

Several NGOs with a background in the Global Justice Movement played a key role in the European mobilization against free trade agreements, providing a common media platform for citizens across the EU. The campaign included various innovative initiatives: more than three million people signed a European Citizen initiative to oppose TTIP, and hundreds of cities across Europe declared themselves TTIP and CETA-free, scaling back from the transnational to the local level. Finally, the mobilization against TTIP and CETA spread not only across borders but also from Green-left political players to the radical right that tried (in most cases unsuccessfully) to co-opt an inherently progressive movement for its own goals (Rone 2018).

Ultimately, TTIP was abandoned by US President Donald Trump, while the European Parliament provisionally ratified CETA as of February 2017. Considering the low level of politicization of subsequent EU trade agreements, it remains to be seen whether the legacy of anti-TTIP and CETA mobilizations will be long-lasting or will remain a flash in the pan.

# European movements between progressive and far-right politics

The European social movements introduced in the previous section of the chapter addressed economic issues mostly from a progressive left-wing political orientation. However, progressive mobilizations went beyond the narrow economic sphere and addressed other relevant contentious issues as well. Among others, it is certainly worth mentioning the feminist movement Ni Una Menos that first occurred in Argentina to tackle violence against women, but then spread rapidly in several European countries where it combined with the local feminist traditions (González and Brochner 2019). This also happened in the case of the #MeToo online mobilizations that developed at first in the United States in 2017: they spread also in other European countries, like Finland, Germany and Portugal although each country saw different interpretations of and level of engagement with

#MeToo (Sweeny 2020). Climate change protests such as Fridays for Future or the more radical Extinction Rebellion were also national movements that spread their networks in various cities across the continent (see Saunders in this volume).

The Black Lives Matter mobilizations that originated in the USA already in 2013 were also able to resonate with the discourses and the traditions of anti-racist movements in Europe (Parti and Wössner 2020). In 2020, after the police killing of George Floyd in Minneapolis, activists mobilized in several countries, including Belgium, France, Italy, Ireland and the United Kingdom. These protests went beyond the expression of solidarity towards the Black Lives Matter activists in the United States. In fact, activists addressed the issues of police brutality linked to racial profiling at the domestic level of many European countries. All these mobilizations speak volumes about the relationship between Europe's movements and social tensions in other countries. In both the case of Ni Una Menos and Black Lives Matter we can see the diffusion, in Europe, of social movements that originated in South America and North America. In the case of the climate change protests, instead, we see how social movement organizations rooted in European countries can resonate worldwide, hence scaling up activists' protests from the European to the global level.

While progressive social movement actors have dominated the European protest scene, the 2010s also saw a remarkable resurgence of far-right social movements (Gattinara and Pirro 2019). These focused above all on migration, the environment and gender politics. In doing so, the European far-right expanded beyond the electoral arena, which it had traditionally preferred (Hutter 2014) and engaged in confrontational dynamics with progressive movements both online and on the streets.

Arguably, the most emblematic far-right social movement of the decade has been the German PEGIDA. For over six years, starting October 2014, every Monday evening citizens have been gathering in the East German city of Dresden in order to protest under the banner of PEGIDA – 'Patriotic Europeans Against the Islamization of the West' (Weisskircher and Berntzen 2019). Far-right actors targeted issues such as immigration and multiculturalism, and promoted climate change scepticism (Forchtner, Kroneder and Wetzel 2018; Kaiser 2019) as well as anti-feminist agendas in some cases (Knüpfer et al. 2020). In both EU and non-EU member states in Eastern Europe, far-right and conservative social movements also mounted an offensive against women's and LGBTQIA+ rights, which are often presented as imposed by a liberal EU against local citizens' democratic will (Ayoub 2015).

Finally, across the continent, far-right movements have also vocally adopted Euroscepticism. They have argued for the European Union's disintegration and the formation of a Europe of nations instead (Caiani and Weisskircher 2020). At the same time, the far right has been active in forging transnational connections and cooperation. Activists from the West, for example, have travelled to the East to participate in commemorative marches and border patrolling (Bjørgo and Mareš 2019).

Far-right social movements connected not only to other social movements across borders but also increasingly engaged with far-right parties and subcultures – both domestically and internationally (Gattinara and Pirro 2019). Far-right activists have been extremely skilful in fostering fringe online subcultures: memes loaded with irony, humour and coded language have increased the attraction of the far-right for younger audiences, providing new mechanisms for identification and community building (Bogerts and Fielitz 2019). Equally importantly, far-right social movements skilfully related also to mainstream media pushing the boundaries of what is acceptable to say and contributing to the normalization and mainstreaming of extreme discourse (Karl 2019).

# Conclusion

In this chapter, we illustrated that beyond the purely geographical fact of being movements in countries from the European continent, many social movements have conceived themselves and acted as explicitly pan-European movements that target EU institutions on topics relevant for the whole union, such as free trade or climate change. However, protests that developed on the European continent are neither necessarily linked to the European Union as a political space, nor are they isolated from mobilizations that occur at the global level.

The last decade's European social movements have, by any standard, shaken up the political system of Europe. While anti-austerity protests in Spain, Italy and Portugal could do little to prevent austerity policies in the immediate aftermath of the crisis, their activism brought about challenger parties and had a long-lasting transformation of their countries' political systems. Challenger parties with roots in social movements, such as Podemos in Spain or Movimento 5 Stelle in Italy, became key players in political life, reaching impressive electoral results and entering government coalitions. In Portugal, a left-block coalition pursued a series of progressive reforms giving hopes for social democracy in decline elsewhere on the continent.

To the right of the political spectrum, social movements such as PEGIDA in Germany successfully pushed centre-right parties' discourse on immigration, to the right. While protest politics has been traditionally dominated by left-wing actors in Western Europe and right-wing actors in the East (Borbáth and Gessler 2020), the last decade has seen a considerable rise of far-right social movements in the West and a slow diffusion of left-wing ideas to the East (Rone 2020). All in all, in the aftermath of a turbulent decade, European politics has become increasingly radicalized and polarized, with a shrinking centre and a rise of Green politics, especially in Germany. At the same time, movements' demand for 'real democracy now' (della Porta 2013) has contributed to democratic innovations of citizen consultations and of decision-making processes within political parties (Wolkenstein 2019).

This chapter has outlined the contours of social mobilization between two big crises – the 2008 economic crisis and the 2020 health and economic crisis caused by the Covid-19 pandemic. Beyond the immediate constraints on protests, the emergency period will certainly have a considerable effect on mobilizations in the long run due to both the increased power of police forces and the pervasive surveillance measures taken by states, often in collaboration with private companies. At the same time, older contentious issues will resurface with renewed strength. The profound economic shock caused by the pandemic will undoubtedly also fuel future mobilizations in Europe that problematize further many of the issues of the 2010s, including precarious work and the rise of the so-called gig economy (Duke 2020), the concentration of wealth in the hands of few powerful economic players and, of course, the environment.

The Covid-19 crisis once again revealed that while social movements in Europe have their own dynamics, shaped largely by both national politics and the institutions of the EU, they are still very much part of global trends and struggles (Bringer and Pleyers 2020). It is thus high time to move away from Eurocentric analyses and to provincialize not just Europe (Chakrabarty 2008) but also the study of European social movements that develop in the European space by focusing more on the connections, both online and offline, between European movements and movements in other parts of the globe. Thus, we can better understand both what is really unique for European social movements and what can connect them to movements elsewhere, allowing us to build true transnational solidarity networks.

# Questions for discussion

1 Can European social movements be discussed in isolation from global social movements?
2 What is transnational mobilization? Did this type of mobilization become more or less relevant in social movement mobilizations throughout the 2010s?
3 What role did digital media play in the 2010s resurgence of far-right mobilization?
4 How did progressive feminist and environmentalist movements in Europe interact with progressive movements in the US and Latin America?

# Recommended for Further Reading

della Porta, D. and Mattoni, A. (2014) *Spreading Protest: Social Movements in Times of Crisis*. Colchester: ECPR Press.

Gattinara, P. C. and Pirro, A. L. P. (2019) 'The Far Right as Social Movement', *European Societies* 21(4): 447–62.

Fominaya, C. F. and Feenstra, R. A. (2019) *Routledge Handbook of Contemporary European Social Movements: Protest in Turbulent Times*. London: Routledge.

González, A. C. and Brochner, G. B. M. (2019) 'The New Cycle of Women's Mobilizations between Latin America and Europe', in H. Cairo and B. Bringel (eds), *Critical Geopolitics and Regional (Re) Configurations: Interregionalism and Transnationalism between Latin America and Europe*, 171–90. London, Routledge.

Rone, J. (2020) *Contesting Austerity and Free Trade in the EU: Protest Diffusion in Complex Media and Political Arenas*. London: Routledge.

# 6

# Climate Change and the Environment

## *Clare Saunders*

In 2012 I co-authored *Politics of the Environment*, 3rd edition (Connelly et al. 2012), in which we claimed that climate change 'has pushed sustainable development aside in the way in which it dominates debates on environmental politics, be it in relation to mitigation (the reduction of greenhouse gas emissions) or adaptation (adapting to the consequences of climate change). This is true for governments at all levels, environmental protestors, private companies and the public at large' (Connelly et al. 2012: 8). Fast forward to 2021 and the situation is little different. Climate change is perhaps the most challenging and pressing of many environmental issues, not least because it intersects with other severe threats to our physical and human environment including plastics, soil degradation, air pollution, water pollution and species extinction. The clock is ticking as time seems to be running out to take action to curtail a climate catastrophe (Doulton and Brown 2009; Hansen 2010; United Nations Framework on Climate Change 2019).

The desperate nature of the situation has been met with a range of increasingly creative responses from the European Union (EU), which has sought to craft out a leadership position on climate change. The EU's leadership on climate change is, however, somewhat fraught as its constituent countries pushback against blanket policy positions not well suited to their geographies and economies. This battle for agency between the EU and member states sits alongside healthy scepticism from environmental NGOs and increasingly radical protest responses on the streets.

Despite minor reductions in global emissions due to the Covid-19 pandemic (IEA 2020), climate change remains a serious concern for European citizens. While the EU's agency has been challenged by countries wanting policies tailored to their own interests, the past two years have witnessed unprecedented climate activism across Europe. A broad array of protesters has engaged in civil disobedience to attempt escalate climate change on political agendas, just as school children have skipped school to draw attention to the need to protect *their* future from climate change (Doherty and Saunders 2021). The Swedish climate activist, Greta Thunberg, founder of Fridays for the Future, has received hitherto unknown levels of access to key international environmental policymaking forums in Europe and beyond (Vavilov 2019). This chapter, then, explores European climate change mitigation policies as a sum of complex struggles for agency among EU member states, which intersects with the demands of environmental NGOs and climate activists.

# European Union climate policies

Until 2009, the EU successfully positioned itself as a world leader in climate change politics. Its leadership has been unravelling from 2009 onwards, partly due to disagreements among member states. The EU has mixed genuine and rhetorical leadership but found the latter easier to sustain.

The EU's overall commitment has been to prevent global warming from increasing more than 2°C above pre-industrial levels and to halve greenhouse gas emissions from 1990 levels by 2050 (Council of the European Union 2007, 2014, cited in Rayner and Jordan 2016). The December 2019 European Green Deal increased this target to zero emissions.

If we unpack the leadership myth, we can get a more accurate picture of how European countries have, together, weakened European climate policy. The EU's own emission targets were set using the principle of burden-sharing, which allowed poorer European countries to make fewer emissions' cuts compared to countries where it was more feasible to make cuts. Under this arrangement, the EU's 1997 targets affected the emissions of only *eight* member states.

There were easy gains to be made in the UK in the dash for gas (upon discovery of North Sea reserves in the early 1990s). The unification of Germany also resulted in the closure of old inefficient industrial plants in what was East Germany. Schreurs and Tiberghein (2008) identify that these UK and German developments meant that the EU's seemingly ambitious 2010 targets were actually easy pickings; they were achievable with little additional effort. Indeed, two of Europe's most powerful nations (UK and Germany) masked real change with political posturing.

Following this contested achievement, EU unity on climate change policies has grown increasingly fractured. The notion of burden-sharing has become harder to deploy as a cohesive force. Currently, we are witnessing a widening gap between Northern European countries, which are generally more environmentally conscious and those in the south, who, under the leadership of Poland are keen to protect their fossil fuel intensive industrial sectors (Rayner and Jordan 2016). This has been challenging for EU climate policy since the EU expanded to include eight new members that were formerly communist, and which have lower environmental standards than in the West (Fischer 2014).

The EU lost a large part of its reputation for climate policy leadership in 2009 when the weak Copenhagen Accord – agreed among five countries – side-stepped EU participation and went ahead without its consent (Bocquillon 2014). Bond (2011: 3) describes the Copenhagen Accord as a 'deliberately vague' document, 'signed in a... backroom by five countries' leaders to the howls of criticism from the general public and the crash of carbon markets'. Moreover, the EU's environmental policies have, for a long time, been criticized for their implementation gap (Parker and Karlsson 2010), which is partially a consequence of the EU's limited capacity to enforce climate change obligations (Jordan and Tosun 2012) or to specify delivery mechanisms (Rayner and Jordan 2016). The picture is even less impressive if we take a quick look inside some of the countries that comprise the EU. Even thinking only in rhetorical terms, we might wonder if it is not the EU itself that is a leader, but the countries that hold the presidency as they seek to position themselves.

A closer look at the national policies of those countries reveals a more mixed picture. Different countries within the EU take climate change mitigation more or less seriously. Their National Mitigation Strategies are 'messy packages', lacking strategic vision, policy integration and the implementation of medium- to long-term strategies. Casado-Asensio and Steurer (2015: 10) therefore conclude that countries' commitment within the EU amounts to '"lacklustre bookkeeping" rather than strategic policymaking'. We could characterize the EU's climate policy aspirations as ecologically modernist: as a win–win situation for the environment and the economy (Barry 2005). The EU's emphasis on ecological modernization in the EU's Europe 2020 strategy further illustrates its loosening grip on its member states. This strategy was launched in 2010, but formerly unveiled in 2008 to the European Parliament where its ecological modernization rhetoric shone through. It was hailed as a 'huge opportunity represented by Europe's transition into a low-emission economy' within the context of 'an effective and competitive industrial sector up to the challenge'. The planned outcome was that 'Europe can be the first economy for the low-carbon age' (Barroso, President of the European Commission 2008).

This climate and energy package (Bocquillon 2014) featured the EU's 20/20/20 headline targets to reduce greenhouse gas emissions by 20 per cent compared to 1990 levels, to achieve 20 per cent of energy consumption from renewables and secure a 20 per cent increase in energy efficiency. These ambitious targets were central to the EU's self-positioning as a leader. But it was by no means an easy process for EU countries to agree to it; agreement only became possible through trade-offs, pay-offs and dodgy handshakes (Skjærseth 2014). Central and Eastern European countries, for example, were given some leeway to continue their coal-fuelled economies to reduce reliance on Russian gas (Boasson and Wettestad 2013).

One way in which the EU seeks to reduce its greenhouse gas emissions is through the European Emissions Trading System (EU ETS), which uses emissions trading to control emissions from energy intensive industries and commercial airlines (since 2012). Central European countries more resistant to climate action were brought on board by being given free allowances for their coal industries. At the same time, they benefited from the co-financing of renewable energy and carbon capture and storage demonstrator plants (Bocquillon 2014).

As always within EU policy, the aspiration to produce 20 per cent of its energy from renewable sources by 2020 distributed renewable energy targets differently across European countries based on their starting point and the potential that their geographical features hold for renewable energy development. The UK aimed to achieve a 15 per cent target but was pushing the EU to increase its renewable target overall to 30 per cent (National Renewable Energy Plan, UK 2010). Sweden, in comparison, had a target of 49 per cent (National Renewable Energy Plan, Sweden 2010). This policy objective is being delivered through a series of market sharing and incentive structures. The success of countries in meeting their renewable energy targets is mixed. The UK (which was a member state until 2020) and the

Netherlands have been among the laggard countries, but some countries have already exceeded their targets.

By 2009, internal dissent was clearly undermining EU climate leadership. Some countries preferred not to sign up to a proposed 30 per cent reduction of greenhouse gas emissions by 2030. Steinebach and Knill (2016) identify a four-year lull in the EU's regulatory activity on climate change from 2010, alongside some softening of previous legislation, together amounting to what they call 'passive policy dismantling'. This is perhaps understandable in the context of the 2008–09 financial crisis and the pressures that came with enlarging the EU. It took until 2014 for European countries to agree on the 2030 Climate and Energy Policy Framework targets of 40 per cent for greenhouse gas emission reductions, and 27 per cent for each of renewables and energy efficiency (Bocquillon 2014). This was only agreed after offering allowances of up to 12 per cent for countries in the EU with below average GDP (Raymer and Jordan 2016).

In 2016, the EU signed up to the Paris Agreement. In doing so, it committed to taking action to prevent global average temperatures increasing by 2°C; fostering resilience to improve its capacity to adapt to the adverse impacts of climate change; and altering finance flows to promote low emissions and climate resilient development (UNFCCC 2015). In the Paris negotiations, the EU failed to persuade other countries to include aviation and shipping in the policies, but it did succeed to introduce 'five yearly review cycles and transparency in the Paris agreement' (Oztig 2017: 920). Another area of controversy is the EU's promotion of biofuels as an alternative to fossil fuels for transport. This has been deemed problematic because of indirect land-use change causing environmental and social harm. In 2013, the EU agreed on policies to prevent competition with food crops (Rayner and Jordan 2016).

Together, these EU policies have had modest effects on the promotion of climate change mitigation technologies. Calel and Dechezleprêtre (2016) found that sectors under the EU ETS achieved a 1 per cent increase in climate change mitigation technologies, compared to those sectors not included under the scheme. Climate change mitigation technologies are particularly useful for increasing the share of energy obtained from renewable sources, with knock-on effects for reducing greenhouse gas emissions overall; but they have little effect on energy efficiency (Bell and Joseph 2016).

As of spring 2021, the EU is negotiating a European Climate Law to realize the aspirations of the European Green Deal to make Europe's economy and society carbon neutral by 2050. Given the tensions within the EU it is difficult to see how this could succeed. Oztig (2017: 198) finds that even though the EU member states have 'curbed greenhouse gas emissions and increased their consumption of renewable energy over the last decade, they have also increased their consumption of fossil fuels'.

Although it seems likely that the EU will meet its five-yearly targets in the short term, it is unlikely to reach zero emissions 'in the foreseeable future' (Oztig 2017: 198). Moreover, one might argue that the EU's climate policies are not directly responsible for falling emissions in recent years (excluding the gains already made from the UK dash for gas and German reunification) due to fortuitous policy gains resulting from reduced emissions as a consequence of the 2008–09 financial crash and the Covid-19 pandemic. Thus, we must be forced to conclude that the EU's promising rhetoric has not transferred into meaningful action (Jordan et al. 2010). The politics, geographies and economies of its member states have doubtless played a role in reducing the ability of the EU to act as a unified actor with the agency to take the types of drastic action required to effectively mitigate climate change.

# European climate activism

Environmental movement actors were among the first to be involved in the construction of climate change as a social problem (Hannigan 2006). Alongside radical scientists involved in the emergence of new ecological ways of thinking, they constructed relevant knowledge frameworks to understand human impacts on the environment (Jamison 2010). More recently, environmental movements have been responsible for constructing the framework of climate justice, which recognizes the unequal contribution and effects of climate change across the world (Jamison 2010)). The fact that – particularly compared to the US – European public support for environmental protection is generally high is in no small measure thanks to environmental movements raising public awareness (Jordan et al. 2010).

In the contemporary era, environmental NGOs and activists are arguably the most vocal critics of European climate policy. Nevertheless, European NGOs have taken a fairly 'soft' approach. They mostly emphasize a reformist/ecological modernist logic, which has 'focused on modifying the EU's ETS [Emissions Trading System], reforming EU budget priorities, and the long-term economic benefits for the EU economy' (Bomberg 2012: 414).

Among the main actors challenging European climate policy are the Green 10, which consists of Birdlife International, CEE Bankwatch Network, Climate Action Network Europe, the European Environment Bureau, the European Federation for Transport and Environment, EPHA Environment Network, Friends of the Earth Europe, Greenpeace EC-Unit, International Friends of Nature and the WWF European Policy Office (Bomberg 2012). These form a sometimes uneasy alliance alongside more radical civil-disobedience networks such as Extinction Rebellion and Fridays for the Future. The Green 10, except for Greenpeace, have consulting status with the EU and receive funding to undertake work for it (Schreurs and Tiberghein 2008).

The work of environmental NGOs and social movements is not confined to the inner corridors of EU institutions. Environmental activists are also present on the streets. NGOs like Friends of the Earth and Greenpeace stage media-attention-seeking stunts outside major climate conferences, radical activists engage in occupations of polluting industries, and Extinction Rebellion activists wilfully seek arrest to draw attention to the realities of climate change.

Despite the global implications of climate change, environmental mobilizations have been relatively small. North (2011) points out that anti-nuclear, anti-war and anti-globalization movements have been able to mobilize around a quarter of a million participants, but even the COP15 mobilization in Copenhagen (2009) – billed by many as 'the last chance to save the planet'– was attended by no more than a hundred thousand people. Is this because climate activism is weak? North (2011) argues that this is rather because climate activism is diffuse and exists at a range of levels and sites from carbon rationing and prefigurative activism – that is being the change you want to see – through to direct action and lifestyles. Each of these sites has important lessons that can 'trickle up' to the EU, or across the broader environmental movement which can learn new frames and tactical repertoires through close engagement.

# The EU climate policy – climate activism nexus

It is important to recognize that the multi-level nature of European governance shapes the advocacy work of climate change NGOs. The soft approach that European environmental NGOs take in their attempts to influence EU policy are arguably an outcome of the nature of the EU and its institutions. On the one hand, there is no EU community, no consistent EU public opinion – perhaps not even an EU public – there is no EU media, and there is perhaps not much sense of EU citizenship. These absent factors are usually central to shaping adversarial forms of protest as we usually know them. On the other hand, the EU is built on slow consensus-driven negotiating processes among a range of countries with more and less developed democracies, and more and less well-developed democracies. Consequently, it appeals to technocratic arguments, and thus oftentimes to lowest common denominator arguments.

The European Parliament provides a forum where a broad range of civil society actors can interact, the EC is open to collaborations, European and G8 summits provide further spaces for collaboration and the EU encourages national, regional and local alliances (Bomberg 2012). The EU also has stakeholder conferences, to which it invites citizens, business representatives, policy makers, scientists and NGOs to help shape policy documents. This 'open door' further encourages the soft approach that European climate NGOs take. Unfortunately, it also means that the higher the number of NGOs being invited to participate the less attention each individual NGO obtains, perhaps weakening their chances of impact (Orr 2016 similarly notes how the dramatically increasing numbers of NGO participants in the United Nations Framework Convention on Climate Change shifted it from an intense discursive forum into a gala atmosphere). These peculiarities in the opportunity structure of the EU shape the activism that targets it. In Bomberg's (2012: 414) words, 'the "upscaling" of advocacy in the EU leads to "downscaling" of radical frames'.

The apparent slowness of action inside the EU, frustrated further by fragmentation of a united Europe, and policy dismantling in recent years (Steinebach and Knill 2016) has arguably been a driving force behind a new wave of climate activism. Time and time again we have seen how an apparently weak and co-opted environmental movement leads to differentiation in the environmental movement as the gap between the pragmatists and the principled widens (Connelly et al. 2012: Ch. 3). Moreover, we can learn from the emergence of anti-roads direct action in the UK in the 1990s that the feeling of reaching a democratic dead-end can lead to a ramping up of action (Saunders 2014). I now briefly discuss two types of radical action that emerged as a result of the climate policy-activism nexus: Fridays for Future and Extinction Rebellion.

In April 2019, the now famous teenager climate activist Greta Thunberg delivered a 12-minute speech to EU leaders at the EU Parliament, Strasbourg, France. Her messaging was powerful:

> Around the year 2030, 10 years, 259 days, and 10 hours away from now, we will be in a position where it will be a set of a chain reactions that will most likely lead to the end of civilization as we know it… You need to listen to us, we who cannot vote… I ask you to please wake up and make the changes required possible. To do your best is no longer good enough, we must all do the seemingly impossible.
>
> (Greta Thunberg's speech during the EU Parliament meeting is available in the appendix of Vavilov 2019).

Thunberg has triggered a widespread movement of school and college students to take Fridays off school to fight for a future not destroyed by climate change. In March 2019, the Fridays for Future climate protests mobilized over 1.6 million participants across the globe, achieving significant youth engagement and receiving impressive media coverage. In March 2020, Greta Thunberg addressed Members of the European Parliament giving them a strong message that it is time to act. She considers that the Climate Law currently being negotiated is too weak, despite its strong promise of climate neutrality by 2050. As she puts it: 'This climate law is surrender because nature doesn't bargain and you cannot make deals with physics' (Thunberg, European Parliament 2020).

Meanwhile, Extinction Rebellion (XR) Brussels has started a network focused on influencing the EU. XR began in October 2018 in Britain, with the aims of persuading the UK government to declare a climate emergency, to make deeper greenhouse gas emission reductions more quickly, and to create a Citizens' Assembly to make decisions for climate and ecological justice. It has sought to engage a broader network of people in civil disobedience to push governments to take seriously these demands. Its principal actions to date have been large-scale occupations of the major arteries of cities, but there are many other smaller creative actions that have taken place within its framework for action. The XR EU group has attempted to mobilize activists by pointing out that the EU's climate targets and Green Deal are, in its view, likely to be inadequate. Interactions with the EU extend beyond the contentious. In May 2019, founder member Roger Hallam and eight other XR activists stood as candidates in the European Parliament elections for London and the Southwest on a climate emergency ticket.

Climate activism is not only shaped by European climate policy; it also shapes it. Schreurs and Tiberghien (2008) argue that the EU's commitment to Kyoto in the first instance was in part due to European NGO's precautionary approach to climate change. The EU European Emissions Trading System, and the belated decision to include aviation in the scheme, were not policy initiatives that developed in vacuum, but were rather the result of NGOs cooperating with industry, think tanks and European Commission officials (Skjærseth and Wettestad 2010). Climate activism matters even in Eastern Europe, where the NGO sector is well known for being weak and distrusted by the public in a post-communist context (see, for example, Fagan 1994, on the Czech Republic case).

Climate NGOs have also shaped norms of environmental policymaking, particularly the relation to the linkage between climate change and energy security goals. The two concepts of security and climate change are now conceived as obvious joint goals for energy policy (Bomberg 2012; Bocquillon 2014). Moreover, a significant consortium of environmental NGOs, including Greenpeace, WWF, RSPB and Friends of the Earth (alongside Oxfam) worked to shape the EU's policy restricting the use of biofuels in transport. As Pilgrim and Harvey (2010: para 5.2) put it: 'Policy changes, review processes, target reductions, and novel sustainability regulation were all found, at least in part, to have been a consequence of NGO campaigning'.

Although the demands of the more radical environmental organizations might be out-of-kilter with the slow consensus-based compromising approach to decision-making in the EU, it is at least the case that activist groups like Fridays for Future and Extinction Rebellion have the effect of making the most radical demands of their more reformist counterparts appear acceptable through the radical flank effect (Haines 2013). Radical environmental organizations are right to judge that serious action to prevent dangerous climate change is required very urgently, but we must not despair. The anticipated failure of EU governance on climate change has a safety net found in the diversity of climate activist groups (North 2011) that also support carbon rationing, lifestyle changes and transformation of their local environments.

# Conclusion

The desperate need to deal with climate change has resulted in ambitious climate change policy aspirations in the EU. However, this chapter has illustrated that these ambitions translate into rhetorical leadership rather than leading by example. Indeed, the climate policies of the EU might be overly ambitious given pushback among member states that are constrained by either their economies or geographies to deliver zero carbon targets.

The urgency of the climate situation, brought into sharp relief by the slowness of progress to mitigate climate change, has been reacted to by NGOs that work throughout Europe to attempt to push the EU and its member states in the direction of more dramatic climate action. These NGOs are mostly described as being somewhat 'soft'. The open nature of the EU – the very same thing that encourages it to bow down to member states' requests to weaken their climate change policies at the domestic level – has meant that the voice of each individual NGO is weakened, such that they are deemed relatively toothless. This has led to a stalemate between NGOs and the EU, which is being responded to by new, more radical, groups and networks of climate activists like Extinction Rebellion and Fridays for the Future.

These, and other lifestyle networks, are at the vanguard for change for effective climate change policies. Although disruptive protests, like those organized by Extinction Rebellion, are inconvenient for people who find their everyday life disrupted by them, a climate catastrophe would doubtless be worse. The EU, its member states, NGOs, activists and everyday citizens must urgently do what they can to help avert such a catastrophe.

# Questions for discussion

1  Why is climate change often considered to be the most pressing environmental policy priority? What effects could the emphasis given to climate change have on other important environmental issues?
2  Why does the European Union struggle to retain a leadership position on climate change policies?
3  In which ways has it been difficult for European environmental NGOs to influence European climate policy to much effect?
4  Is European climate policy's ecological modernization rhetoric a success or failure in terms of generating effective climate change mitigation policies?

# Recommended for Further Reading

Borghesi, S. (2021) 'A Room with a View: A Special Issue with a Special Perspective', *Environment and Development Economics* 26(3): 205–10.

Fay, M., Block, R. and Ebinger, J. (2010) *Adapting to Climate Change in Eastern Europe and Central Asia*. Washington: The International Bank for Reconstruction and Development.

Haug, C., Rayner, T., Jordan, A., Hildingsson, R., Stripple, J., Monni, S., Huitema, D., Massey, E., van Asselt, H. and Berkhout, F. (2010) 'Navigating the Dilemmas of Climate Policy in Europe: Evidence from Policy Evaluation Studies', *Climatic Change* 101(3): 427–45.

Huitema, D., Jordan, A., Massey, E., Rayner, T., Van Asselt, H., Haug, C., Hildingsson, R., Monni, S. and Stripple, J. (2011) 'The Evaluation of Climate Policy: Theory and Emerging Practice in Europe', *Policy Sciences* 44(2): 179–98.

Tagliapietra, S. and Veugelers, R. (2021) 'Fostering the Industrial Component of the European Green Deal: Key Principles and Policy Options' *Intereconomics* 6: 305–10.

# 7

# Capitalist Varieties under One Roof: Coping with Diversity in the European Union

## *Vera Scepanovic*

The 2010s were a rough decade for Europe and the current one – ushered in by the Covid-19 pandemic – promises to be just as challenging. The global financial crisis of 2008/9 had shaken economies around the world, but only in the European Union did it lead to sovereign debt crises that seriously slowed down the recovery. The sputtering economy led to bitter fights over economic policies and fed the flames of nationalism and populism around the continent. All of this threatened to undermine the EU's ability to tackle in a unified way the burning questions of the new century: the energy transition, economic relations with China, and the recovery from Covid-19.

What made the management of this 'polycrisis' (Zeitlin et al. 2019) especially difficult was that its effects varied across EU member states. In many countries of Northwestern European the crisis weakened the banks, but their governments managed to shore up the financial sector without increasing the costs of public borrowing. Meanwhile, in Southern Europe, attempts to protect the banks led to skyrocketing yields on government bonds, bringing some of these states to the brink of insolvency.

Why did we see such divergence? Whether they blamed profligate governments unable to control their spending (see Dooley 2014; Khan and McClean 2017) or labour market institutions failing to contain inflation and maintain competitiveness (Hancké 2013; Johnston and Reagan 2016), most analysts found explanation in the underlying differences in national economic governance. The subsequent years have therefore seen a flurry of measures to align economic policies and institutions of all EU member states towards an ideal roughly modelled on Germany: export-oriented, fiscally prudent and equipped with a skilled and flexible labour force as well as mechanisms to keep wages pinned to productivity (Johnston and Reagan 2018; Perez and Matsaganis 2018; Jones 2021). These measures include tightening the limits on fiscal deficits, introduction of constitutional 'debt breaks' and 'watchdog councils' to monitor spending, and in-depth scrutiny by the European Commission of a wide range of economic indicators – wages, employment, education, housing prices – accompanied by recommendations for institutional reform (Verdun and Zeitlin 2018). The same monitoring mechanisms and reform conditionality have also been built into the post-Covid-19 recovery funds.

While the EU's efforts to foster institutional convergence among its members may seem like a logical response to the unevenness of crisis, this chapter argues that they have been – and are – unlikely to work. The reason is that capitalist diversity in the European Union is not merely a quirk of history or a failure of national governance in certain countries that can be 'fixed' though a bout of institutional engineering but is itself largely a product of past integration. Decades of harmonization of European markets and institutions have not only failed to produce convergence but have in fact actively encouraged the development of different production and growth models. This point is frequently under-emphasized even in the scholarly theories of capitalist varieties, but its implications for the efforts to address the EU's polycrisis are serious.

If diversity is a product of integration, as will be argued here, then more pressure for convergence is unlikely to eliminate it, or its potential costs. But also, if the economic impact of integration is going to be uneven, the EU needs to take more responsibility for managing its costs.

The chapter makes this argument in several steps. The first section reviews two dominant strands of literature on capitalist diversity – the 'production models' and 'growth models' – to highlight the mechanisms through which international integration contributes to the persistence of capitalist variety in Europe. Section two then draws on the experience of the East European members to highlight the challenges to top-down institutional convergence. The concluding section revisits the debate about the need for convergence in the EU and argues for an alternative policy approach.

# Why so different?

The policy push for institutional convergence decades after the launch of the Single Market and the European Monetary Union may appear surprising. One reason clearly is that it took an existential crisis to give the EU the authority to demand such reforms from its member states. Another is that in the heydays of integration optimism many believed that convergence would result more or less automatically. Bringing diverse economies under a set of common market rules was supposed to push them into regulatory competition that should have weeded out inefficient institutions, and the loss of control over monetary policy should have forced labour market adjustments in order to prevent inflation (Verdun and Wylie 2002). And yet, more than three decades later, diversity of economic institutions as well as outcomes continues.

Attempts to explain this persistence have led to a flourishing of comparative political economy as a discipline and produced many different typologies and labels: the 'Anglo-Saxon' vs. the 'Rhenish', 'Nordic' and 'Mediterranean' capitalisms (Albert 1993; Amable 2003); the 'coordinated', 'liberal' and 'mixed' market economies (Hall and Soskice 2001; Hancké et al. 2007); as well as 'export-oriented' and 'debt-oriented' growth models. Yet more varieties have been identified among the post-socialist economies in Europe: 'dependent market economies' (Nölke and Vliegenthart 2009), 'neoliberal', 'embedded neoliberal' and 'neocorporatist' economies (Bohle and Greskovits 2012), as well as 'oligarchic', 'patrimonial' and various state-authoritarian types (Myant and Drahokoupil 2010).

These typologies emphasize different aspects of the economy and highlight different elements of the institutional subsystems – welfare institutions, the role of the state more than others. Most can, however, be grouped into roughly two camps which I will call *production models* and *growth models*.

## Production models

The literature that relates the institutional structure of an economy to its production specialization has a long pedigree, including attempts to explain different pathways towards industrialization, or the link between dependence on commodity exports and authoritarianism (e.g. Gerschenkron 1962; Karl 1997).

More recently, the research into production models in industrialized economies has focused on uncovering the ways in which domestic institutions shape divergent responses of countries to globalization (Streeck 1991; Hollingsworth and Boyer 1997; Hall and Soskice 2001). The main argument, broadly speaking, is that domestic institutions supply individual companies with inputs they need to compete in the international markets – finance, skills, technology – but do so in very different ways.

This argument is formulated most strongly by the Varieties of Capitalism (VoC) approach which sees these cumulative differences as amounting to a country's *comparative institutional advantage* (Hall and Soskice 2001). Thus, a company in say Germany can count on highly trained and cooperative industrial workforce, patient, long-term funding from banks and close relations to both competitors and suppliers that facilitate diffusion of new technologies. This is an environment well suited to production of goods that rely on quality and gradual innovation, such as engineering products and complex consumer goods like automobiles. It also allows German companies to retain a competitive age in the face of increased competition, but in exchange binds them to institutions that ensure that the necessary inputs continue to be produced: dual vocational training in which firms take an active part, largely at their own expense; higher levels of employment protection to compensate workers for the risks involved in acquiring industry-specific skills; collective bargaining, which prevents companies from 'poaching' workers from one another and gives employee organizations a say in how companies are run; and participation in industry and employer organizations that facilitate coordination between companies (Hall and Soskice 2001; Iversen and Soskice 2001).

A very different set of constraints faces a firm in the UK or Ireland. Here companies more frequently raise capital on the stock market, which are more likely to finance original, high-risk ventures than are banks. But the stock markets also make company financing less stable. To remain flexible, firms therefore need to be able to hire and fire workers more easily too. This leads to a more adversarial relationship with the unions and practically rules out the kind of long-term cooperative employment relations that facilitates investment in industry-specific skills. At the same time, individuals have an incentive to invest in their own education – as evidenced also by the private costs of higher education in UK and Ireland compared to the continent – because the absence of collective bargaining means less wage compression and greater returns to those whose skills are in high demand.

These stylized accounts represent what the VoC literature calls 'coordinated' and 'liberal' market economies – the first represented by a cluster of countries in Northwestern Europe (Germany, Austria, Belgium, Netherlands, Sweden, Finland, Denmark), and the latter by UK and Ireland in Europe, as well as other Anglo-Saxon economies (US, Canada, Australia, New Zealand) (Hall and Soskice 2001). The VoC does not argue that these different types were created through mutual competition – various authors have explored at length the role of history, path dependence and politics in the formation of Europe's capitalist varieties (Thelen 2004; Iversen and Soskice 2009). Yet the core claim remains that the persistence of diversity has been reinforced by global, and especially European market integration. As integration eliminates economic barriers and sharpens competition, some features of the system might change, but the domestic producer groups will rally to protect those institutions that allow them to remain competitive (Hall and Soskice 2001; Hassel 2014).

The logic of institutional comparative advantage could thus explain why, for instance, trade liberalization accelerated the decline of manufacturing in the UK, but less so in Germany, and why employers in the Netherlands continue to support collective bargaining even in the face of falling union membership. The implications for the broader question about the desirability, and the likelihood of institutional convergence in Europe are also clear-cut. Institutions are protected by powerful cross-class coalitions and are resistant to change. Moreover, as institutions provide specific advantages to firms, forcing change may undermine their comparative advantages and make an economy less successful.

However, the binary of coordinated and liberal market economies does not do justice to the breadth of capitalist variety in Europe, and in fact leaves out most economies in East and Southern Europe that have been the main subjects of reform pressures in recent years. From the point of view of the VoC, both regions are home to different combinations of 'liberal' and 'coordinated' institutions. The southern economies have indeed been dubbed 'mixed' market economies (Molina and Rhodes 2007) to describe the contrast between high levels of coordination that prevail in the capital markets and some parts of industry, and the more liberal and adversarial relations in the rest of the economy.

Similar fragmentation in the modes of coordination has been observed in East European 'dependent' market economies (Nölke and Vliegenthart 2009), but here the division rather runs along ownership lines. In Eastern Europe, fragmented domestic capital with weak financial and business institutions and contentious relations with the state stands in contrast to a highly organized and coordinated network of foreign firms that rely on external connections and public support to secure their supply chains, finance, and even skills (Nölke and Vliegenthart 2009; Scepanovic and Bohle 2018; Ban 2019).

The implications of the existence of these mixed types for the prospects of institutional reform and convergence in Europe are also less obvious. The early VoC effectively argued that institutions across different sub-systems reinforced one another, and that such 'complementarities' were at the root of institutional comparative advantage. The less coherent, 'hybrid' institutional systems would lose out, and end up adjusting either towards the more liberal or the more coordinated pole (Hall and Gingerich 2009). It would appear that the EU's policy responses in the aftermath of the financial crisis were inspired by similar logic. Liberalization of labour markets, decentralization of collective bargaining and breaking up of the links between state, industry and banks all signalled adjustment towards the more liberal model (Hall 2018).

As argued in the introduction, this policy approach has been far from successful. Moreover, the subsequent fierce debates over the relative merits and demerits of different institutional systems in Europe helped to reveal just how much the 'coordinated' economies of the core have themselves been changing. The notion of institutional complementarities increasingly came under fire, and the field of comparative political economy saw the emergence of an entirely different paradigm, that of growth models.

# Growth models

The focus on production models proved a useful tool to explore different pathways to competitiveness within one integrated market. However, by highlighting the institutional systems that support the production models of the lead export sectors, this approach overlooked the trends that were under way in the rest of these economies and which, unfortunately for the approach, ended up in the eye of the storm.

The most important of these trends was an explosion in private household borrowing that affected economies across Europe. The overexposure of Irish, Spanish and Greek banks made headlines in the crisis, but the expansion of private credit affected just as much some of the coordinated 'core'. Denmark, Sweden and the Netherlands have in fact some of the highest levels of per capita household debt in Europe. Nor were the changes limited to finance. Most of these economies have been experiencing rapid growth in service sector employment, away from their traditional specializations in high value-added manufacturing. This was accompanied by changes in the educational systems, employment relations and social policy (Hassel and Palier 2021). In other words, even as some countries fought to preserve the core features of their comparative institutional advantage, others showed signs of looking for alternative sources of growth.

The 'growth models' perspective departs from the microeconomic supply-side view of institutions as providers of essential assets to competing firms, and looks at the institutional structures from a macroeconomic perspective, as ways of supporting different sources of demand (Baccaro and Pontusson 2016). Reliance on exports, or external demand, is only one option. Another one is to build up domestic demand, either through rising wages, public expenditure or loans.

What does this have to do with European integration and the prospects of convergence? In the postwar period most of Europe relied on domestic consumption. Trade and capital restrictions meant that capital owners had to get majority of their profits from the domestic market, so wage growth had a positive effect on investment as long as the cuts in profits due to higher labour costs could be offset by expanding production. Welfare systems, expansion of education and coordinated wage bargaining all served to support this growth in demand. However, market opening since the 1970s, and in Europe radical liberalization of product and capital markets since the mid-1980s, meant that capital was free to seek lower production costs and higher investment returns elsewhere, and wage growth increasingly came to be seen as an obstacle to investment (Lavoie and Stockhammer 2013).

European countries adapted in different ways. Some, like Germany, shifted to an export-based growth model, which required keeping wages firmly in line with productivity. In the large export-oriented sector this meant using collective bargaining to ensure wage moderation, but also investments into the training of low-skilled workers. It also meant, however, preventing wage inflation in the growing service sector from undermining these competitive gains, and this was partly accomplished through changes in the employment legislation that allowed for increase in precarious and low-paid jobs (Hassel 2014).

In many other countries, including southern ones, such as Spain and Italy, manufacturing sectors fought to keep wages in check but lacked clout to impose the same kind of discipline on others. Wages continued to grow in the public sector, and in sectors that relied on domestic demand – tourism, construction, retail, as well as in the growing 'knowledge economy'. Much of this demand expansion was now fuelled by credit, but a number of countries managed to turn growth in the domestic service sectors into a new source of competitiveness in high value-added finance, ICT and business services (Thelen 2021). For some, like the UK, this also meant rapid erosion of manufacturing exports, but in others, like Sweden, the conflicting logics of consumption-led growth in services and profit-led growth in manufacturing continue to battle, leading to institutional compromises and a more balanced growth model (Baccaro and Pontusson 2016).

Like the production models theories, then, the growth models approach offers a sceptical view on the prospects of institutional convergence in Europe, although for different reasons. In this view, institutions are not functional solutions to the problems of international competitiveness, protected from change by cross-class coalitions of producers and by inter-institutional complementarities. Instead, institutions are seen as products of political struggles, in which certain dominant social blocks can for a time impose their preferences, but where these compromises are in constant dangers of being challenged from inside and outside by actors seeking a larger portion of wealth.

This also implies a more complex view of the impact of European integration on different countries' institutions. Integration is no longer viewed merely as an external structure that exerts competitive pressures on local firms. It is now also perceived as a source of opportunities for various actors to explore new strategies of wealth accumulation and change their bargaining power, which in turn allows them to reshape domestic institutional arrangements. This allows us to explore, for instance, how the expansion of credit that re-directed some southern countries towards consumption-led growth was facilitated by the deep integration of the European financial markets. It also allows to see how the success of German export industries was made possible not only by the efficiency of domestic wage-setting institutions but also by the euro area shielding them from currency pressures that such success may have otherwise engendered (Jones 2021).

The emphasis on politics, internal conflict and multiplicity of pathways thus makes the growth models perspective a potentially promising tool for the study of institutional change in transnational context. Much of this work is, however, still in early stages, as the early literature focused on explaining the changing growth models of the 'core'. To see more clearly how the transnational agency shapes institutions of the EU member states, we turn next to the closest the EU has to an experiment in institutional transfer: the experience of East European member states.

# Lessons from the East

Both the transition from socialism as well as the accession to the European Union required an overhaul of economic institutions in this region. The EU played an active role in this, with the Commission providing guidance, training and funding for the construction of market-supporting institutions (Bruszt et al. 2020). Similar to the current efforts in the south, these policies did not necessarily reflect a consensus distilled from the existing institutional systems of the 'old' EU members – these, as we saw earlier, remained quite diverse. Rather, they reflected the prevailing ideological preferences for liberal market arrangements at the time of the 'Washington consensus', as well as suspicion towards the old state-connected elites. The result was a spate of reforms that insulated monetary policy, encouraged privatization, liberalized labour markets and weakened union bargaining power, promoted investments in general and higher education to support the transition towards 'knowledge economy' and invested in the development of domestic stock markets, among other by encouraging privatization of pensions (Ther 2016).

Yet none of this turned the East European countries into textbook 'liberal market economies', at least as far as development of comparative institutional advantages was concerned. Even in the Baltic states, which structurally came closest to the liberal model, no burgeoning services sector replaced labour-intensive manufacturing as a source of export earnings (Bohle and Greskovits 2012; Bohle 2018). A complicating factor was that constructing certain domestic institutions could not ensure that they fulfilled their function, especially if European integration offered an alternative mechanism. Investment financing is a good example. Despite all efforts at reform, neither the domestic stock markets nor the overwhelmingly foreign owned banking sectors played a big role in company financing (Scepanovic and Bohle 2018). Instead, the bulk of capital came from direct foreign investment.

The FDI itself offered another potential pathway for institutional transfer. East Central European countries, for instance, had become prime destinations for German capital investing in relatively capital intensive and high value-added industries. These companies brought with not only capital and technology but also entire networks of suppliers. They also established own associations that actively lobbied governments for policy changes, including revival of vocational training (Drahokoupil 2009; Ban 2019). Nevertheless, this propitious combination of export specialization and institutional culture did not lead to the transplantation of the 'coordinated' model to East Central Europe. Investors were eager to secure in-house cooperation with employees but eschewed higher-level collective bargaining. They demanded legal changes that allowed them to employ very young trainees through the systems of dual education but refused to contribute to the training schemes beyond the needs of their own companies. Above all, the institutional systems of these 'dependent market economies' (Nölke and Vliegenthart 2009) remained deeply fragmented between sectors dominated by export-oriented foreign firms and domestic capital mostly focused on the national market.

In sum, neither top-down institutional engineering nor import of entire economic sectors resulted in convergence of the East European institutional systems with those of the older EU members. What we saw instead was evolution of distinct sub-types, each shaped by its specific pattern of integration into the wider European economy: export-oriented manufacturing in East Central Europe, finance-led reorientation towards services in the Baltics (Bohle and Greskovits 2012). While this does to some extent confirm the VoC thesis that different economic specializations are underwritten by different institutional systems, the East European capitalist varieties by no means represent stable, self-reinforcing 'models'. Instead, and more in line with the expectations of the growth models literature, these are based on fragile political compromises, and depend heavily on the stability of various mechanisms that link them to the larger EU market.

The financial crisis made this readily apparent. The Baltic states, which had amassed huge amounts of private household debt, were in fact the first economies in Europe to buckle – Latvia requested a bailout as early as 2008. But while Baltics' ready embrace of harsh austerity was held up as an example to the more recalcitrant bailout recipients, their recovery was due just as much to other, less advertised factors.

For one, the East European economies were saved from the crippling costs of rescuing private banks because the banks were foreign owned to begin with, and because the EU's competition policy, as well as direct negotiations between the EU institutions and private banks, made sure they remained put instead of repatriating capital out of the region. The same was true of the subsidy schemes to West European manufacturing, which also helped along the recovery in East Central Europe. Another factor had to do with massive labour emigration. According to the Eurostat, the number of working-age citizens living abroad nearly doubled for all eastern member states, and in 2018 remittances outpaced both foreign investment and EU funds as a source of external finance in these countries (Bohle 2018).

Finally, even though deep integration into the EU's capital, goods and labour markets provided a lifeline in the immediate aftermath of the crisis, the crisis itself, and the difficult recovery since, had prompted political realignments and a rethinking of the regional growth models. The banking systems may have been saved from collapse through transnational intervention, but lending was severely curtailed, bringing the Baltics debt-led growth model to an abrupt stop. In East Central Europe, too, foreign investment became more volatile, and the wage convergence ground to a halt. International financial institutions began to warn that without serious investment in innovation the region will be heading into a middle-income trap (EBRD 2017).

The slowdown also offered domestic capital an opening to challenge the dominance of the foreign-led export growth model. Loud denouncements of rapacious foreign banks and 'economic colonialism' by Western firms have become the staple of populist politics in Poland and Hungary. While it is unclear to what extent there is really a shift to a different growth model (Bohle and Greskovits 2018; Scheiring 2020), a search is definitely under way.

# Conclusion

This chapter argued that the EU economic integration, far from promoting convergence, has in fact been part of the reason that capitalist diversity persists in Europe. Indeed, the review of the two currently dominant perspectives in comparative political economy shows that they both recognize the fundamental role played by international market integration in perpetuating diversity, although they do so in different ways. The Varieties of Capitalism literature grounded in the production models approach views institutional difference as part of developing competitive specialization in an integrated market. The growth models perspective rather sees transnational market integration as altering the structure of opportunities for different actors to earn higher returns on their assets, and thus pushing countries to look for different sources of growth.

Even as they acknowledge the role of integration, however, both perspectives treat it as a starting point, a background structure that too easily fades from focus as the analysis zooms in on the importance of domestic institutions, politics and ideas. This may not be surprising for a discipline that is above all preoccupied with comparisons of national systems, but an excess of methodological nationalism has meant that European comparative political economy has largely ignored the role of the EU and has until very recently had relatively little to say about how the EU could, or indeed should, manage this internal diversity.

Studying the evolution of capitalist institutions in the East European member states can prove instructive in this regard, as this is where the most extensive experiments in institutional engineering have taken place in recent decades. The literature makes it clear that such efforts did not result in replication of the core states' institutional models, but instead lead to different and more unstable patterns of 'dependent' institutional development and economic specialization that have left these economies highly vulnerable to external shocks.

One may argue, a little cynically perhaps, that the success of this experiment depends on one's measure of success. From the point of view of the EU, or at least of its net contributor states, it may not matter very much that Slovakia or Lithuania have not yet found a reliable road to structural and economic convergence with the 'core' EU members. What matters is that these countries' institutional systems allow for achieving price flexibility that renders extensive EU 'bailouts' unnecessary. Yet a closer look at the much-praised crisis responses in the Baltics and East Central Europe shows that this flexibility was due not only to radical austerity, but to significant transfers accomplished through an informal banking union, revenues from structural funds and massive labour emigration: mechanisms that are not readily available for the larger southern economies.

Most of all, therefore, research into Eastern European capitalisms helps to highlight the extensive transnational entanglements of Europe's institutional systems. Understanding those, and their role in continuing capitalist diversity, could help to break new ground not only in the study of comparative political economy but also in the design of EU-level policy. If we think of EU member states not as discrete economic units that must all live by the same rules, but as one integrated economy that is shaped by the interaction of local institutions and transnational market actors, it becomes clearer that we cannot really expect all its national parts to function in exactly the same way. This also suggests that instead of attempting to 'fix' the periphery, the EU as a whole might need to look for a growth model that accommodates better its different parts.

The struggle over the Covid-19 recovery funds shows both the potential and the difficulties of such an approach. On the one hand, the emphasis on ambitious investment goals and the green economy suggests a willingness to move towards a growth model more focused on internal demand and investment. On the other hand, the fact that funding for individual members' investment plans remains conditional on structural reforms in the public sector and labour markets suggests that the EU is finding it hard to let go of its bias towards export-led growth (Johnston and Reagan 2018). The tension between the two is likely to mark the EU politics for years to come. Which of the two prevails may in the end depend as much on the outcome of internal political battles as on changes in the global economic environment.

# Questions for discussion

1 What are the main drivers behind the diversity of capitalist economic models in Europe?
2 What role does the European Union have in managing the internal diversity of economic models? How has this role evolved in the last decades?
3 What explains the delay of East European member states to become what is generally understood as 'liberal market economies'?
4 How does the Covid-19 crisis affect European economic integration? In what way could the advent of the health crisis influence political realignments and a rethinking of regional growth models?

# Recommended for Further Reading

Ban, C. (2016) *Ruling Ideas: How Global Neoliberalism Goes Local*. Oxford: Oxford University Press.
Ban, C. and Bohle, D. (2021) 'Definancialization, Financial Repression and Policy Continuity in East-Central Europe', *Review of International Political Economy* 28 (4): 874–97.

Streeck, W. (2017) *Buying Time: The Delayed Crisis of Democratic Capitalism.* New York, NY: Verso.

Tooze, A. (2021) *Shutdown: How COVID Shook the World's Economy.* New York, NY: Penguin.

Vachudova, M. (2019) 'The EU's Eastward Enlargement and the Illiberal Turn', *Current History* 118 (806): 90–5.

# 8

# Worlds of Welfare Regimes

*Kimberly J. Morgan*

Welfare systems are of central importance to European politics and societies. In many popular understandings, comprehensive, generous welfare programmes help define what it means to be a European country (as opposed to one located in North America, for instance). Welfare programmes are also mainstays of contemporary political debate: much of what political parties and candidates spar over during elections is who is best positioned to protect these programmes or bring about reforms to them. However, the politics of reform can be treacherous, as existing social benefits and services often have strong constituencies behind them. Governments who threaten these programmes have thus faced mass protests, a precipitous decline in popularity and loss of power in the next election.

To get a handle on European welfare systems, we first need to dispense with some myths about them. Although we may be tempted to think of European welfare systems as state-run monoliths, there are considerable differences in how much they rely on public, private and hybrid modes of delivery. Taking these many differences into account, we can identify distinct worlds of welfare. These worlds have their roots in over a century of social, political and economic developments. In reviewing those developments, we can both understand how we arrived at the point where we are today, as well as some of the forces that are shaping current debates and decisions about reform. This chapter will treat these questions as follows: first, offering an overall characterization of welfare regimes; second, reviewing the forces that have shaped cross-national differences in these regimes; and third, discussing recent debates about the future of these systems.

# Characterizing welfare regimes

The term 'European welfare state' may call to mind large, state-run programmes that provide for social needs from cradle-to-grave – from childcare to nursing homes, and all the benefits and services covering each life stage in between. In reality, welfare systems in Europe vary considerably in their size, coverage and the significance of private funding and provision. Given these differences, scholars of welfare systems often describe them as welfare *regimes*, drawing attention to the fact that all nations provide for human welfare through four spheres: states, markets, the voluntary sector and families. Analysing welfare regimes requires us to examine the interrelations and division of labour between these spheres.

One way to capture differences in the role of the *state* in welfare provision is to look at how much governments spend in this area. European welfare regimes vary considerably on this measure (see Figure 8.1): on average, these countries devote over 20 per cent of gross domestic product (GDP) to social spending, but the French state spends twice as much on social benefits and services as the Irish one. What counts as social spending? In this measure, social spending includes benefits and services related to old-age, disability, unemployment, health, family, housing and income support or anti-poverty initiatives. However, while education is not included here,

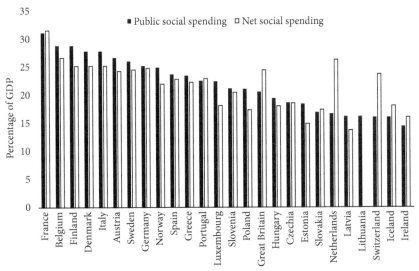

**Figure 8.1** Spending on European welfare regimes as a percentage of GDP.
Compiled from OECD SOCX.

many scholars do see education as an important part of welfare systems. For instance, vocational education programmes that prepare or retrain people for paid work are essential features of labour market policy that, alongside programmes such as unemployment benefits, affect workers' income security.

Another limitation of this measure is that it misses the role of private funds and actions in the delivery of social benefits and services in both *markets* and through the *voluntary sector*. We can start to correct that through another figure collected by the OECD – net social spending (Figure 8.1) – which takes into account the effects of tax systems and private spending on social provision. Some countries subsidize private welfare delivery through the tax code, as in fiscal subsidies for the purchase of childcare or to hire caregivers for the disabled. Some also levy taxes on benefits as they do other forms of income; in countries with high tax rates, this can significantly reduce the total amount spent on social programmes. Finally, governments in some countries mandate private social spending, requiring that employers provide benefits such as health care or pensions to their employees, for instance. But employers also can voluntarily provide such benefits, thus adding to the total resources that societies devote to social welfare. Once we take into account tax systems and both mandated and voluntary social spending, gaps between countries in their total spending on welfare shrink.

Capturing meaningful differences in welfare regimes requires us to go beyond spending figures, however, and look at the entities that deliver benefits and services. In many European countries, for-profit actors are less significant in this regard than the voluntary sector, which includes non-profit organizations, churches, mutual aid societies, cooperatives, volunteer service groups, foundations and trade unions. These entities may receive public subsidies to provide for welfare needs, but also often rely on volunteer or below-market cost labour, fundraising and other philanthropic support, and/or fees. In other words, through their own activities and marshalling of people and funds, the voluntary sector can contribute significantly to overall welfare effort. In the Netherlands, for instance, the majority of primary school students are in publicly funded but privately run schools, and many social services are delivered through non-profit organizations that receive public funds.

Finally, *families* play a vital role in providing care and support to their members. For much of the twentieth century, the expansion of welfare systems was guided by gendered assumptions about family care – namely, that women were available to look after young children and ageing relatives, thus obviating the need for state assistance in these domains. Strong economic growth and rising wages in the post-1945 period enabled many families to be organized along these lines, with men as the primary breadwinners and women the main caregivers who were in paid work at most part-time or intermittently. Even in communist countries, where women were both expected and enabled to be in paid work by state-provided childcare services and old-age care, a 'second shift' of household labour often awaited them at home. By the close of the twentieth century, however, rising rates of solo parenthood and women's employment made the male breadwinner–female caregiver model increasingly obsolete across Europe, spurring the expansion of public supports for the care of children and ageing relatives. That said, women generally do more of the unpaid labour (care, cleaning, etc.) in the home than men, and families remain an important source of financial support for their members.

To make sense of the tremendous differences in how states, markets, families and the voluntary sector provide for social welfare, scholars have sought to identify clusters of commonly structured welfare regimes, largely by building upon the foundational typology of sociologist Gøsta Esping-Andersen. He developed his typology in the last two decades of the twentieth century and identified three worlds of welfare in Western Europe and some other English-speaking democracies: a social democratic model found largely in the Nordic countries; conservative regimes, present in continental Western Europe; and the liberal market systems of the English-speaking countries, such as the UK and Ireland (1990). At the core of the typology is the concept of decommodification – the idea that social protection can improve the conditions under which workers make themselves 'commodities' in the sense of selling themselves as workers in the marketplace. A limited welfare system results in a high degree of labour commodification, such that when individuals are sick, disabled, old or pregnant, for instance, they remain dependent on employment for their incomes and may not be able to forgo work.

By contrast, decommodification is when benefits and services cushion people from the vagaries of markets and risks over the life course, thus providing sickness pay, pensions and parental leave, corresponding to the examples given above. Decommodification does not entail workers ceasing to work entirely, but rather it reduces their dependence on employment as a source of income in times of need. Esping-Andersen further analyses welfare regimes according to the significance of public or private provision, and the extent to which welfare programmes break down or reinforce economic and social hierarchies. These hierarchies reflect whether programmes are universally available or segmented by a person's occupation or income.

Welfare benefits and services in the social democratic world (mainly in the Nordic countries) are generous, widely if not universally available, largely publicly provided and mostly financed through general taxation. The result is a high degree of decommodification, low poverty rates and diminished economic or social inequalities and hierarchies. In the liberal market regimes of the UK and Ireland, by contrast, benefits are less generous while markets deliver much welfare provision. Not only is labour commodified through the more limited public supports but also through dependence on employers for benefits. With so much reliance on markets, there is greater income inequality and higher poverty rates than in the Nordic countries. Finally, the continental Western European approach to social welfare emerged out of societies historically divided into guilds and other occupational groupings that tended to the welfare of their own members. While these welfare regimes are more generous and de-commodifying than the liberal market regimes, they reflect and reproduce some of these divides, with benefits delivered by social insurance funds, often linked to one's occupation, to which individuals pay contributions. The voluntary sector also is involved in social provision in many of these countries. Poverty and inequality are lower than in the liberal welfare systems, but higher than in the social democratic ones.

Adopting a gendered perspective on these worlds of welfare leads to some qualifications of the typology but also reinforces it. The male breadwinner model was the norm during the initial development of these regimes in Western Europe and was reflected in benefits enabling male workers to support families on one income (Lewis 1992). But many social democratic regimes abandoned the male breadwinner model early – starting in the 1970s – and, with the aim of supporting mothers' employment, began developing generous parental leave benefits, affordable and highly quality childcare, and public facilities for old-age care. Some liberal regimes also had the effect of promoting mothers' employment, as the lesser generosity of these welfare systems made it difficult for families living on one income to make ends meet. Supports for mothers' employment have been slower to develop, however, leaving workers reliant on markets and employers for such assistance. Many countries in the conservative world of welfare in continental Western Europe hewed longest to male breadwinner model and subsidized it through wages and benefit systems, while neglecting the development of care services. There have been some major shifts in these policies over past two decades, however, as is discussed later in this chapter.

These worlds of welfare are rough approximations and scholars have often pointed to countries or policy areas that do not fit well in these categories. In some cases, this inspired the articulation of additional worlds, with some scholars arguing that Southern Europe is a world of welfare on its own (Ferrera 1996), characterized by particularly high pension spending, low public support for families and a pronounced divide between labour market insiders and outsiders – the former with access to generous social benefits while the latter have more fragmented access or none at all if employed in large underground economies. Central and Eastern European countries also fit uneasily in the existing typology: they had welfare systems under communism in which the state provided for most major needs. The transition to democratic polities and market economies initially brought retrenchment and privatization but was followed by expansions in some programmes and efforts to improve the quality of public services. There is some debate among scholars about whether post-communist welfare regimes make up a coherent world of welfare, but many emphasize the hybrid nature of these regimes, as policymakers in each country have incorporated elements of social democratic, liberal and conservative welfare regimes into their own (Cook and Inglot 2021).

There also are some policy areas that fit less well within the conventional typology, such as health care. One basic divide in health care systems is between national health service and social insurance-based systems. In the former, care is not only publicly financed but also delivered by public hospitals and clinics as well as state-salaried physicians. In the latter, social insurance funds cover costs but the auspices of providers are more varied: hospitals may be public, private or run by voluntary organizations, while physicians and other providers tend to operate private practices. National health services tend to be found in Northern and Southern Europe, as well as in the UK regime, thus scrambling the conventional typology. Many continental European countries, including those in Central and Eastern Europe, finance coverage through social insurance funds, while the provision of care is done largely by private practitioners (although in some, such as France, hospitals are publicly operated). There are even some countries (the Netherlands and Switzerland) whose health care systems resemble 'Obamacare' in the United States, whereby individuals purchase insurance from a market of competing private insurance plans.

Finally, Esping-Andersen's typology was developed and refined during the last two decades of the twentieth century. Since that time, demographic change, financial crises and long-term economic developments have put pressure on these systems, spurring continual demands for reform. But before we can get a handle on these reforms, we must first understand why these systems look the way they do.

# Explaining welfare regimes

To explain the size and contours of European welfare regimes, some researchers highlight the role of labour unions and left political parties in developing universalistic and generous welfare programmes (Huber and Stephens 2001). By the start of the twentieth century, industrialization had spurred a mobilization by trade unions and left political parties across much of Europe to improve working conditions, redistribute wealth and income, and empower workers through expansion of the suffrage. As workers and their representatives gained footholds in politics, they created or expanded welfare programmes, with some of the most generous systems in the Nordic countries where social democratic parties governed for decades. Further to the East, communist parties that gained power through revolutions after the Second World War went a step further in socializing the means of production. Social democratic and labour parties in the West, by contrast, sought to work through democratic politics to mitigate the economic shocks and inequalities resulting from capitalism, rather than overthrowing capitalism itself. In countries where left parties were less powerful, they could nonetheless shape welfare provision during periods of serving in government, as was the case of the UK's National Health Service that a Labour government created in 1948.

Although the working class and its representatives were key progenitors of welfare states in many countries, they were not the only ones. The middle classes also came to see merit in systems of social insurance – of paying contributions into funds that would later pay out benefits to contributors as needed (Baldwin 1990). Religious forces provided yet another set of arguments in favour of redistributive initiatives: in many European countries, Christian trade unions and movements coalesced into political parties that would become powerful conservative parties. Their support for welfare programmes reflected doctrinal commitments to caring for the poor as well as their own interests: churches and related charitable organizations were important providers of education, health and other social supports (van Kersbergen and Manow 2009). In countries where middle-class or religious interests were more dominant in shaping the development of welfare states, social provision was often more segmented, as in the conservative or liberal welfare states described earlier, or solicitous of market or voluntary actors.

Democracy would contribute to the ability of these varied forces to shape the worlds of welfare. Certainly, autocracies can also develop welfare programmes: in communist Eastern Europe, for instance, state provision covered many needs, including housing, healthcare, education, food assistance and old-age support, but often at a basic level (Cook and Inglot 2021). In seeking to understand why social provision expanded so markedly in the postwar decades in Western Europe, one can point to democratization of many countries following the end of the Second World War, with further waves of democratization and welfare expansion coming in the 1970s in parts of Southern Europe. In Central and Eastern Europe, after a period of welfare state contraction during the transition to both democracy and market capitalism in the 1990s, welfare spending grew in many countries in the 2000s.

Going beyond democracy as a means of channelling popular support for redistributive programmes, some scholars have highlighted the role of particular features of electoral politics that help translate the pro-redistributive sentiment of the mass public into governing agendas. Proportional electoral systems are widespread in Europe and some scholars argue they have facilitated the development of social democratic parties and governments that favour redistribution (Iversen and Soskice 2006). That is because proportional representation facilitates coalition governments of multiple parties that often represent 50–60 per cent of the electorate, whereas in winner-takes-all electoral systems, governments are often elected with only a plurality. In more recent years, scholars point to electoral competition for voting blocs as a key source of policy dynamism, as parties jostle to show they are most responsive to redistributive preferences of key constituencies (Green-Pedersen and Jensen 2019).

Those constituencies have been evolving across Europe since the latter decades of the twentieth century, with the decline of trade union power in many countries, expansion of the middle class, secularization and mobilization of new social groups, including advocates for gender equality and disability rights. These social-structural changes and mobilizations have drawn attention to needs that had not been taken into consideration during the initial period of welfare state expansion. For instance, rising education levels, especially among women, and a concomitant rise in female workforce participation helped put the issues of childcare, parental leave, working time flexibility and old-age care more centrally on the political agenda.

The result would be considerable policy dynamism to promote mothers' employment, even in the conservative world of welfare that had long cherished the male breadwinner model (Morgan 2013). In Germany, for example, reforms in the 2000s dramatically expanded early childhood education and care and created a more generous parental leave system. The Netherlands also abandoned the male breadwinner model starting in the 1990s, as signalled by the development of broadly available childcare services and a universal right to part-time work. In the Nordic countries, governments in recent years have built on their already generous systems to not only help mothers work but also to help fathers care by creating 'use-it-or-lose-it' months of parental leave that are reserved solely for fathers. Not all countries have adopted policies that support and encourage mothers' employment, however. In Central and Eastern Europe, some conservative governments instead allowed communist-era childcare centres to close and have encouraged mothers of young children to leave the labour market and care for their own children at home for several years, supported by public benefits.

In many countries, the expansion of the middle class has changed the calculus of politicians about how to deliver benefits and services. Middle-income people are often comfortable with market-based provision in that they have the resources to purchase goods and services in the marketplace and may prefer to do so rather than pay higher taxes for public programmes. Seeking to cater to these preferences, while also holding down public spending, governments in many countries have created vouchers or tax subsidies to encourage the purchase of private services (Gingrich 2011). Sweden, for instance, instituted a system of school vouchers in the 1990s that allows parents to choose between competing public and private schools. The goals of promoting consumer-choice has also influenced policies for the elderly or disabled (Da Roit and Le Bihan 2010). Thus, Germany and Austria are among a number of countries with long-term care allowances that individuals can use to fund institutional care (such as nursing homes or assisted living facilities) or else to pay home care providers of their choice, including family members.

Finally, a number of scholars seeking to explain patterns of social provision have emphasized how they fit within the broader economic context of European countries. Strong economic growth during the decades following the Second World War was one precondition for the development of broad-based social programmes, but welfare systems in turn helped support the continued flourishing of capitalist economies. For example, generous social programmes enabled countries to progressively liberalize trade relations in the latter half of the twentieth century, as redistributive programmes cushioned workers in these countries from the destabilizing effects of global economic competition. Moreover, social democratic and some conservative welfare regimes (such as in Austria, Denmark, Germany, Sweden and the Netherlands) emerged in countries characterized by a considerable degree of bargaining between well-organized trade unions and employers' organizations over wages, working conditions and the like. In addition to fostering the social peace that supports the functioning of market economies, these types of negotiations have often laid the foundation for the development of welfare programmes that mesh in supportive ways with labour market conditions. For example, in the Danish 'flexicurity' model, job loss triggers comprehensive income supports alongside retraining and other measures to help individuals find employment. With these types of guarantees in place, firms are allowed greater latitude by the government to fire employees, enabling them to make decisions that maximize competitiveness rather than being hemmed in by restrictive labour laws.

The liberal welfare regime also fits with features of liberal market economies – including weaker trade unions, uncoordinated employers and highly decentralized bargaining over wages and working conditions. These countries therefore have more flexible labour markets, with easier hiring and firing and greater labour mobility, but also more wage stratification. The result is a certain level of economic dynamism of firms reliant on cheaper and flexible labour, but also a higher degree of poverty, inequality and insecurity. It is important to keep in mind these differences in the nature of capitalism when considering prescriptions for policy reform. The generous welfare policies of Germany and Sweden, and concomitantly high tax burden, may be more sustainable where educated, healthy, well-trained workers may be expensive to hire, but operate at a high level of productivity. In liberal market economies, by contrast, a certain amount of production is rooted in cheap labour that is enabled by labour market deregulation, lower taxes and a high degree of inequality.

Given these underlying economic differences, the policy prescriptions for one world of capitalist market economies may not be suitable for another one. For example, reforms that would make labour more expensive to hire and harder to fire in the liberal market context might clash with a production model based on highly flexible labour markets. Workers may gain greater security but at a cost of more unemployment. In countries such as Germany or Austria, where the economic production model is based on firms investing in the skills of workers who then stay with those firms for the long-term, efforts to flexibilize labour markets could disincentivize such investments, thus diminishing the overall skill level of the workforce.

# Debates and reforms

Claims about the imminent demise of welfare regimes are a perennial feature of politics in many European countries. Right-leaning critics see welfare systems as unsustainable given ageing societies and pressures to keep tax burdens low, while some on the left see neoliberal prescriptions as destroying social programmes despite ever-growing need. In general, however, welfare programmes have displayed remarkable staying power, a reflection of their strong public support. That does not mean they have been immobile, however, as demographic and economic pressures have brought about significant changes and spurred ongoing debates about future reforms.

One source of concern about the long-term sustainability of welfare regimes in Europe is demographic ageing, owing to both greater life expectancy and fertility rates below population replacement levels. Europe is the site of four of the top five countries in the world as measured by the percentage of the population sixty-five and over – Italy, Germany, Portugal and Finland – and that proportion is projected to rise in the European Union from 19.8 per cent in 2018 to 31.3 per cent in 2100 (Eurostat 2020). These trends diminish the numbers who work and pay taxes while increasing the demands placed upon the welfare system, particularly on pensions and health care, which are typically the largest social expenditures. Ageing societies also face strongly growing demand for old-age care.

Economic volatility and structural change also strain welfare systems. Welfare spending is a short-term macroeconomic stabilizer, supporting incomes during economic downturns, but there are some limits on public spending even in times of recession. High debt loads can spook creditors, who may fear governments will not be able to pay them back, and European Union member states have agreed to limits on public deficits and debt (the UK opted out of that requirement and has since left the EU). Whether or not countries should adhere to such limits during times of economic downturn has been hotly contested, but the 2007–2009 Great Recession induced some governments to institute significant cuts in social programmes (Taylor-

Gooby et al. 2017), particularly in Southern European countries that were hardest hit by the crisis and under the most pressure from the European Union and International Monetary Fund to institute austerity measures.

Long-term economic transformations also are changing the context within which welfare regimes operate. The creation and expansion of many social programmes in Western Europe took place in a context of rapidly growing manufacturing economies in which unemployment was low and tax revenues were plentiful. The shift to post-industrial, knowledge-based economies has generally brought slower growth and higher unemployment, even though some countries have experienced periods of economic buoyancy (e.g. Germany, Ireland, Portugal and the UK). Well-remunerated manufacturing jobs have disappeared in many countries, and some argue that digitalization is hollowing out the middle class, generating well-paid jobs for the highly educated as well as jobs at the bottom of the wage ladder (in care and personal services, for example), while automation eliminates many jobs in the middle (Palier 2019). Related to this is the phenomenon of dualization, whereby labour markets become segmented between those with well-paid jobs covered by social insurance programmes and/or employer-provided benefits, while others with part-time, short-term and other atypical work contracts have less entitlement to social protection (Emmenegger et al. 2012). Another development is the liberalization of labour markets, as many forms of work become de-standardized and less protected by wage laws or labour standards – a trend some scholars see as widespread in Central and Eastern Europe, as well as in the UK and Ireland.

In the face of these challenges, neoliberals in academia, think tanks and governments argue that the answer lies in cutting taxes, de-regulating labour markets, reducing the burdens on the public sector and augmenting the role of markets in providing for human welfare needs. These views have influenced pension reforms in some countries: Sweden and Norway instituted private retirement accounts alongside public pension systems, for instance, while during the post-communist transitions in Central and Eastern Europe, the World Bank pushed many of these countries to institute partial or full privatization of their pension systems while creating private pension accounts (Appel and Orenstein 2016). Neoliberals also argue that generous welfare programmes burden the economy with the taxes needed to pay for them while undermining incentives for people to seek employment. These types of concerns have underpinned initiatives to 'activate' the non-employed by reducing the tax burden on employers while cutting disability, unemployment and other welfare benefits.

An alternative, social investment perspective also favours activating those disconnected from paid work but argues this is best achieved through potentially *more* spending, not less. The social investment logic has roots in the focus of Scandinavian welfare states on promoting full employment and high levels of human capital, but it has gained momentum in recent years through the work of both academics and policy thinkers in the OECD and European Commission (Morel et al. 2012). The logic is that, in post-industrial knowledge-based economies, social policies should aim to develop the skills and capacities necessary for inclusion in paid work. Social investment advocates thus argue that welfare regimes need to be recalibrated from sustaining consumption to investing in human capital. With this in mind, advocates favour prioritizing spending on early childhood education and care, lifelong learning initiatives and other active labour market policies that involve retraining and skill development.

Critics of both neoliberal and social investment perspectives argue that they lose sight of continuing and, in some countries, growing problems of poverty and social deprivation. Poverty rates across the European Union declined between 2008 and 2017, to an average of 22.4 per cent, but countries still vary markedly on this measure, ranging from a low of 12.2 per cent (Czech Republic) and to as high as 38.9 per cent (in Bulgaria) (Eurostat 2019). The overall downward trend in poverty also masks growing poverty rates in a number of countries, such as Greece, Italy and Spain. Given these realities, scholars and activists in some countries have pushed for an unconditional basic income so as to ensure that everyone has a certain level of resources. Some activists have worked transnationally by creating an international non-profit organization – Unconditional Basic Income in Europe – that seeks to mobilize support for basic income policies.

All of these reform prescriptions run up against a key barrier: the stickiness of the status quo, as creating new programmes often means taking money from old ones. Existing programmes often have constituencies behind them that will mobilize strongly against any loss of benefits or services to which they are accustomed. For defenders of welfare regimes, this is good news, as neoliberal prescriptions for privatization and massive cuts to the state are unlikely to get very far (Pierson 1996). On the other hand, advocates for major expansions of existing programmes or the creation of new ones also face considerable barriers. More commonly, governments adopt incremental reforms that can, over time, add up to significant change, but the basic contours of welfare provision bear strong continuities with the past.

# Conclusion

Welfare regimes are central to European politics and societies. Historically, these systems often emerged out of democratic politics, reflecting the power of political actors that championed distinct visions about how state, market, family and voluntary sector should provide for human welfare needs. Welfare regimes vary markedly across Europe, but all countries devote significant budgetary resources to these benefits and services. That ensures that welfare programmes are often at the heart of political debates. Although policymakers continually wrestle with how to adapt their welfare systems to shifting economic structures – with economic and demographic sustainability a key concern – the broad popularity of these programmes has helped protect them from the budgetary axe and will likely do so in the years ahead.

# Questions for discussion

1  What are the main 'worlds of welfare' and how do they differ from each other?
2  What explains the differences between welfare regimes?
3  What are the main challenges facing welfare systems today?
4  Can welfare regimes be reformed? What obstacles stand in the way of change and how could they be overcome?

# Recommended for Further Reading

Béland, D., Leibfried, S., Morgan, K. J., Obinger, H. and Pierson, C., eds (2021), *The Oxford Handbook of the Welfare State*, 2nd edn. Oxford: Oxford University Press.

Emmenegger, P., Kvist, J., Marx, P. and Petersen, K., eds (2015) 'Special Issue: 25 Years of "Three Worlds of Welfare Capitalism"', *Journal of European Social Policy* 25(1): 3–134.

Hassel, A. and Palier, B.(2021) *Growth and Welfare in Advanced Capitalist Economies: How Have Growth Regimes Evolved?* Oxford: Oxford University Press.

Kenworthy, L. (2020) *Social Democratic Capitalism*. New York, NY: Oxford University Press.

Lynch, J. (2021) *Regimes of Inequality: The Political Economy of Health and Wealth*. New York, NY: Cambridge University Press.

# 9

# Gender, Women and Politics

## Lisa A. Baglione

Although the World Economic Forum (WEF) has reported improved gender equity throughout Europe over the past twenty years, the whole continent does not deserve a reputation for high levels of gender empowerment (WEF 2020). In fact, the pattern of equality is varied. To understand differing levels of women's status in European states, we first need to explore the concept of gender. Because it is a sociological construct, gender orders the expectations and aspirations of individuals and is embedded in structures. Gender then affects how women and men engage in politics and the economy.

One important indicator of women's political power is their level of representation in national parliaments. Political recruitment is the key concept for illuminating how women candidates, political elites and voters react to women's electoral ambitions. A variety of gender-influenced factors – cultural values, social structures, political institutions and external pressures – combine to explain why women are less likely to be elected to legislatures. Not surprisingly, the variation in women's representation in European national parliaments reveals a configuration related to embedded gender cultures.

This regional pattern is visible not only in politics but also in the economy, where a comparable set of obstacles hinder women's empowerment. Gender conditions women's participation in the work force and how they balance familial roles with their desire and need to earn wages and achieve professional goals. Throughout the continent, women typically make a variety of 'choices' that constrain their economic advancement. Again, these outcomes tend to appear with regional regularity and correspond to prevailing national gendered expectations and institutions.

Because economic advancement feeds back into political power and overall empowerment, women in European countries still have a way to go before equality is achieved, even in the best performing states. In less egalitarian places, gender equity is a faraway ideal. Moreover, Covid-19 creates new obstacles blocking and even reversing progress. Thus, the levels of equity achieved prior to Covid-19 are not guaranteed to prevail, and the impact of the crisis is likely to set equality back in countries that take a gender-blind view to addressing the pandemic.

# 'Seeing' women and understanding gender analysis

Gender theorists insist that scholars, policy makers and citizens notice how political outcomes vary by gender, and how social norms regarding appropriate behaviour for women and men diverge by time, place and social delimiters like class, race, ethnicity, religion, sexuality and other characteristics. Underpinning gender analyses are three core insights from feminist theory: for centuries, most human societies refused to see and define women as a) fully *human*, b) *worthy* of education, ownership of property or legal responsibilities, and c) *capable* of behaving in public as adults. Despite contemporary popular culture's views, the vast majority of feminists don't see achieving women's equality as zero sum. They argue that traditional gender stereotypes also hurt men by forcing them into a box that is not fully human, either (Pateman 1988; Grant 1993; Okin 1998).

Political science has often ignored the importance of gender and the complexity of self. A key reason for this inattention has been the discipline's focus on the public sphere and dismissal of the private as a place that is apolitical, i.e. where no power is wielded. Therefore, traditionalists insist the home is beyond the scope of the field (Okin 1998; Owens 2016). While that assumption makes sense for male theorists thinking as men about men, feminists have understood the pervasive power that privileged men wield over 'their' women and others in private (Pateman 1988; Owens 2016). Although historically male 'heads of households' had enormous control, theorists in the 'canon' have imagined these 'kings of their castles' to be benevolent dictators who had the best interests of all in their hearts. The reality was much grimmer for their subjects, including wives, children, dependent relatives, servants and enslaved peoples. Still, this assumption of 'harmony' in the private sphere, along with notions of female inferiority, led to the ideas that men were the only ones who need to vote, serve on juries, stand for election and go out into the world as 'breadwinners' (Okin 1998; Tickner 2014).

Once the notion of the apolitical private sphere is eroded and the social construction of gender is acknowledged, the impact of ignoring other markers becomes clear. Understandings of appropriate behaviour across time and place for women and men are affected by class, race, ethnicity, sexuality and other socially relevant attributes. Intersectionality – the idea that privilege or disadvantage comes from these multiple characteristics – reveals new sources of oppression. In the 1970s, the feminist slogan 'Sisterhood Is Universal' advanced by primarily white, wealthy, heterosexual, Global North feminists frustrated and angered others who didn't share their advantages. These sloganeers experienced privilege in *every other* social category besides their gender and were often tone deaf to the multiplicity of obstacles other women (within their own societies and from around the world) faced; in other words, discrimination based on biological sex was only one of an intersecting set of structural constraints facing women (Crenshaw 1991; Enloe 2016).

After unpacking gender and intersectionality, observers can see and then explain why public sphere changes (e.g. giving women the right to vote or opening schools and professions to them) have not resulted in closing the gender gap in politics or in the economy. Even if legal changes remedy public sphere inequalities, new freedoms infrequently liberate women from social constraints and economic realities that restrict them and particularly hinder less privileged ones. To account for these continuing challenges, gender scholars have advanced two other concepts: political recruitment and the gendered economy.

# The continuing gender gap in political representation

The Political Recruitment Model (PRM) (Norris and Lovenduski 1995; Hughes and Paxton 2017; Chiva 2018) explains how gender interacts with traditionally recognized variables – resources, experience and political institutions – to keep women disproportionately out of politics. The point is that each of these *gendered* factors increases women's tendency to drop out of the electoral politics pipeline. Being elected requires four steps: 1) being allowed to serve, then 2) aspiring and 3) deciding to run, and finally 4) winning the race. Although women have been eligible to run everywhere in Europe for decades, the challenges of the last three steps – wanting to run, competing and being victorious – are still enormous. Barriers emerge from supply and demand pressures on (potential) candidates.

On the supply side, women have to be willing and able to supply themselves or be convinced by others that they should get involved in electoral competitions. Typically, those decisions are based on personal and social assessments of efficacy. These, in turn, are related to an individual's characteristics, access to resources and applicable experiences, as well as electoral rules. What a person can bring to the table and how these assets are perceived are filtered through gendered social, economic and political processes. If a woman has been raised in a highly unequal environment where politics is not considered a place for her, then she is very unlikely to seek to run (supply herself). Even if she has that inclination, she might lack the social and economic resources to compete. Does she have the time and family support to devote to a campaign and a political career if she is successful? Does she have access to funding through her own familial wealth or that of friends, connections and political organizations? Similarly, does she have the kind of occupational experience that many think is appropriate for politics and that provide her with the contacts she needs to be successful? Because gendered assumptions typically affect women's self-perception, control over time and money, and work choices, women fall out of the supply chain at multiple points (Norris and Lovenduski 1995; Hughes and Paxton 2017; Chiva 2018).

Turning to the demand side, women suffer more than men from the competitive political marketplace. Traditionally, neither the public nor political elites have sought women out and viewed their candidacies positively. Voters imagine what politicians look, sound and act like, and they usually aren't thinking of women (Norris and Lovenduski 1995; Hughes and Paxton 2017). These mismatches tend to be most disabling in head-to-head electoral contests. Still, the supply side can change if states or parties adopt new electoral or party rules that require certain percentages of woman candidates or mandate levels of gender representation. Then, party gatekeepers go looking for women and support them through the process.

Over time, such behaviours and women's electoral success can help to naturalize the idea of female politicians, undermining the gendered notions that women 'don't belong' in parliament. In some cases, success begets additional changes, and transformations in demand encourage a virtuous circle on the supply side. Girls and women begin to dream of political careers, and people become comfortable with the idea of female elected officials. With societal acceptance, individuals make decisions about family and career that make women's inclusion in electoral politics more likely. In addition, there can be demonstration effects from neighbouring countries and impacts from global movements and intervening states. More neighbouring women leaders and societal- and state-led pressures legitimate greater supply and demand of women (Hughes and Paxton 2017).

These political marketplace factors help explain not only why women have tended to be underrepresented in parliaments but also when and where they have succeeded. Party leaders know which territorial districts are 'safe' because of skewed voter registrations. Thus, if they want to include more women in parliament, elites can encourage women to run in or choose them for those constituencies. Overcoming biases against women leaders, particularly at the level of national executive, is harder, especially in head-to-head competitions. In parliamentary systems in Europe, however, women members of parliament (MPs) can repeatedly show their abilities in their party and then rise to the top. As head, they can and have led their group to victory. Margaret Thatcher and Angela Merkel are prominent examples, serving in rather women-unfriendly environments when they ascended to the top (Hughes and Paxton 2017; Chiva 2018; Mushaben 2019; Simpson 2019).

Another way of bringing more women into the legislature as well as helping them achieve the leading role is to have quotas for female candidates and use proportional representation (PR) to elect some or all parliamentary seats. In proportional representation with fixed lists, parties create their slate of candidates and rank order them *prior to the election*. Thus, parties that seek or are forced (by quota rules) to advance women can easily do so by slotting them appropriately. For instance, if a party desires or electoral rules mandate equal representation of men and women, parties can create zippered lists, alternating women and men. Parties can also abuse the spirit of the quota but abide by the letter. If requirements state that women must be a certain *percentage of candidates*, parties lacking a commitment to increased representation of women can put all the necessary-for-quota women near the bottom. Since parliamentarians are chosen off the list in rank order, those down below are less likely to be elected (Hughes and Paxton 2017; Chiva 2018).

Insights from the PRM – the roles of norms, resources, experience, institutions and global forces in creating the supply of and demand for women in politics – help us to interpret electoral outcomes. Table 9.1 shows

**Table 9.1** Average share of women legislators in national parliaments

| Year (per cent) | 1997 | 2000 | 2005 | 2010 | 2015 | 2019 |
|---|---|---|---|---|---|---|
| | | | *Lower House* | | | |
| World | 12.4 | 13.5 | 16.1 | 19.1 | 22.4 | 24.6 |
| Europe and OECD | 12.3 | 13.3 | 16.9 | 19.9 | 23.7 | 28.1 |
| Nordic Countries | 35.9 | 33.8 | 39.9 | 42.1 | 41.5 | 44.0 |
| | | | *Upper House* | | | |
| World | 10.1 | 13.2 | 15 | 17.9 | 20.5 | 24.3 |
| Europe and OECD | 8.8 | 14.1 | 16.9 | 19.7 | 24.3 | 28.5 |

Source: Interparliamentary Union, 'Women in National Parliaments: Regional Averages', various.

the share of women serving in parliaments in Europe as compared to world averages over the last two or so decades. For perspective, in 1945, the global average for women in parliament was under three per cent. By 1975, that figure was 10.9 per cent, and in 1995, women were still only 11.6 per cent of members of parliament (MPs). Thus, 2020's 25.2 per cent share of lower house seats worldwide is a significant improvement, but still far from parity (IPU n.d.a; IPU 2020).

At first glance, perhaps the most striking data in Table 9.1 are how far ahead the Nordic states have consistently been relative to the rest of the world. Interesting, too, is that Europe's performance, minus the Nordic states, tracks relatively closely to global averages, particularly in the lower house.

Disaggregating the data in Table 9.2, we see the interplay of those gendered factors that the PRM highlights and variable regional progress. For instance, the formerly state-socialist countries on average tend to elect fewer women to parliament. The Baltic states score close to those in Southern Europe, an area that, except for Italy, also has newer democracies than the others in the West. Also interesting, especially to US eyes, is that all countries have some form of quota. The mandatory ones are typically set as a percentage of the PR list seats (maybe 25 per cent, 40 per cent or even 50 per cent) for women (IDEA n.d.). For the optional ones, parties have a choice regarding whether to employ set-asides, although EU members must as of 2020 take positive steps to right the imbalance (European Commission 2020). An interesting development is that *voluntary* quotas in Nordic states translate into above average rates of women in parliament. In other areas choice seems ineffective. The relatively low levels of women in states lacking

**Table 9.2** Average share of women legislators in European national parliaments

| Regional Group and Country | Per cent | Mandatory Quota or Party Choice? |
|---|---|---|
| *Visegrad 4* | *19.6* | *Mixed, more party choice* |
| Czech Republic | 18.7 | Choice |
| Hungary* | 12.1 | Choice |
| Poland | 26.4 | Quota |
| Slovakia* | 21.3 | Choice |
| *Southeastern Europe* | *26.0* | *Mixed, more mandatory quotas* |
| Bosnia and Hercegovina | 31.4 | Quota |
| Bulgaria* | 26.7 | Choice |
| Croatia* | 19.2 | Quota |
| Montenegro* | 29.6 | Quota |
| Romania | 18.3 | Choice |
| Serbia* | 37.6 | Quota |
| Slovenia* | 18.9 | Quota |
| *'Core' Europe* | *34.3* | *Evenly split* |
| Austria | 37.7 | Choice |
| Belgium | 42.8 | Quota |
| France | 36.4 | Quota |
| Germany | 33.7 | Choice |
| Ireland | 27.1 | Quota |
| Luxembourg* | 30.0 | Quota |
| Netherlands | 36.0 | Choice |
| United Kingdom | 30.5 | Choice |
| *Baltic States* | *27.6* | *All party choice* |
| Estonia* | 28.7 | Choice |
| Latvia* | 30.0 | Choice |
| Lithuania* | 24.1 | Choice |
| *Southern Europe* | *34.3* | *All mandatory quotas* |
| Greece* | 20.7 | Quota |
| Italy | 35.1 | Quota |
| Portugal* | 40.0 | Quota |
| Spain | 41.5 | Quota |

| Regional Group and Country | Per cent | Mandatory Quota or Party Choice? |
|---|---|---|
| *Nordic Countries* | *42.4* | *All party choice* |
| Denmark* | 39.7 | Choice |
| Finland* | 46.0 | Choice |
| Iceland* | 38.1 | Choice |
| Norway* | 41.4 | Choice |
| Sweden* | 47.0 | Choice |

Note: * indicates unicameral system.

Source: Interparliamentary Union, 'Women in National Parliaments: Regional Averages', various.

the mandatory obligations raise questions as to whether many parties opt out of ensuring women are on the ballot or place them (in districts or on lists) disadvantageously.

Considering the data, we can see patterns emerging by region, defined as the *Visegrad Four*: Czechia, Hungary, Poland, Slovakia; *Southeastern*: Bosnia, Bulgaria, Croatia, Montenegro, Romania, Serbia, Slovenia; *'Core'*: Austria, Belgium, France, Germany, Ireland, Luxembourg, Netherlands, UK (this data is pre-Brexit); *Baltic*: Estonia, Latvia, Lithuania; Southern: Greece, Italy, Portugal, Spain; *Nordic*: Denmark, Finland, Iceland, Norway, Sweden. Table 9.2 presents the countries alphabetically by region, with yellow bars meaning mandatory quotas and blue indicating party choice in a country. The table also shows average percentages of women in parliament in each region and communicates the extent to which mandated quotas prevail per zone.

Nordic countries have the most impressive (but not fully equitable) performance with a regional average of 42.4 per cent of women in parliament. While some might chalk this superior performance up to wealth levels, other states in Europe and the world with similar development scores do not match the Nordic countries' achievements on women in parliament, and some poorer ones, like Rwanda and Mexico, now exceed the Nordic states (IPU 2020). Thus, the impact of overall societal resources is complex.

Unlike other parts of Europe, Scandinavia is known for gender progressivism in redressing family responsibilities, distributing benefits to parents regardless of their gender. Thus, women and girls in Nordic states are particularly well positioned on both the supply and demand side of the pipeline to dream of running for office. Although critics blame the Scandinavian welfare state for perpetuating gender biases (Sanandaji 2018), these data seem to suggest that superior resources and experiences make the reality of their election more likely than it does for women elsewhere (Wood 2018; IPU 2020).

The context is very different in former communist countries. They had a past, under Soviet (direct or indirect) or Yugoslav domination, in which state-socialist feminism predominated. Women were supposedly liberated because they were expected to work for pay outside the home. This equality was false, as private sphere burdens and anti-woman stereotypes didn't change. Moreover, women found their 'equality' exhausting, as they were often given the hardest types of work, earned less, remained primarily responsible for care, shopping and cleaning, and lacked conveniences to make these domestic tasks easier (Einhorn 1993).

Eastern women also had more political responsibilities than Western ones (Einhorn 1993; True 2003). Some were selected for 'representative' bodies at the local or higher levels. By the 1970s, communist women held about 30 per cent of the seats in their national legislatures. These parliaments, however, were rubber stamps for decisions made in party bodies where women were virtually absent. They held a very small share of party central committee posts; from 1948–89, only three non-Soviet women ever served in a national Politburo (the top decision-making body) in the former Warsaw Pact states.

Thus, the legacy of women's 'political empowerment' among post-communist citizens is that women elected officials are tokens (Einhorn 1993; True 2003). Only in the Baltic states is the average for women in parliament equal to the former communist level; in the Visegrad Four, regional performance is the worst in Europe. Southeastern European parliaments average a 26–74 per cent split in favour of men.

In other parts of the continent, however, women have made progress compared to the past, and we can see that mandatory quotas have played an important role. Particularly notable are France, Spain and Italy, none known for their gender-progressive cultures. Whether these changes in political institutions will have feedback effects on values and help to create additional supply and demand for women legislators is still unclear. Also uncertain is whether these changes will bring more women into the highest levels of leadership in more European countries (IPU 2020; IDEA n.d.). Will more women lead governments? Although not legally mandated, French President Emmanuel Macron intentionally created a cabinet with 50 per cent women in 2017, giving them valuable executive experience. Although most of these women serve in traditionally 'feminine' posts, Macron did name Sylvie Goulard as Defense Minister (Turkington 2017).

Thus, when comparing today's performance with that of three decades ago, some parts of Europe have made significant gains in electing women, although states where women were previously selected to serve have not all reached their historic highs. Because the majority of the included European countries are democratic, the achievements are noteworthy, but parts of Europe are facing creeping authoritarianism. The contemporary appeal of populism – growing after the 2008 financial and 2015 migration crises – has eroded the democratic centre. Far-right and left movements have emerged, and in much of Europe, the right seems the greater threat to democracy and gender parity (Kantola and Lombardo 2017; Art 2018). Some parties have adopted extreme nationalist, anti-feminist and anti-democratic positions that seek to retreat from the forward steps made in recruiting women into politics. This trend is dangerous for equality, particularly given Covid-19. Unfortunately, experience with other crises suggest that women's gains will recede, and traditional gender norms will return to the detriment of women's political, economic and social empowerment (Einhorn 1993; Waring 1999; Bjørnholt and McKay 2014; Kantola and Lombardo 2017).

# Gendering the economy: Pink collar obstacles to equality

In addition to affecting political representation, gender influences the economy, which then feeds political recruitment. With respect to supply, social structures affect the ideas, resources and experiences women have and condition where all imagine women belong in the economy. Other elements of identity – class, race, ethnicity, religion, immigration status, intersect with gender and affect employment choices.

When traditionally gendered economies predominate, women see themselves and are perceived by others as having a primary career related to family role: as mother, wife, daughter and/or grandmother. That private sphere job often limits their abilities to take advantage of training and compels them to seek flexibility so that they can handle their caretaking and family responsibilities (Enloe 2016; Malgesini et al. 2017). Of course, forgoing these opportunities has negative impacts on women's ability to amass the necessary resources (experiences, skills, connections and wealth) to succeed in politics.

Thus, various 'personal decisions', conscious and unconscious, affect women's job market participation and, relatedly, political recruitment.

Interestingly, societal messages telling women they are primarily caretakers misrepresent just how much time women spend in paid employment and how much less day-to-day flexibility they usually have in their jobs (Table 9.3). Other norms and practices constrain women's ambitions and advocacy for equality in pay and opportunities. Women who seek such 'privileges' are deemed problems, aggressive, unnatural and sometimes even coded 'unmarriageable' (Enloe 2016). Thus, gender conformity disadvantages women's earning and professional accomplishments over the short and long term, thereby impeding their amassing supply- and demand-side resources for political success.

Just as with representational quotas in politics, societies can take affirmative steps to bring women into 'untraditional' jobs through targeted recruitment, training programmes and employment benchmarks. In fact, at the elite level, many European countries have instituted quotas to put women on private and public corporate boards. The 2019 EU average has women accounting for 26.4 per cent of such boards, and legal mandates deserve credit for that accomplishment. Perhaps not surprisingly, former state-socialist countries are the least likely to have such rules in place, and much lower levels of women are found on East European boards and in

**Table 9.3** Gender differences in employment in the European Union

| Indicator | Women | Men |
|---|---|---|
| Full-time equivalent employment rate* | 40.8 | 56.9 |
| Duration of working life in years | 33.4 | 38.3 |
| Employed people in education, health and social work* | 30.3 | 8.3 |
| Workers able to take personal time off during working hours* | 22.8 | 27.3 |
| Career prospects index (likelihood of losing a job in six months) | 63.7 | 62.6 |
| Employment in science, technology, engineering and mathematics* | 7.0 | 33.0 |
| EU employment rate, ages 20–64* | 67.0 | 79.0 |
| Mean monthly earnings (purchasing power standard) | € 2249 | € 2809 |
| Not at risk of poverty* | 82.9 | 84.5 |

Note: * is per cent.

Source: European Institute for Gender Equality, 'Gender Equality Index: Time in the European Union, 2019' and 'Gender Equality Index: Money in the European Union, 2019'.

executive suites. Continent-wide, at the very top of the corporate ladder, women hold fewer than 8 per cent of both CEO positions and board chairs (Rankin 2020).

Without affirmative programmes, women have 'pink-collar' jobs, positions consistent with stereotypes about a 'woman's nature', 'responsibilities', 'skills' and assumed secondary earning status, although women are often single heads of households. Even when working in factories, women-centric industries are typically referred to as 'light', to signify their inferiority to 'heavy', male-dominated work. When women do work in 'heavy' industries, they are often relegated to positions which are less well paid and are considered less skilled (Waring 1999; Enloe 2016). Because of gendered expectations and pay inequities, women are also more likely to leave the workforce for caretaking responsibilities. These 'choices' affect possibilities for advancement, training and earnings, as well as retirement savings and pensions (Malgesini et al. 2017).

The gendered economy imposes obstacles to women's advancement and lifelong earnings which, in turn, affect the supply- and demand-side resources they need to compete successfully in politics. In addition, just because women live in economically comfortable households, they might not have access to an equitable share of the earnings and wealth to finance their political ambitions (Malgesini et al. 2017). How far women can advance is also affected by other family members and the extent to which partners and relatives are willing to take on equitable shares in various reproductive roles. These include caretaking, shopping, food preparation, cleaning and other labour. Time use and public opinion data reveal that women have far more household responsibilities and less leisure time than men. Even in 'progressive' Europe, women are seen as far more emotional, and more than 40 per cent of all respondents think men's most important role is as breadwinner and women's is as home and family caretaker (EC 2017; EIGE 2019).

Looking into country-level data shows diversity in achievements in gender equity vary in predictable ways. The Nordic states have the most egalitarian behaviours and attitudes, the state-socialist the least progressive. 'Old' Europe is somewhere in the middle. Especially interesting is how much more strongly East Europeans lack faith in women political leaders and believe women belong home with their children (EIGE 2019). Not surprisingly, these economic and social factors feed into the gendered electoral outcomes we have seen.

With the pandemic, women's accomplishments are endangered, and status is at risk. They have higher rates of unemployment, although their relative disadvantage in the eurozone is less than in the OECD overall. Still, European government programmes implemented to revive the economy are insufficiently sensitive to women workers' current and future needs. In addition, during economic crises, pressures tend to mount at home, and gender-based violence has correspondingly increased (Moscovenko 2020; Taub and Bradley 2020).

These developments are not surprising; during crises, stereotypes resurface, as solutions for regaining 'normalcy' at the expense of gender equity gain popularity. Thus, women usually lose jobs because of either explicit state policies or their 'choice' to go home to pick up the increased burdens. In economic downturns, they typically see their living standards and physical well-being deteriorate more than men (Bjørnholt and McKay 2014; Kantola and Lombardo 2017; Moscovenko 2020; Taub and Bradley 2020). The PRM suggests that today's economic hardships, along with the rising tide of right-wing populism, will negatively affect women's political empowerment. We should not expect significant improvements in gender equity gains in the economy or politics any time soon.

# Conclusion

Socio-political factors and the gendered economy highlight how social, economic and political structures interact and create a gender gap in politics. Although Europe still suffers from gender inequalities, in places it has implemented affirmative measures to promote women's political and economic empowerment. In terms of the continental average, women's representation has increased, although some parts of Europe, particularly most post-communist states, have registered losses compared to decades ago. Everywhere political parity is lacking, and women's workplace achievements and opportunities are still short of men's (European Commission 2020).

While recognizing improvements is important, so too is realizing that progress is not irreversible. The histories of East European states underline both the negative impacts of pursuing a false liberation and the complexity of maintaining equity gains in the face of economic dislocation and rising nationalism, challenges that are now continent-wide. With Covid-19, advances will likely come under renewed attack. Feminist researchers and global policy makers remain convinced, however, that gender parity benefits everyone by producing better governance, less violence and more human-centred and sustainable economies (UN 2015; Hudson et al. 2020). Gender equality is, therefore, an outcome very much worth achieving and maintaining.

# Questions for discussion

1 What is gender? What do we mean when we say that gender varies across time and geographic space? Give examples of the chronological and geographic patterns that are visible on the European continent.
2 What is the Political Recruitment Model (PRM)? How does the PRM explain how women are disadvantaged when running for political office? What are the necessary systemic changes to see more women elected to office at the national level?
3 How do you expect Covid-19 to affect women's performance in future elections? Are best performing European political systems likely to behave differently from the poorest performers?
4 In what ways is the political economy in Europe gendered? What are the impacts of that gendered political economy on both the supply of and demand for women parliamentarians? How might we expect the pandemic to affect the gendering of the economy?

# Recommended for Further Reading

Gwiazda, A., ed. (2019) 'Special Issue: Politics and Gender in Eastern Europe', *Politics and Gender* 15(2).

Meserve, S. A. et al. (2020) 'Gender, Incumbency and Party List Nominations', *British Journal of Political Science*, 50(1): 1–15. http://dx.doi.org/10.1017/S0007123417000436.

Valdini, M. E. (2019) *The Inclusion Calculation: Why Men Appropriate Women's Political Representation*. New York, NY: Oxford University Press.

Wiltse, E. C. and Hager, L. (2021) *Women's Paths to Power: Female Presidents and Prime Ministers, 1960–2020*. Boulder: Lynne Rienner.

Xydias, C. (2016) 'Discrepancies in Women's Presence between European National Legislatures and the European Parliament', *Political Research Quarterly* 69(4): 800–12. http://dx.doi.org/10.1177/1065912916663655.

# 10

# The Comparative Politics of Migration Governance in Europe

## *Regine Paul*

The sudden and sustained movement of high numbers of displaced people from Syria to Europe since 2015 forcefully situated the issue of migration centre stage in European politics. While most people found rescue in the Middle East region, the popular interpretation of the events as a refugee 'crisis' highlights a widespread sense of overwhelming administrative, institutional and political challenge (Paul and Roos 2019). But not all political answers to the perception of crisis were restrictive: Germany introduced a 'track change' model, in 2019, which allows rejected asylum seekers to regularize via a job, albeit with much conditionality. The EU Commission pursues a similar model for its Blue Card meant to attract high-skilled workers. Russia's invasion of Ukraine in early 2022 has set off large refugee movements at the heart of the continent in early 2022. This development will further push European governments to search for political strategies to deal with migration and mobility. Indeed, tensions between impulses for openness vs. closure, between liberalism and protectionism, have been at the heart of Europe's dealings with migration since the continent birthed the modern nation-state; and they have informed a highly selective migration and mobility governance ever since (Torpey 2000; Anderson 2013; Follis 2021).

The overlapping pressures for openness and closure foreclose any generic expectation of wholesome liberalization of policies in Europe since the Second World War (unlike suggested with the 'liberal constraint' thesis in migration policy studies, cf. Joppke 1998). Neither has the democratic transformation in the 1990s for Central and Eastern European (CEE) countries lead to more liberal migration policymaking – in the sense of easier access and more rights for migrants – across the board. Attempts to pigeonhole European countries as 'liberal' or 'restrictive' must hence be met with caution. A recent comparative study (de Haas, Natter and Vezzoli 2018) suggests that variation between countries does not easily map onto their position in democracy measures nor on the length of their migration transition; an initial phase of 'accelerated liberalization' in Europe since 1945 has given way to 'decelerated liberalization' since the 1990s; and there are co-existing forms of liberal and restrictive migration policies *within* each country (for example more liberal labour migration vs. more restrictive border control or asylum policies).

To map the comparative politics of migration governance in Europe more systematically, this chapter examines the specific conditions which shape liberal and restrictive elements in countries' migration policymaking. To provide an overview, I discuss *three sets of interacting terrains* on which European states navigate the relative openness or restrictiveness of their migration policies: political economy, domestic politics and interactions with(in) the EU. I show the variation in how different states are situated on these terrains, and the factors that shape their relative position, with – necessarily cursory and selective – illustrations from across Europe.

# Variable political economies of governing migration in Europe

Europe's open economies have arguably shaped comparably liberal approaches to migrant admission policies across the board (Menz 2009). Economic competitiveness goals feature explicitly in the EU's approach to 'managed migration', developing since at least the early 2000s, which outlines a 'more economistic and demographically sanguine thinking on migration' (Favell and Hansen 2002: 598; cf. Carmel and Paul 2009). Some have even claimed that 'market-driven migrant selectivity is irrevocably becoming a major determinant of migration flows in the EU' (van Houtum and Pijpers 2007: 301) and that EU citizenship itself hinges upon neoliberal interpretations of utilitarian belonging (Hansen and Hager 2010).

And yet, patterns of divergence persist amidst these economic convergence pressures. First, variable (labour) migration policy arrangements seem to be related to different forms of capitalism. Dominant production strategies in different economies (cf. the classic twofold typology by Hall and Soskice 2001) shape which labour migrants businesses require and lobby for. Firms in the coordinated market economies of Germany, Austria, Switzerland and arguably also the Scandinavian and Benelux countries, will advocate a focus on 'highly skilled well-trained labor migrants that can be easily integrated into the high-value-added production pattern' (Menz 2009: 261). The liberal market economies in the United Kingdom and Ireland, with their radical innovation strategy, tend to produce business advocacy for a 'steady supply of labour migration into … low-skill and low-wage … positions' (Menz 2009: 261; for a comprehensive summary, see Paul 2015).

A larger comparative study confirms this basic capitalist variety to play a role for the relative openness of nineteen EU countries (in a sample of forty-six countries overall) for migration at different skill levels (Ruhs 2013). This study also highlights, however, that because giving migrants access to territory and labour markets also grants them access to socio-economic rights in liberal democracies, countries tend to limit the rights of migrants in low-skill/low-wage jobs or curtail their access altogether (cf. Paul 2012). This economic logic of 'the price of rights' (Ruhs 2013) has been outdone more recently, when Sweden responded to the large-scale arrival of refugees from Syria with a withdrawal from the sound finance dogma (that also governs the eurozone): the central government increased its spending and thus boosted both refugees' socio-economic integration *and* formerly depopulated local communities' rejuvenation (Hansen 2021).

Mixed market economies in Southern Europe feature a stronger role for state intervention – most obviously so in France's 'dirigiste' tradition – but also a dual labour market where 'high-tech islands' coexist with 'seas of low-skill assembly' and employer advocacy for migrant admissions is equally dualized (cf. the typology in Hancké, Rhodes and Thatcher 2007; Menz 2009: 236–41). Political and economic elites in the Baltic and CEE countries, by contrast, would believe in 'radical free market economics', arguably nourishing pressure for openness to migration after the post-Communist transformation (Woolfson 2009; another study associates the Baltic states with arm's-length state-economy relations similarly to the UK: Hancké, Rhodes and Thatcher 2007). For example, with 9 per cent Hungary has the lowest corporation tax in the EU and its privatization and deregulation agenda has been drastic (Elliesen, Henkel and Kempe 2019). Such neoliberal rationality is oddly merged with elements from contrasting types of market coordination, including government intervention, in most CEE economies (Hancké, Rhodes and Thatcher 2007: 290–3; Menz 2009: 218–21).

Second, we need to account for the role of segmented (migrant) labour markets (Cohen 2006; Ruhs and Anderson 2010; Papadopoulos 2011). On the one hand, segmentation dynamics exist in any European country, for example where seasonal migrant workers in the low-waged hospitality and food sector fill dire shortages (for the UK, see Ruhs and Anderson 2010). It is no coincidence that Western and Northern European governments brought in migrant workers on charter flights to harvest strawberries and asparagus in the middle of the 2020 Covid-19 lockdown. On the other hand, the economic and political salience of informal employment shapes considerable pressures for countries to grant legal statuses and more generous rights to irregular migrant residents (Geddes and Scholten 2016). In the late 1980s and throughout the 1990s, the 'endemic presence of irregular migration' in the large informal economies of Southern Europe led to a 'reactive, rather than proactive, framework for immigrant integration' (Peixoto et al. 2012: 136), including the frequent, but then widely uncontested, use of amnesties. More recently, Southern European countries developed more pro-active immigration and migrant integration policies which mark a departure from the bureaucratic politics of post-hoc regularization. An example is a liberal citizenship reform in Greece in 2015 credited to the proactive advocacy by migrant NGO's advocacy and SYRIZA's left-leaning government (Geddes and Scholten 2016).

The post-hoc integration of irregular migrants in Southern Europe, including pathways towards citizenship, differs considerably from a politics of 'wilful negligence' in the UK, where large-scale migrant informality has been politically tolerated despite harsh talk of control and where residual social protection cements the vulnerability of irregular migrants (Wilkinson and Craig 2011). For 2008, Papadopoulos (2011: 33, cf. table 2.3) estimates a 17.5 per cent share of irregular migrants among the relatively large foreign population in the UK. This share might even have grown after successive British governments closed down regular paths for entry since 2010.

A similar pattern seems to have emerged in the CEE and Baltic countries. Aggregate estimates suggest especially high shares of irregular migrants as part of the overall foreign population in those countries, except for Latvia, 'ranging from 11.5 percent in Slovenia to more than half the foreign population (54.5 percent) in Slovakia' in 2008 (Papadopoulos 2011: 33f). But the pressure to address irregular residence politically was comparatively low across Central and Eastern Europe: unlike Southern Europe, the CEE countries experienced relatively low levels of migration until recently (with the Czech Republic being a forerunner in the migration transition). CEE governments felt neither compelled to pro-actively promote migrant integration (Drbohlav 2012; Geddes and Scholten 2016), nor to liberalize their restrictive citizenship regimes (see the next section).

Third, profound differences in countries' location in the global division of labour affect the salience of immigration versus emigration policymaking. Countries in Northwestern Europe count as 'old countries of immigration' with persistently high numbers of newcomers since at least the end of the Second World War and by now comprehensive policies for integrating settled migrants (Geddes and Scholten 2016). These countries actively recruited foreign workers to re-build their economies after the war and then saw a 'second wave' of migration when family members joined their 'guest worker' spouses (Castles 1986). This second wave was unexpected at the time but drew support after the fact when courts gave a liberal interpretation to human rights norms (Joppke 1998). The Southern European countries followed a similar pattern with some delay, moving rapidly from emigration to net immigration countries in the late 1980s and 1990s as their informal economies attracted labour (Geddes and Scholten 2016). In Spain, for example, 'in only twelve years the size of the inflow increased by a factor of 55: from 17,000 arrivals in 1996 to 921,000 in 2007' (Peixoto et al. 2012: 109).

Yet, it would be deeply flawed to portray Europe as a labour-importing and integrating continent (Weinar 2019: 38). There are large asymmetries in net population and labour force gains and losses across Europe. While some CEE countries have become recent immigrant destinations (Hungary, the Czech and Slovak Republic, more recently also Poland), most countries in the region have experienced net emigration since the post-Communist transition and feature relatively low shares of foreigners within their population. Emigration is particularly high in Romania and Bulgaria, but also for the Baltic states, and primarily reflects labour exports to Northern and Western Europe. Labour mobility across the EU might be an asset from the perspective of the common market's competitiveness, EU citizens' upward social mobility and their ability to send remittances to countries of origin (cf. debate at the time: Favell and Hansen 2002); yet, it also raises serious issues of brain-drain, depopulation, demographic ageing, social deprivation and identity loss for exodus regions. In addition, emigration puts pressure on sending countries to protect the rights of their citizens abroad and engage in diaspora relations (for Romania, see Baldwin-Edwards 2007). Such political pressures might return to Southern Europe, as the financial and sovereign debt crisis of 2008–09, austerity measures and soaring unemployment created an environment in which thousands of (especially young and educated) workers turned their backs on their home countries, once more, in search for jobs and prosperity in the richer European North (Geddes and Scholten 2016).

# The variable domestic politics of migration governance in Europe

Political economy alone cannot explain why policies tend to be more restrictive for low-wage workers (Ruhs 2013; Paul 2015) or why some countries with 'liberal' market economies have overhauled their formerly very liberal labour migration approaches altogether (for the UK, see: Paul 2012, 2016). Patterns of liberal reception and restriction do not easily map onto types of economy or region either: while Portugal scores 80 out of 100 points overall in the 2014 Migrant Integration Policy Index (MIPEX), just like integration 'forerunner' Sweden, and Spain scores a leading 90 points for family reunion rights, Italian migrant integration policies have been much more restrictive (scoring only 62 points for family reunion and only 58 points overall).

As liberalism and democracy 'seem to work in different directions when it comes to immigration', we observe a coexistence of economically driven openness and a domestic politics of closure with the latter usually being 'ascribed to elections cycles, party politics, and public opinion' (Natter 2021: 114). So how do domestic politics shape migration governance and which patterns emerge in Europe?

Much research turns to right-wing populist and extreme parties' role in different political systems to answer this question (for an effective review see Lutz 2019). Right-wing cabinets in Europe have arguably realized 'a change of course towards more restrictive and assimilationist immigration and integration policies since the 1990s' (Akkerman 2012: 523). However, their influence varies by migration policy domain. A comparison of seventeen national cabinets between 1999 and 2017 – either featuring a far-right party in government (in Austria, Italy, Norway and Switzerland) or its explicit support (in Denmark, the Netherlands and Norway) – shows that these parties exercise little influence on admission policies, even when in government, but very much shape integration policies (Lutz 2019: 518).

This variation in influence may be because governments manage immigration policies through partisan consensus while the integration policies remain deeply partisan. As centre-right parties are divided between 'cultural conservatism and economic liberalism' and left-wing parties struggle over 'the protection of domestic workers and the universal principles of justice and equality', they compete for votes in 'the middle' with moderate immigration positions (Lutz 2019: 522). This is different for integration policies where 'mainstream parties align along a socio-cultural divide, with the left advocating policies that are more liberal and the right advocating policies that are more restrictive' (Lutz 2019: 522f). This nuanced analysis of migration politics explains *both* the liberal dynamics of migrant admission policies, especially for workers, and the more restrictive stances on integration (and potentially also asylum and border enforcement). Of course, the moderate dynamic for admissions wanes in cases like Hungary, where Victor Orbán's right-wing populists have reigned with large parliamentarian majority for three terms (Elliesen, Henkel and Kempe 2019).

The fear of losing voters to parties with an anti-immigrant agenda arguably also pushes more moderate (even left-leaning) parties towards policy decisions and discourse which highlight their willingness to control migration (Guia 2021). Examples include the inability of the Italian Democratic Party, in 2015, to push through *ius culturae* citizenship, which would enable migrant children who attended Italian schools to gain citizenship eventually (vocal protests by the Lega stopped the endeavour); the 2010 electoral campaign of the British Conservative Party which came into office on a 'reducing net migration' ticket that clearly targeted UKIP voters; the restriction of the traditional stronghold of *ius soli* citizenship in France under the influence of an influential Front National; the Dutch debate about revoking dual citizenship; or the German Chancellor's U-turn on her initially humanitarian approach to refugee migration from the Middle East in 2015 given fierce struggles of her own party family to position itself on the electoral market against an increasingly successful AfD (cf. Guia 2021).

The relative influence of far-right and populist parties is also shaped by the degree of politicization and successful mobilization of an anti-immigrant discourse in elections and – as Brexit infamously highlights – referendum polls. Politicization is not straightforward though as there is 'extreme fluctuation in the intensity of the political conflict over immigration' (Grande, Schwarzbözl and Fatke 2019: 1459). As the experience of Southern European countries indicates, neither high numbers of migrants nor economic grievances among potential voters explain politicization. These geographical location of these countries at the outer EU border and a lack of solidarity of other EU member states (see the next section) results in heightened arrivals, enormous socio-economic grievances, administrative challenges and political debate, especially for the much-affected Greece.

Yet, this geographic vulnerability has not automatically led to more restrictive policies. The higher degree of anti-immigration mobilization in Italy (Geddes and Scholten 2016: 198) correlates with the long-standing electoral successes of parties such as the Lega, which has first been part of a coalition government in 1994. A 2018 coalition of the populist Cinque Stelle movement with Matteo Salvini's Lega campaigned almost exclusively on an anti-immigration ticket and went on to pass the openly xenophobic 'Salvini Decree' which strips anyone without refugee status off basic humanitarian protection rights such as shelter (D'Ignoti 2019). Right-extreme parties have been much less successful in Portugal, Spain and Greece. For example, though the right-extreme and neo-fascist Chrysi Avgi ('Golden Dawn') party of Greece has been in parliament from 2012–19 and feeds the expression of anti-immigrant sentiments in public discourse, Greek migration policies have developed in more liberal ways under the left-wing SYRIZA-led government since 2015, including a liberal citizenship reform (Geddes and Scholten 2016: 222).

The limited explanatory power of market liberalism alone, and the role of anti-immigrant politicization, has become highly palpable with Brexit. Indeed, while Euroscepticism is no new phenomenon in Britain and has created a higher politicization potential around EU mobility than elsewhere in Europe (cf. Roos 2019), a discursive 'fusion' of the country's EU membership with the immigration and mobility issues helped in mobilizing Eurosceptics at the polling station far beyond core UKIP votership (Dennison and Geddes 2018). In Britain, the conflict between openness and closure rages, it seems, more fiercely than elsewhere because the country's laissez-faire neoliberalism contradicts a historical dedication to tough migration control more forcefully than would, for example, the German and French variants of a coordinated or even 'dirigiste' market economy (Paul 2015, 2016).

Another variant of this ominous combination can be observed in some CEE and Baltic countries, where an elite-driven radical neoliberalism has interacted with an exclusionary ethno-politics of migration after the democratic transition (for Hungary: Rusu 2011; Elliesen, Henkel and Kempe 2019; for Latvia: Woolfson 2009). Latvia, for instance, has experienced a strong revival of ethnic-nationalist ideas of belonging after decades of Soviet occupation (Woolfson 2009). The sense of a 'precarious national identity' (Woolfson 2009) has arguably increased further with the large-scale exodus of mobile workers from the Baltic states, Poland and, more recently, Bulgaria and Romania towards Western European labour markets. Such ethno-politics might explain the rather unfavourable citizenship policy in the thirteen newer EU member states (33 points vs. 59 for the EU-15 in the 2014 MIPEX) and the outright exclusionary approach to migrants' political participation (16 vs. 60 points); and have nourished the impression of 'big bad Visegrad' countries where 'extreme' anti-immigrant voices have established a place inside increasingly 'illiberal' governments (*The Economist* 2016).

Some scholars suggest that outright migrant exclusion might wane over time alongside countries' migration transition – as was the case for the former 'guest worker' countries in the North and more recent Southern European destinations (Peixoto et al. 2012; Geddes and Scholten 2016). They might, however, also foreshadow a darker era in which resilient ethno-political ideas of belonging, sustained and aggravated by rising anti-immigrant rhetoric and steady electoral successes of radical right and populist parties, counteract any economic or constitutional pressure for liberal migration governance in Europe far beyond 'illiberal central Europe' (*The Economist* 2016).

# Variable interactions with the European Union in migration governance

Migration governance in Europe is 'not a story of various national exceptionalisms or of countries just doing their own thing' (Geddes and Scholten 2016: 13). For one, the creation of a common market with free movement for EU citizens has dramatically changed migration patterns in Europe, by layering or replacing existing (often postcolonial) migration systems (Paul 2013) and by creating large disparity between those who receive and send mobile people (Recchi 2015). In addition, the EU has become an active source of migration and integration policies since the 1990s. This is true, for instance, for family reunification or the long-term residence of non-EU migrants in member states (Geddes, Hadj-Abdou and Brumat 2020), where EU minimum requirements translate into above average scores in the migrant integration policy index (MIPEX) even in otherwise restrictive CEE countries. Similarly, deteriorating conditions in reception centres in Greece, but also in Italy, led the European Court of Justice and the European Court of Human Rights to rule, in several cases, that refugees must *not* be returned to the countries of first entry without guarantees of human treatment (Trauner 2016: 314).

Nevertheless, the EU migration governance regime is partial at best and creates a 'complex stratification' of migrant rights rather than any predictable hierarchies of belonging (Carmel and Paul 2013): Brussels does not regulate all forms of migration and integration to the same extent, and even where admission standards have been Europeanized – for example with regard to high-skilled workers – this is mainly per Directive with quite some leeway for national transposition and considerable implementation disparities (Cerna 2013). Most importantly perhaps, sovereignty-concerned member states have jealously guarded their power to define volumes of migrant admissions (Boswell and Geddes 2011; Geddes, Hadj-Abdou and Brumat 2020).

The interactions national governments have with the EU level shape their migration policies – but such 'shaping' varies in several ways. First and foremost, whether countries experienced coercive pressure during their EU accession matters: the need to adopt the *acquis* on migration, border control and integration explains why CEE countries developed migration policies 'in the absence of migration' (Geddes and Scholten 2016: 197). Increasing cooperation with the CEE countries on migration admissions and external border management – and making cooperation conditional for accession – was (and still is) part of a Western European strategy of creating a 'buffer zone' against feared 'mass' movements from poorer regions of the world (Lavenex 1998). Besides creating a power asymmetry between 'older' and 'newer' EU member states that backfired during the 2015 negotiations over refugee relocation, the one-sided pressure to adopt the EU *acquis* has arguably implied a neglect for other pressing migration policy issues in the CEE region: dealing with large-scale emigration and brain-drain or resolving the tensions between economic neoliberalism and ethno-cultural politics (for Romania: Baldwin-Edwards 2007).

Second, a country's relative socio-economic and geopolitical position in the EU migration system matters. Since the Dublin Regulation (first established in 1990) requires asylum seekers to launch their applications in the first country of entry and that only one member state be responsible for examining asylum claims, the challenge of managing arrivals was bound to be highly uneven across Europe as the 2015–16 migration phenomena exposed

(Trauner 2016: 320). While 'frontier states' in the South and Southeast of Europe, transit countries, especially on the Eastern Mediterranean corridor, and Northern European 'destination countries' experienced high levels asylum migration, their administrative and fiscal capacities for managing heightened levels of newcomers varied (cf. Geddes and Scholten 2016 for individual country reports). For example, implementation problems and reception standards in Greece – already an issue for EU-internal debate – magnified beyond manageable when the sovereign debt crisis hit in 2008/9 and triggered tight budgetary constraints (Trauner 2016: 312) and they became dramatic when the Covid-19 outbreak hit already overcrowded and ill-equipped refugee camps in 2020.

Lastly, the relative influence of a country's domestic policy preferences on other member states reflects asymmetric power relations among EU member states. Negotiations of the Common European Asylum System (CEAS) before and after 2015 expose member states' variable ability to shape policies (Zaun 2018). Germany, Austria and Sweden, with their long-established reception procedures, imposed blueprints for a reform of the CEAS on Southern European countries which lacked a regulatory approach at the time (Zaun 2018). Such policy-shaping by the 'old' EU-15 countries has not gone uncontested. In Italy, the Interior Ministry – much before being run by radical right party leader Matteo Salvini – has threatened to release migrants to other member states without prior registration if no more support and burden-sharing would come their way (Trauner 2016: 315).

The vocal role of Hungary, Poland, Slovakia and the Czech Republic in opposing a relocation mechanism for 160,000 asylum applicants from Greece and Italy to other member states, in September 2015, equally evidences the CEE countries' transition from policy-takers to policy-shapers (Geddes and Scholten 2016: 212). The EU Council may have outvoted Visegrad countries on this one-off relocation, but a long-term sustainable reform of the CEAS with a quota for relocating asylum applicants seems doomed against such fundamental opposition. In this case, the dominance of a domestic (electoral) politics of anti-immigrant mobilization in parts of CEE creates 'asymmetrical interdependence' within Europe: small countries with low numbers of asylum applicants have little incentive to act more solidaristically with large receiving countries but do wield power to bloc reform for all (Zaun 2018: 44). Of course, the securitization of the Schengen borders predates the CEE countries' EU accession. Ironically perhaps, the countries now portrayed as 'big bad Visegrad' (*The Economist* 2016) were once drawn into the EU's restrictive border control approach – with coercive accession conditionality – long before they became restrictive migration policy-shapers in Europe in their own right.

# Conclusion

This chapter highlighted that to frame Europe as a liberal or restrictive immigration continent conceals more than it reveals. Instead, we need to comprehend just how the conceptually unresolvable conflict between openness and closure towards migration (and residents with migration background) plays out in the interaction of countries' variable political economies, domestic politics and their relative position and interdependencies in the EU. We also need to comprehend how such interactions change over time. The chapter's overview character forecloses any systematic comparative conclusions, but its discussions condense into three focal points for future research and public debate on the politics of migration in Europe:

First, restrictive migration governance is by no means limited to the illiberal democracies of Hungary or Poland. Sure, these countries display exclusionary integration regimes, a high salience of anti-immigrant politics and they also have blocked reforms of the Common European Asylum System. More recent developments in policy and discourse in Britain and Italy – or Denmark for that matter – highlight, however, that they are not alone in such orientations. Nor did CEE countries invent them, but they inherited a restrictive refugee reception and border control agenda with the *acquis* when joining the EU. It seems futile then, both from the perspective of effective policy coordination among member states and from a migrant rights lens, to name and shame Eastern Europeans without *also* explicating, beyond stereotypes, how ostensibly more liberal European democracies manage the tension between openness and closure impulses and on what normative footing they sieve 'desired' from 'undesired' migrant.

Second, if anything, the CEE story – if there is only one – on migration governance, sends out a warning to the rest of Europe. The combination of untamed neoliberalism (including a laissez-faire approach to informal migrant work) with ethno-cultural interpretations of the nation (provoking highly exclusionary migrant integration policies) not only forges an especially hostile environment for migrants. It also nourishes a breeding ground for the electoral success of right-wing populist and right-extreme parties which can spiral itself beyond liberal-constitutional control.

Last, but not least, debate over how (the history of) socio-economic and geopolitical asymmetries on the continent shape – and ought to shape – migration governance in any one country or across the European Union should intensify. As long as a burning refugee camp in Moria during a global pandemic is perceived as pretty much a Greek problem, the recruitment of numerous young unemployed Spaniards into (short-staffed) vocational training as a German strike or the withdrawal of European citizenship from millions of Brits a mere technical effect of Brexit, a more solidaristic migration governance in Europe – both among member states and with migrants – seems out of reach.

# Questions for discussion

1   How useful is it to map European migration policies as *liberal* or *restrictive* for comparative analysis? What does such categorization reveal and hide?
2   How do *varieties of capitalism* shape diverse migration policy approaches in Europe? What are the shortcomings of this perspective for explaining policy variation but also labour market realities in Europe?
3   How dangerous are ethno-cultural trends in migration politics for liberal democracy in Europe?
4   How do countries' variable political and economic interactions with, and their geographical positioning within, the EU shape the governance of migration in Europe? How do these complex interdependencies affect efforts to develop common EU policies for migration?

# Recommended for Further Reading

Carmel, E., Lenner, K. and Paul, R., eds (2021) *Handbook on the Governance and Politics of Migration*. Cheltenham: Edward Elgar Publishing
Consterdine, E. and Hampshire, J. (2019) 'Convergence, capitalist diversity, or political volatility? Immigration policy in Western Europe', *Journal of European Public Policy* 27(10): 1487–505.

Geddes, A. (2021) *Governing migration beyond the state: Europe, North America, South America, and Southeast Asia in a global context.* Oxford: Oxford University Press

Geddes A, Hadj-Abdou L and Brumat L (2020) Migration and Mobility in the European Union. 2nd edn. London: Red Globe Press.

# 11

# Populism and Extremism

*Léonie de Jonge*

Populism and extremism have become important political forces in contemporary European politics. Over the past three decades, populist, far-right and far-left parties have more than tripled their vote share from around 10 per cent in the early 1990s to 30 per cent in 2020 (Rooduijn et al. 2020). In particular, support for far-right parties such as Matteo Salvini's League in Italy, Marine Le Pen's National Rally in France or Viktor Orbán's Fidesz in Hungary has increased substantially.

The rise of populist and extremist forces constitutes one of the most dramatic changes in European politics in the postwar era. From Sweden to Spain and from Britain to Bulgaria, the electoral fortunes of populist and extremist parties have coincided with the decline of the traditional party families that long dominated European politics. The appeal of such alternatives illustrates the 'thawing' of European party systems that had long been declared 'frozen' (Lipset and Rokkan 1967).

This chapter traces the evolution of populism and extremism in Europe in the last decades. The electoral performance of populist and extremist parties is often conceptualized as a marketplace, where success and failure are contingent on 'public demand' and 'party supply'. In line with existing studies (e.g. Mudde 2007; van Kessel 2015; de Jonge 2021b), I argue that the success of these parties is best understood by the complex interplay of demand- and supply-side variables.

The first section defines populism and extremism and discusses the relationship between these two essentially contested concepts (Rooduijn 2019). The second section investigates the main explanations for the success of populist and extremism parties in Europe. I first discuss demand-side explanations, which highlight factors that create a breeding ground for populist and extremist parties, such as socio-economic or political conditions. I then turn to supply-side theories, which include factors that enable populist and extremist parties to translate lingering demand into actual votes, such as the electoral system and the media landscape. The conclusion reflects on the wider implications of the success of populism and extremism and asks what the future of these parties might look like in light of recent developments, notably the outbreak of the Covid-19 pandemic.

# Defining populism and extremism

There is widespread confusion on labelling and characterizing populist and extremist parties. In media and academia alike, these terms are often used interchangeably to denote a host of different phenomena and actors at different time periods and in different parts of the world. In particular, the term 'populism' has become a popular buzzword to designate any type of movement, party or politician that challenges the status quo. It has long been acknowledged that there is no consensus in the literature on how to define populism. In fact, '[i]t has become almost a cliché to start writing on populism by lamenting the lack of clarity about the concept and casting doubts about its usefulness for political analysis' (Panizza 2005: 1). Scholars have variedly sought to characterize populism as a style (Moffitt and Tormey 2014); a strategy (Weyland 2001); a discursive frame (Aslanidis 2016); or a moralistic imagination (Müller 2016). While the concept remains highly contested, some consensus has emerged around the so-called 'ideational approach', which maintains that populism (however 'thin' it may appear) is ultimately based on a set of ideas (Rooduijn 2019; see also Mudde and Rovira Kaltwasser 2017; Moffitt 2020). This approach refers to Cas Mudde's seminal definition, according to which populism is best described as an ideology that considers society to be divided into two homogeneous, antagonistic groups (i.e. 'the people' and 'the elite'), and which argues that politics should be an expression of the general will of the people (Mudde 2004; see also Canovan 1999).

Populism is 'chameleonic', in the sense that it can change appearance depending on the political context in which it occurs (Taggart 2000: 10). This characteristic helps explain why it can appear in many different guises and across the political spectrum. The slippery nature of the concept has led scholars to define populism as a 'thin' ideology (see Fieschi 2020: 23–41); in other words, one that merely sets up a framework and thus cannot provide answers to all societal questions. Contrary to more comprehensive ('thick') ideologies such as liberalism or socialism, populism 'is diffuse in its lack of a programmatic center of gravity, and open in its ability to cohabit with other, more comprehensive, ideologies' (Stanley 2008: 99–100). In other words, populism rarely exists in isolation; indeed, it typically attaches itself to a 'host ideology', notably nationalism or conservatism on the right, and socialism on the left. As a result, political parties may be classified as right- or left-wing populists, but ideologically, they can rarely solely be described as 'populist'.

Accordingly, there is great ideological diversity among populist parties in Europe. On the right end of the political spectrum, populist parties share two core ideological features: authoritarianism and nativism. Authoritarianism refers to 'the belief in a strictly ordered society, in which infringements of authority are to be punished severely' (Mudde 2007: 23). This belief is built on the appreciation of compliance, discipline and rigid social norms (Carter 2018), and exemplified by their advocacy for stricter border controls as well as a strong emphasis on security and law and order. Nativism is best defined as a xenophobic form of nationalism, 'which holds that states should be inhabited exclusively by members of the native group ("the nation") and that non-native elements (persons and ideas) are fundamentally threatening to the homogenous nation-state' (Mudde 2007: 19). These two core ideological features often translate into an anti-immigration agenda, which continues to be a key characteristic of all (successful) right-wing populist parties in Europe. Examples of such parties include, among many others, the Partij voor de Vrijheid (Party for Freedom or PVV) in the Netherlands, the Fremskrittspartiet (Progress Party) in Norway and Fidesz in Hungary.

The strong proclivity to exclusionism differentiates right-wing populist parties from more inclusionary left-wing populist parties (Mudde and Rovira Kaltwasser 2013). Although populism in Europe was long exclusively associated with the (far) right, the success of movements such as SYRIZA in Greece, Podemos (We Can) in Spain, Levica (The Left) in Slovenia and La France Insoumise (Unbowed France) suggests that left-wing populism is no longer a marginal force in Europe (Katsambekis and Kioupkiolis 2019).

While both left- and right-wing populists share a Manichean view of society that glorifies the 'people' and vilifies the 'elite', left-wing populists tend to define the elite in economic terms, whereas right-wing populists view the elite as 'agents of an alien power' in the sense that they allegedly favour the interests of non-natives, including immigrants and minorities (Mudde and Rovira Kaltwasser 2017: 14). Right-wing populist parties demarcate outsiders by highlighting cultural differences, left-wing populist parties tend to emphasize egalitarianism and inclusivity (March 2011). And, whereas right-wing populists are opposed to immigration, left-wing populists criticize globalization and neoliberalism. By channelling the language of social justice, left-wing populists aim at addressing 'the diverse forms of subordination around issues concerning exploitation, domination or discrimination' (Mouffe 2018: 61). More generally, left-wing populist parties are concerned with socio-economic issues, whereas right-wing populist parties tend to focus on ethnic identity (March 2017: 286).

Because of this tendency, populism (especially its right-wing variant) is commonly conflated with extremism. This is a misconception. While populism rejects some features of (liberal) democracy (e.g. pluralism and minority rights), extremism rejects the essence of democracy, notably majority rule and popular sovereignty (Mudde 2019: 7). Contrary to extremists, populists are not anti-democratic, nor do they typically resort to militant (let alone violent) forms of protest. This explains why the German Alternative für Deutschland (AfD) is generally considered a populist radical right party, whereas Neo-Nazi movements are seen as extremist. In practice, however, the boundaries between radical and extremist politics have become increasingly blurred (Mudde 2019).

The relationship between populism and democracy is complex. While some scholars suggest that populism is entirely incompatible with non-democratic forms of politics (Mouffe 2018), others argue that populism can open pathways to authoritarianism (Urbinati 2019). A third strand of scholarship suggests that populism is neither good nor bad; instead, populism should be understood and evaluated in relation to the ideological and normative political project to which it is attached (De Cleen et al. 2018: 654). As Benjamin Moffitt has observed, whether or not one perceives populism as a threat or a corrective to democracy ultimately depends on which subtype of democracy one prefers: proponents of liberal democracy tend to see populism as a clear menace to checks and balances, whereas radical democrats see populism as a powerful tool to open up channels to democratize and recalibrate the political order (Moffitt 2020: 94).

For the purposes of this chapter, it is sufficient to remember that populism refers to the antagonistic relationship between a pure and virtuous people and a corrupt and evil elite, and that it is critical of liberal democracy but generally accepts democratic rules and procedures. Extremism rejects democracy altogether. While populism is widespread in Europe, extremism remains a relatively marginal phenomenon – although the Covid-19 pandemic could boost the rise of violent extremism in Europe (Davies et al. 2021).

# Explaining the rise of populism and extremism in Europe

Having provided some conceptual clarity, the remainder of this chapter considers factors that help explain the recent increase in electoral support for populist and extremist parties in Europe. Before doing so, however, three caveats are in order.

First, it is important to note that socio-political contexts vary greatly across the European continent, giving rise to a plethora of different populist movements. While the rise of populist and extremist parties is commonly seen as a Europe-wide phenomenon, this generalization disguises the fact that there are noteworthy regional characteristics and patterns. For instance, right-wing populist parties in Northern and Western Europe tend to be more socially progressive (by supporting same-sex marriage and LGBTQIA+ rights), whereas comparable movements in Southern, Central and Eastern Europe are generally more socially conservative. Furthermore, left-wing populism is more prevalent in Southern Europe, whereas in Scandinavia, populism is exclusively a right-wing phenomenon. This is also the case in Central and Eastern Europe, where experiences with communism have generated widespread hostility towards leftist movements (Abăseacă and Piotrowski 2018). In this region, populism and extremism did not emerge from the fringes of the political spectrum but from the very centre. Parties such as Fidesz in Hungary started their political lives as mainstream parties, leading some scholars to conclude that it may be more accurate to describe them as 'radicalized mainstream parties' (Buštíková 2018). The illiberal turn in this region is one of the biggest challenges the European Union (EU) is currently facing, as democratically elected governments are undermining institutions by disrespecting the rule of law and dismantling institutional checks and balances (Jenne and Mudde 2012).

Second, the disproportionate attention that successful populist and extremist parties receive tends to obscure the fact that they have not been (equally) successful in all European countries. If we omit to acknowledge the failures of these parties, their success 'appears to be almost natural, and even theoretically uninteresting' (Art 2011: 5). Therefore, it is important to bear in mind that there is great variation in the electoral performances of such parties across the continent. Whereas far-right parties have formed part of national governments in some countries including Austria, Estonia, Italy and Switzerland, they have been unsuccessful in rallying broad popular support in countries such as Ireland, Lithuania, Luxembourg and Portugal.

We can also identify important regional differences in the electoral trajectories of far-right parties. Belgium is a case in point, where such parties have historically been more successful in Flanders (the northern, Dutch-speaking part) than in Wallonia (the southern, French-speaking part) (de Jonge 2021a). The Belgian case is an important reminder that the development of populism and extremism in Europe has been a story of failure as well as success.

Third, in light of this variation, it is difficult to generalize about the reasons behind the electoral success of populist and extremist parties in Europe. Studies have shown that populist attitudes are relatively widespread (Akkerman et al. 2014). Many Europeans believe that ordinary people are neglected and exploited by a corrupt elite. The reasons behind these sentiments differ widely across the continent. Over the past decades, many European countries have witnessed various kinds of domestic political upheaval, which has contributed to a growing sense of dissatisfaction with mainstream politics. While the 2008 global financial crisis and the ensuing Great Recession generated momentum for left-wing populist movements, the influx of immigrants and asylum seekers during the so-called 'refugee crisis' in 2015 created fertile soil for the far right.

Although it is difficult to synthesize the root causes of populism and extremism, some broad patterns can be discerned. The following sections provide an overview of demand- and supply-side explanations. Demand-side theories highlight broad structural and societal changes that fuel public demand for populist and extremist parties, while the supply considers factors that enable parties to harness lingering demand.

# Demand-side explanations: Creating a breeding ground

In Central and Eastern Europe (CEE), the rise of populism and extremism is often seen as a backlash against the liberal policies associated with European integration. According to this line of reasoning, citizens perceive the EU as a top-down project that did not socialize citizens and elites in the region to accept the philosophical rationale that underpins liberal-democratic institutions (Dawson and Hanley 2016). By contrast, some commentators have argued that the illiberal turn in CEE is the result of the failures of liberalism to deliver economic prosperity and social justice (Krastev 2016).

We do not have any conclusive empirical evidence to connect the rise of populism with the claim that citizens are disenchanted with liberalism. Although differences in social values continue to persist, CEE citizens support the basic model of liberal democracy to a degree similar to those in traditional democracies (Anghel 2020). Yet, some populist parties may have temporarily profited from the frustration of voters with incumbents as well as low levels of party identification and loyalty (Stanley 2017). More generally, public sentiments against neoliberal economic policies and the perceived immigrant threat have been at the centre of elite manipulation strategies (Vachudova 2020). This is broadly in line with studies of public attitudes in Western Europe (Ivarsflaten 2008).

While the newly established parties and party systems were slow to consolidate in the post-communist setting, traditional party families in Western Europe failed to appeal to ever larger swathes of the electorate. In the West, the rise of populism can broadly be attributed to a crisis of representation (Mair 2013; Halikiopoulou and Vasilopoulou 2018). The growing disenchantment with mainstream politics has been attributed to the cartelization of politics (Katz and Mair 2009). Specifically, the erosion of parties' representative function has contributed to a sense of alienation between voters and political parties, thereby generating demand for alternative challenger parties (Grzymala-Busse 2019).

The decline of traditional 'mass parties' (i.e. parties that were characterized by large memberships) was accompanied by widespread social changes including secularization and class de-alignment, which, in turn, helped pave the way for political de-alignment. At the same time, broad changes in the international environment (e.g. immigration, globalization, economic crises) made people feel less secure about their lives (Mudde 2007: 223), thereby giving rise to a broad range of grievances. As traditional social structures such as religion or class degenerated, individuals lost a sense of belonging, making them more susceptible to the attraction of populist parties.

Studies have shown that the so-called 'losers of the modernization process' tend to be most inclined to vote for populist parties (Kriesi et al. 2012). This typically includes people working in certain industries that are vulnerable to foreign competition, small business owners and other working-class people

(Arzheimer and Carter 2006). In times of economic recession, competition over scarce resources such as jobs and access to public services increases, which can contribute to a heightening sense of insecurity. It is important to note, however, that these grievances at the voter-level are not solely driven by economic factors but also by cultural processes (e.g. immigration) and political changes (e.g. European integration) (Halikiopoulou and Vlandas 2020).

In this insecure environment, voters moved away from moderate parties at the centre to seek answers in the narratives of populist parties, which promised an identity as well as protection against an ever-changing world (Mudde 2007: 223). This helps explain why populist parties on the left and right attract voters that can be characterized as socially and economically vulnerable (van Kessel 2015). Using survey data from nine European countries, Steven Van Hauwaert and Stijn van Kessel (2018) found that populist voters on both sides of the political spectrum are generally more interested in politics but have lower levels of satisfaction with democracy. In addition, they are similarly sceptical about the EU (Rooduijn et al. 2017).

Despite these parallels, however, the underlying motivations for supporting right- versus left-wing populist parties are very different. For instance, radical right voters tend to have lower levels of education than radical left voters as well as diverging views on immigration 'the radical left shows marked signs of cosmopolitanism and the radical right clear nativism' (Rooduijn et al. 2017: 555).

Studies have shown that anti-immigrant attitudes are the single most important factor in explaining demand for far-right parties (Ivarsflaten 2008). Yet, while support for far-right parties has increased over the past decades, people's attitudes towards immigration have remained relatively stable (Rooduijn 2020). This begs the question why support for the far right has increased so substantially over the past decades. More generally, assuming that there is a reservoir of potential voters for populist and extremist parties in *all* European countries, why is there such great variation in the electoral performances of these parties across the continent? To answer this question, we need to take into account supply-side explanations.

# The supply side: Exploiting fertile soil

Focusing exclusively on the demand side of populism does not give us a complete picture about the reasons why these parties are successful in some countries but not in others. The supply side, therefore, considers the various ways in which parties mobilize voters, including the agency and characteristics of populist and extremist parties themselves. After all, '[i]rrespective of how favorable the breeding ground and the political opportunity structure might be to new political parties, they merely present political actors with a series of possibilities' (Mudde 2007: 256). In the end, it is up to the parties whether they can actually benefit from these possibilities.

There is widespread consensus in the literature that populist parties are more likely to succeed if they can present themselves as credible alternatives to mainstream parties (van Kessel 2015). Several factors influence a party's credibility, notably party organization as well as party leadership. These two features are closely linked, as charismatic leaders can be instrumental in both rallying public support and holding their parties together.

The supply side considers not just the behaviour of parties themselves but also the political opportunities available to them. For instance, the fiscal transfer system of the EU appears to have inadvertently sustained and perpetuated the authoritarian turn in CEE by enabling populist leaders to solidify their position of power (Kelemen 2017). Moreover, proportional representation (PR) electoral systems are more 'permissive' than disproportional majoritarian systems and make it easier for new parties to gain parliamentary representation, thereby favouring multipartyism (Duverger 1954). In general, countries with PR electoral systems (e.g. the Netherlands) are known to offer more opportunity for smaller parties than countries with majoritarian electoral systems (e.g. France).

Another supply-side factor relates to the political space available to populist and extremist parties. This depends to a large extent on the positioning of mainstream parties. If mainstream parties gravitate towards the centre of the political spectrum, there is more space at the fringes of the political spectrum for radical parties to emerge. In particular in Western Europe, the ideological convergence between centre-left and centre-right parties has given rise to a number of centrist coalition governments. Political convergence generally forces parties to compromise their ideals by agreeing on a lowest common denominator. This is likely to frustrate voters, who feel that they are being robbed of a real choice.

As Bartek Pytlas (2015) has shown, however, competition between radical and mainstream parties should not just be studied in spatial but also in discursive terms. In Central and Eastern Europe, the ideological boundaries between challengers and mainstream parties are more blurred. Here, the diffusion of radical right ideologies and narratives into the mainstream political discourse has increased the salience of the (issues of the) populist radical right, thereby contributing to the normalization of far-right narratives (see Mudde 2019). More generally, mainstream parties play a crucial role in the electoral trajectories of populist and extremist parties (Heinze 2018; Meguid 2005).

A final factor that can help explain the variation in the electoral performances of populist and extremist parties in Europe is the media (de Jonge 2019). In CEE, particularly in countries where populist authoritarian parties are in power, key liberal institutions including the media have come under attack (Surowiec and Štětka 2020). In Western Europe, media outlets used to be tied to political parties, churches and trade unions; from the 1960s onward, however, the media started to gain political independence (Hallin and Mancini 2004). The dual forces of privatization and commercialization launched a 'struggle for readers and viewers and, consequently, a focus on the more extreme and scandalous aspects of politics' (Mudde 2004: 553).

There is a growing consensus in the literature that the 'mediatization of politics' has contributed to the rise of populism (Kübler and Kriesi 2017). Political competition increasingly consists of a battle over media attention that is acted out on a public stage, with the electorate assuming the role of an audience in a theatre (Koopmans and Muis 2009: 644). On the one hand, the media can set the agenda by addressing issues and making them salient. On the other hand, the media can play an instrumental role in exacerbating lingering political dissatisfaction, for instance by amplifying voters' fears about immigration. As such, the media can play a key role in mobilizing voters and disseminating the populist message, which, in turn, can contribute to making these parties and movements appear more socially acceptable. Particularly in the earlier phases of a party's development, the media is a crucial asset to generate visibility (Ellinas 2010).

The reasons behind the electoral success (and failure) of populist and extremist parties in Europe are many and complex. As mainstream parties and politicians struggle to deal with the profound upheaval that the continent has experienced over the past decade, the breeding ground for populist and extremist movements has become increasingly fertile.

# Conclusion

At the onset of the global public health crisis brought about by outbreak of Covid-19, pundits were quick to suggest that it could take the wind out of the sails of populist movements. First, it was believed to expose the incompetence of populists (especially those in power) and bring to the fore the importance of expert knowledge, thereby dampening the anti-elitist sentiments that were rampant before the pandemic. Second, in some countries, it triggered a 'rally round the flag' effect by generating increased (albeit often short-lived) popular support for governments and political leaders. This could harm populists (notably those in opposition) by empowering the establishment. Third, it could shift the public focus away from identity politics, for instance by decreasing the salience of immigration.

At the same time, however, lessons from the United States indicate that the coronavirus can also easily be weaponized and absorbed into existing social cleavages. Moreover, the ensuing economic crisis is likely to provide fertile soil for populists. Indeed, the pandemic not only contributes to deepening inequality but also brings into focus the importance of the welfare state. This, in turn, could provide renewed momentum for left-wing populist movements. Perhaps most importantly, the underlying issues listed above that gave rise to populism have not magically disappeared. On the contrary, these issues are likely to be exacerbated in times of crises. If anything, the pandemic risks amplifying anti-government resentment, which, in turn, could accelerate the spread of extremist ideologies, particularly online (Davies et al. 2021).

While crises are often seen as a trigger for populism, it is important to bear in mind that populists are remarkably good at 'performing' crises. As Benjamin Moffitt has observed, 'populist actors actively participate in the "spectacularization of failure" that underlies crisis, allowing them to pit "the people" against a dangerous other, radically simplify the terms and terrain of political debate and advocate strong leadership and quick political action to stave off or solve the impending crisis' (2015: 191). In an era where Europe seems to be stumbling from one crisis to the next, this tactic is likely to continue to bear fruits in the future. In short, populism is here to stay.

# Questions for discussion

1 Why do right-wing populist parties generally outperform left-wing populist parties in Europe?
2 What role does gender play in the rise and spread of populism in Europe?
3 How has social media contributed to the dissemination of populist and extremist ideologies in Europe?

**4** Should populists be opposed? Are there reasons to consider populists more favourably?

# Recommended for Further Reading

Berezin, M. (2009) *Illiberal Politics in Neoliberal Times: Culture, Security and Populism in the New Europe.* Cambridge: Cambridge University Press

Donà, A. (2020) 'What's Gender Got to do with Populism?' *European Journal of Women's Studies* 27(3): 285–92.

Miller-Idriss, C. (2018) *The Extreme Gone Mainstream: Commercialization and Far Right Youth Culture in Germany.* Princeton, NJ: Princeton University Press.

Nissen, A. (2022) *Europeanisation of the Contemporary Far Right: Generation Identity and Fortress Europe.* Abingdon: Routledge.

Wodak, R. (2015) *The Politics of Fear: What Right-Wing Populist Discourses Mean.* London: SAGE.

# 12

# Integration and Disintegration

## Nicole Lindstrom

Since European states signed the European Union (EU) into being in 1992, it has been considered a largely stable system. That is, formally equal sovereign states have willingly agreed to transfer authority to supranational institutions to coordinate and regulate trans-border issues to an unprecedented level and scale. The EU has faced many crises in its history. But the process of European integration has appeared, if not at times under significant pressure, irreversible.

Starting with the 2008 global financial crisis, multiple crises including (but not limited to) the eurozone crisis, refugee crisis and Brexit have prompted questions of whether we are witnessing a process of European disintegration. 'The risk that the EU will disintegrate', claims one observer, 'is a clear and present danger' (Krastev 2012: 23). Some scholars argue that traditional approaches to the study of the EU, which have tended to assume the EU is built to last (Kelemen 2007) are poorly equipped to analyse whether and why, as Zielonka (2014: 1) puts it starkly, 'the EU is doomed'.

This chapter argues, in contrast to these most pessimistic scenarios, that European politics have always been defined by interrelated processes of regional integration and disintegration. The EU is not doomed to disintegrate. But this disintegrative moment, like other crises it has faced, will arguably leave it transformed.

How can we define disintegration in the EU context? Douglas Webber (2019) sets out three dimensions, which can be viewed as mirror images of integration:

- reducing the formal or treaty-based authority of supranational institutions;
- diminishing the range of common issue areas over which the EU has competence; and,
- decreasing the number of member states.

Brexit remains the sole instance of the third dimension. Some argue that responses to the refugee crisis, such as rejection of common asylum policies and suspension of Schengen, is characteristic of the second dimension. But to date we have not witnessed the kind of reversal of formal authority through renegotiated treaties associated with the first. We can also add to these definitions a dimension of 'perpetual disintegration' (Rosamond 2019: 39) in which the system is preserved but affected by continual disintegrative dynamics.

What drives disintegration? Traditional theories of European integration offer different explanations of what moves the process forward. But they have devoted less attention to why it slows, stops or even reverses. Moreover, governance approaches, which analyse the EU as a political system comparable to nation-states, identify challenges of governing complex multi-level entities but have had say little about their possible dissolution.

Liesbet Hooghe and Gary Marks' (2009) post-functionalism account offers an important exception. It points to the growing disjuncture between the deepening and widening of European integration since Maastricht, and the strengthening of political appeals to defend territorially sovereign national identities against Europeanizing pressures. As EU issues become more politicized domestically, Hooghe and Marks (2009: 21) argue, the more we can expect 'downward pressure on the level and scope of integration'. The eurozone, refugee and Brexit crises each involved mass domestic politicization. Yet one of the most pertinent questions in EU studies is the extent to which this politicization – which is manifested differently across issue areas – is leading to further European integration, disintegration or something in between.

The following chapter examines different developments in European studies seeking to understand disintegration in the post-2008 crisis period. The first section considers traditional approaches to understanding theories of European integration, neofunctionalism and liberal intergovernmentalism, and shows how the former has been more analytically attuned to disintegrative dynamics than the latter. The second section goes on to examine the governance turn in European studies. It suggests that analysing the EU as a stable political system has left most governance approaches, except post-functionalism, poorly equipped to understanding the potential for disintegration. The third section narrows in on Brexit as the most ostensible case of European disintegration by Webber's (2019) criteria. It suggests that while Brexit offers a very compelling example of how the domestic politicization of European issues can result in a radical transformation of a member state's relationship with the EU, five years after the Brexit vote disintegration is a more likely scenario within the UK than the EU. The final section considers how we can understand European (dis)integration in times of crisis, prompting new ways of analysing integrative and disintegrative dynamics transforming the European project.

# Theories of European integration and disintegration

Since the first European institutions were established in the 1950s, theories of European integration have sought to explain what drives the process forward. Today the EU can be defined as something more than an international organization, given that it has legal jurisdiction over member states with the authority to monitor and enforce rules, but falls far short of a federal United States of Europe since its member states remain sovereign entities.

Neofunctionalism and liberal intergovernmentalism offer two different explanations for this outcome. Neofunctionalism suggests that cooperation in one area continues to spill over into others due to functional necessity. Liberal intergovernmentalism argues that integration has been a rational choice of sovereign states. Both approaches assume that while integration can slow at times and speed ahead at others the process never fully reverses. While neither approach offers an explicit account of disintegration, the following section suggests that neofunctionalism has traditionally been more attuned to disintegrative dynamics than intergovernmentalist accounts.

Neofunctionalists argue that integration is driven by a rational necessity for cross-border cooperation. The concept of 'spillover' captures how action to achieve one goal, such as the free movement of goods across borders, creates a situation in which that goal can only be achieved by taking a further action, such as the harmonization of food and safety standards.

These 'converging practical goals', Ernst Haas (1968: xix) argues, provide the 'leaven out of which the bread of European unity' is baked.

Neofunctionalists never identify a specific end to this process. But, following neofunctionalist logic, governments and citizens should gradually shift loyalties and activities to the supranational level as they recognize the benefits of cooperation. Reflecting on his theory in the second edition of *The Uniting of Europe* (1968: xix), Haas pondered how 'a single charismatic Frenchman' could 'stop the [spillover] process'. French President Charles de Gaulle withdrawing his representatives from European negotiations to protest against the expansion of qualified majority voting in the Council marked the first major threat to European integration.

The so-called empty chair crisis prompted neofunctionalists to modify their approach to consider possibilities that 'spillover' could be accompanied by 'spillback'. In other words, and mirroring Webber's (2019) first and second definition of disintegration, the scope and institutional capacities of supranational institutions could retract as well as expand (Lindberg and Scheingold 1970). Phillipe Schmitter (1971) suggests that disintegrative acts by purposive actors, such as de Gaulle leaving an empty chair at the bargaining table, could have specific consequences, such as slowing the integration process. Indeed, the 1966 Luxembourg compromise resolved the crisis by giving member states a veto over any supranational decision deemed to threaten their national interest, which came to significantly slow the pace of integration.

But such acts did not necessarily lead to the collapse of the whole system (Rosamond 2019: 37–8). These disintegrative moments could also lead to deeper integration or other forms of differentiation to cope with crisis. Schmitter (2012: 39) reminds us that 'there is nothing new about crises in the process of European integration'. Indeed, as he and neofunctionalists argued five decades ago, crises can accelerate, slow or transform integration.

Liberal intergovernmentalism, the main theoretical challenger to neofunctionalism, should, in theory, offer a more straightforward account of disintegration. According to this approach, member states cooperate at the European level only insofar as it helps achieve national preferences. If states cannot achieve their preferences through supranational institutions, then they would theoretically try to reduce the scope and level of supranational authority or exit altogether. But Andrew Moravcsik (1993) argues that regional cooperation within conditions of complex interdependence is a positive-sum game. In other words, domestic producers, dependent on integrated supply chains and cross-border trade, lobby their elected officials to promote their interests at the European level. And governments, in turn, use different strategies at the EU bargaining table to try to maximize their preferences. Member states may not always get what they want. But every state can accept what Moravcsik (1993: 522) calls 'lowest common denominator' outcomes that satisfy the greatest number of member states and, by extension, domestic economic interest groups, to make everyone marginally better off.

Neofunctionalism and liberal intergovernmentalism identify different drivers of integration. Insofar as they address the possibility of disintegration, they seek to explain why states have periodically threatened to throw a wrench in the European integration process. For neofunctionalists 'spillback' is contained to specific rules or policy areas rather than the disintegration of the entire political system. Liberal intergovernmentalists like Moravcsik have considered the shadow of the veto or the threat of exit more an effective bargaining strategy than a realistic possibility due to ever-increasing economic interdependence amongst European states.

When states signed up to the most ambitious European integration project to date in Maastricht in 1992, the newly named European Union appeared so secure that the question of why states cooperate, the question that motivated European integration scholars, gradually declined in relevance. Scholars turned their attention to studying the EU as stable political system comparable in most fundamental ways to sovereign nation-states. If traditional theories of European integration struggle to explain disintegration, a key challenge for the so-called governance turn is whether it can still take for granted the stability of the EU as a state-like system and whether governance frameworks can capture post-crisis disintegrative dynamics.

# Governance approaches and European disintegration

The primary focus of European governance approaches is how relatively stable rules and practices shape the behaviours of actors situated within a multi-level European system. Each leading governance approach is based on the largely unquestioned assumption, in other words, that European integration has progressed to the point of creating a European-wide polity where the formal and informal rules of the game are, despite not being codified in a formal constitution and subject to ongoing modifications, largely fixed. Ben Rosamond (2019) argues that the governance turn has left EU scholars poorly equipped to analysing the potential for crises to fundamentally change the nature of the EU as a political system.

The following section examines three prominent governance approaches – multi-level governance, institutionalism and Europeanization – to examine how they can help us understand disintegration. It suggests that while governance approaches may indeed be inadequate in accounting for substantial changes in EU competencies and membership, which Webber (2019) argues characterizes disintegration, they offer important insights into more day-to-day disintegrative tendencies.

Multi-level governance (MLG) argues that European integration reallocates authority upward, downward and sideways from central states, with interlinked actors sharing policymaking authority across a range of issue areas. Operating within such a multi-level governance system, a key insight of MLG approaches is that member state governments cannot always control political or policy outcomes (Hooghe and Marks 2003). Critics of MLG argue that the approach overstates the extent to which European integration diminishes the autonomy of the central governments. Ian Bache (1999) suggests, for example, that central governments act as gatekeepers in allocating EU funding for underdeveloped regions, which can strengthen rather than weaken their hand vis-à-vis sub-national entities.

With respect to more fundamental issues related to the territorial integrity of member states EU leaders have traditionally been reluctant to intervene. When Catalonia declared independence in 2017, for example, then President of the European Council, Donald Tusk, made the EU's position clear: 'For EU nothing changes. Spain remains our only interlocutor' (Kostaki 2017). MLG raises important insights into how European integration can empower sub-national actors to demand more formal authority and competence over policy areas. But it provides a more limited account of under what conditions multi-level governance spurs disintegration with the EU and its member states.

Institutionalists, meanwhile, analyse how European integration constrains and enables different sets of actors across time. Rational institutionalists consider how individuals or groups pursue their preferences within institutional structures, expanding liberal intergovernmentalism's focus on treaty negotiations to more day-to-day EU decision-making. Historical institutionalists argue that preferences are not fixed but shaped by the formal and informal institutions in which they operate. Member states governments might face domestic pressure to pursue significant changes at the EU level, for example, but sunk costs, accumulated policy constraints and unintended consequences of earlier decisions make it difficult for governments to significantly change course (Pierson 1996).

Sociological institutionalists bring to the analysis of institutions the importance of ideas and norms. Actors immersed in the 'ways of doing things' in the European system, they argue, will resist change out of convention or loyalty to the European project (see Jupille, Caporaso and Checkel 2003: 7). Institutionalist accounts of the EU are more focused on how actors operate within existing institutions than questioning the stability of the institutions themselves. But they can still provide important insights into integrative or disintegrative dynamics. Rational institutionalists turn our attention to domestic actors seeking to constrain or enable supranational institutions to pursue their interests, historical institutionalists to the importance of critical junctures in altering integration trajectories and sociological institutionalists to how loyalties can shift.

Finally, Europeanization frameworks analyse why, given the same external pressures on member states (or aspiring members) to adapt to EU rules and norms, we see different degrees of change in national polities, policies and politics. The most prominent of Europeanization frameworks, top-down analyses take a fixed set of EU rules and norms and then compare the level and speed of compliance across member states.

Europeanization frameworks are particularly well equipped to understanding an additional dimension of disintegration: non-compliance with EU rules. For example, Tanja Börzel and Thomas Risse (2000) suggest that EU adaptational pressure can lead to domestic transformation, where an institution or policy becomes fully Europeanized. But adaptational pressure can also result in inertia, whereby EU pressures lead to little real change, or retrenchment, where a policy area become less Europeanized due to political resistance.

Retrenchment differs from disintegration, however. Europeanization scholars tend to understand Europeanization as a kind of feedback loop. That is, resistance to top-down pressures can spur governments and domestic actors to pursue bottom-up changes to those rules through the normal EU legislative process. Europeanization scholars have not typically considered, however, the possibility of inertia or retrenchment fundamentally challenging the EU's treaty-based authority or competence over a policy area.

# Brexit and European disintegration

A key assumption underlying both traditional European integration theories and governance approaches is that European elites have largely enjoyed a permissive consensus on EU matters. Since Maastricht voters have rejected important treaty-making decisions in referendums at times slowing integration momentum, such as French and Dutch voters rejecting the 2005 Constitutional Treaty. However, given the technocratic nature of most EU decision-making, EU issues have commonly been considered too removed from voters' everyday concerns to make European integration a salient political issue.

Hooghe and Mark's (2009) post-functionalist approach suggests that member state governments increasingly face a constraining dissensus on European matters. That is, governing elites no longer enjoy a relatively free hand in pursuing decisions at the EU level but must consider how these decisions can be politicized domestically. Post-functionalism offers an important approach to understanding disintegration since, as Hooghe and Marks (2009: 21) argue, domestic politicization of EU issues, and around a national/international divide, places the kind of steady 'downward pressure on the level and scope of integration' that Webber (2019) argues is indicative of disintegration. Post-functionalism also comes closest to accounting for why member state could decide to leave the EU altogether.

The July 2016 Brexit referendum, where 52 per cent of votes cast favoured the UK leaving, sent shock waves across Europe and beyond. Some EU scholars predicted soon after the vote that Britain's complete exit from the EU was unlikely. Moravcsik (2016), for example, had already dismissed Cameron's renegotiation of the UK–EU relationship prior to the referendum as a 'masterclass in political theatre', a 'great Brexit kabuki'. After the referendum Moravcsik (2017) went on to predict that 'in theory, Britain could ultimately carry out its threat to leave the European Union, but in practice, more will remain the same than change'. In 2020 the UK officially exited the EU and in 2021 signed an EU–UK Trade and Cooperation Agreement (TCA) that fundamentally changes Britain's relationship with the EU.

Moravcsik's interventions show how Brexit defied liberal intergovernmentalist assumptions. Most major British producer groups, for example, warned leaving the single market would have devastating effects on British businesses and the wider economy. But these powerful domestic interests ultimately failed to prevent a referendum, sway the vote towards remain or successfully lobby the UK government to remain in the European single market. Moreover, if Cameron's so-called political theatre was indeed a bargaining strategy, it backfired, resulting in his immediate ousting as Conservative Party leader and, in liberal intergovernmentalist terms, arguably left both the UK and the EU economically worse off, at least in the short term.

Hooghe and Marks' (2009) post-functionalist framework captures many relevant political dynamics leading to Brexit. Many observers suggest that Cameron's call for a renegotiation and referendum was driven more by the need to solve domestic political problems than to exert change at the European level. That is, Cameron used the referendum to appease the Eurosceptic faction of the Conservative Party and stop the haemorrhaging of votes to the UK Independence Party (UKIP).

British Eurosceptics had been successfully mobilizing voters around identity-based concerns since the 2004 eastward enlargement led to a massive increase of new EU citizens. The combination of anti-EU and anti-immigration sentiments culminated in the Leave campaign, which combined the slogan 'take back control' with images of refugees under the headline declaring the UK was at a 'breaking point'. The continued mass politicization of European issues continued to limit British leaders' room for manoeuvre in negotiating Britain's future relationship with the EU (Menon and Wager 2020). The national versus international cleavage has, as Hooghe and Marks (2009) suggest, defined British domestic politics leading up to and following the Brexit vote.

Neither the UK nor the EU will remain the same after Brexit. But the question remains whether it will place downward pressure on the level and scope of integration. The EU's negotiating position has been united and clear: protect the integrity of the single market and ensure a level playing field. The EU made explicit, as it did during Cameron's pre-referendum renegotiation, that it would not allow the UK to pick and choose access to the single market, such as opting out of free movement of persons while opting in on free movement of goods.

Some British critics complained the EU's perceived intransigence in Brexit negotiations was designed to punish the UK to deter other states from leaving. EU negotiators argued, however, that they were fulfilling the obligation with which they are tasked: to uphold the mutually agreed rules underlying the single market and the EU more generally. By 2021, any contagion effect – or, in other words, Brexit spurring Grexit, Czechzit, Italexit or Frexit – has become a distant prospect. Indeed, perhaps due to observing the destabilizing impact of Brexit, most nationalist-populist parties have modified their anti-EU rhetoric to changing the EU from within instead of destroying it (Webber 2020).

Brexit could ultimately have a more significant impact on the integrity of the UK than the EU. The Scottish National Party (SNP) remains committed to holding another referendum on Scottish independence. If passed, the UK's exit from the EU could be followed by Scotland's exit from the UK. The EU would be placed in a difficult position in such a scenario. Spain and other member states facing secessionist demands will not want to make Scotland's re-entry an easy process. Another outstanding issue relates to Northern Ireland.

Once the UK left the EU, the border between Northern Ireland and the Republic of Ireland ceased to be an internal EU border. Constructing a hard border between Northern Ireland and the Republic of Ireland threatens the peace reached in the 1998 Good Friday Agreement, while creating a border between Northern Ireland and the rest of the UK in the Irish Sea risks undermining the integrity of the United Kingdom of Great Britain and Northern Ireland. The EU–UK Trade and Cooperation Agreement leaves these fundamental border issues unresolved. Disintegration of the UK in terms of nations seceding or, short of that, increasing their authority vis-à-vis London has become one of the most salient British political issues post-Brexit.

# Future dimensions of European integration and disintegration

Brexit reduced the number of member states, one of Webber's (2019) three dimensions of disintegration, but the EU-27 appears intact for the foreseeable future. With respect to Webber's two other dimensions – reducing the formal or treaty-based authority of supranational institutions or diminishing the range of common issue areas over which the EU has competence – the eurozone and refugee crises provide an opportunity to assess under what conditions crises can lead to integrative or disintegrative outcomes.

In his comparison of European responses to the two crises, Frank Schimmelfennig (2018: 970) suggests that the eurozone and refugee crises share important features: they are a result of an exogenous shock, expose significant deficiencies of integration, spur intergovernmental conflicts over who should bear the costs of crisis and lead to high levels of domestic politicization. He concludes that the eurozone crisis has led to *more* integration, expanding rather than reducing the level and scope of supranational authority, while EU responses to the refugee crisis exhibits more disintegrative tendencies.

Schimmelfennig's (2018) intervention suggests that mass politicization does not necessarily exert downward pressure on the level and scope of integration, and, indeed, can be consistent with further integration. If mass politicization is a necessary but insufficient condition of disintegration, then post-functionalism can be considered a mirror image of European integration theories insofar that it identifies important drivers of disintegration but struggles to explain why and how mass politicization can lead to 'integrative' or 'neutral' outcomes (Webber 2019: 1143). Schimmelfennig (2018) argues that the eurozone crisis triggering more integration and the refugee crisis less can be explained by a higher level of transnational interdependence in the case of the eurozone crisis and a more active role of supranational actors, namely the European Central Bank (see also Niemann and Ioannou 2015).

A closer examination of responses to the refugee crisis can expose ways in which it was integrative, such as the creation of a new autonomous EU border force that has been granted authority to implement EU policies designed to manage forced migration flows. Some argue that the EU is most accurately described as a system of differentiated integration: integrating further in some policy areas than others, and sensitive to increased politicization, but neither significantly expanding nor significantly diminishing the common issue areas over which it has competence (Schimmelfennig, Leuffen and Rittberger 2015).

Rosamond (2019: 39) suggests, however, that if we view disintegration, like integration, as a process rather than an outcome, we can look for disintegrative dynamics or signs of perpetual disintegration. Governance approaches are well equipped to helping scholars look beyond formal institutional arrangements to examining how they work in practice. One important sign of perpetual disintegration, for example, is widespread non-compliance with EU rules. As discussed above, Europeanization scholars examine whether and why states comply with EU rules that they have agreed at the EU level.

Some scholars go beyond formal indicators of compliance, such as correct and timely transposition of EU rules into domestic legislation, to investigate how EU rules are implemented. Batory (2016) finds, for example, that while the European Commission uses single market rules to try to penalize governments such as Hungary or Poland's for violating fundamental rights, in practice governments have shown they are adept at complying creatively: doing just enough to avoid formal sanction but continuing an illiberal path (see also Lindstrom 2020). Enough evidence of passive resistance to EU rules, in the form of inertia, or active resistance to EU rules, whether through creative compliance or outright defiance, can signal a gradual form of disintegration whereby the EU retains formal competence, but its authority and legitimacy required to exercise it is steadily diminished.

# Conclusion

In response to multiple crises facing Europe since 2008, the EU has managed to date to avoid disintegration as defined by Webber (2019): its formal authority has not been significantly reduced, the number of policy areas it governs has not been diminished and it has limited the reduction of member states to one (the UK). Yet the political divisions and popular discontent that have threatened to tear the EU apart over the last decade remain (Vollard 2014).

The EU continues to find itself in what Zielonka (2014: 58) terms a 'technocratic-populist trap' (Zielonka 2014: 58–9). EU leaders continue to 'govern by rules and rule by numbers' (Schmidt 2020: 1) while populists demand 'the people' (most often defined in exclusively national terms) take back control over political economic decision-making. Critics of European integration on the right and left argue that the sovereign nation-state is the only legitimate site for economic and political decision-making and advocate the reduction of both the scope and level of European integration. But others point to continued crises to argue that nation-states remain deeply immersed in a globalized world in which managing the flow of money, goods, people or viruses require the kind of transnational coordination at the heart of the European project.

Understanding European (dis)integration as a process rather than an outcome allows us to examine ways in which responses to crises transforms the EU (Bartolini 2005; Rosamond 2019). The UK's withdrawal from the EU, for example, is often portrayed as radical rupture, spurring five years of tumultuous negotiations and political uncertainty before signing the TCA. But understanding Brexit as an ongoing process draws our attention to ways that Brexit will continue to transform European and British political economies, inviting scholars to analyse whether and how it spurs greater integration or disintegration within the EU-27 and UK-1. Moreover, understanding the European political system as one of differential integration points to how integration can proceed further in one policy area than another.

Yet understanding differential integration as a process encourages us to go beyond comparing responses to crises as discreet outcomes to understanding dynamic change across policy areas and over time. For example, suspending Schengen and resisting burden-sharing at the height of the 2015 refugee crisis were disintegrative moments but prompted further integration by expanding the EU's competence to police its external border. Finally, scholars of European (dis)integration must be attuned to ways in which passive or active forms of non-compliance with EU rules and norms can lead to a consequential, if not always as easily discernible, form of perpetual disintegration.

# Questions for discussion

1  How have crises shaped the history of European integration?
2  What is perpetual disintegration? Is it more or less important that other dimensions of disintegration as identified by Webber (2019)?
3  Why are some EU policy areas more prone to disintegration than others?
4  Some consider Brexit a sign of European disintegration. Can you think of reasons in favour and against this claim?

# Recommended for Further Reading

Gänzle, L., Benjamin, L. and Trondal, J. eds. (2019). *Differentiated Integration and Disintegration in a Post-Brexit Era*. London: Routledge.

Greer, S. and Laible, J. (2020). *The European Union after Brexit*. Manchester: Manchester University Press.

Schmidt, V., Coman, R. and Crespy, A., eds (2020) *Governance and Politics in the Post-Crisis European Union*. Cambridge: Cambridge University Press.

Vollard, H. (2018). *European Disintegration: A Search for Explanations*. London: Palgrave.

Webber, D. (2018). *European Disintegration? The Politics of Crisis in the European Union*. London: Bloomsbury.

# 13

# Terrorism and Organized Crime

## Rosa Maryon and Simone Tholens

Terrorism and organized crime (OC) are transnational and opaque phenomena operating in the shadows of a deeply interconnected Europe. European counter-terrorism and counter-organized crime strategies form part of distinct sets of security practices. But they are also related and intersecting. Even if the co-existence of terrorism and organized crime are observed to occur only 'in some marginalised places' (Europol 2020: 21), European responses to these threats operate in the same policy space where competences often overlap. This makes it difficult to evaluate one without taking into account the other – or *others* – as generally, 'disaster management' can be conflated in several policies and mechanisms (cf. Rhinardt, Boin and Ekengren 2007; cf. also Argomaniz, Bures and Kaunert 2015). In this chapter we will treat terrorism and organized crime as manifesting similar security policy patterns.

EU cooperation in dealing with terrorism and OC has grown significantly since the turn of the century, but preferences for national and bilateral strategies remain salient. European states and regions differ in the security threats they face as well as in their political will for European cooperation in the realm of security. National security agencies across the continent have different cultures, ways of operating and standards to which they hold themselves. Yet European-level integration in the area of security is decisively expanding and is a key development in the last decade.

In the 2003 European Security Strategy, terrorism and organized crime were listed as two of the main threats facing European peace and security. The Strategy identified the serious risk from the combined threats of 'terrorism committed to maximum violence, the availability of weapons of mass destruction, organised crime, the weakening of the state system and the privatization of force' (Council of the EU 2003: 5). With the shift to viewing transnational threats as the main focus of European security strategies, the neat internal–external security distinction collapsed, leaving scope for European ownership of an expanded portfolio of activities. This allowed the EU, spearheaded by the European Commission, to step out of the mainly economic area of cooperation, and assume competencies in areas traditionally the responsibility of member states.

This shift fostered a people-centred – as opposed to a state-centred – era of security making. Such 'biopolitics', where the relationship between governments and people is increasingly concerned with sifting out risks among the population (Vaughan-Williams 2015: 7), is at the centre of European responses to 'a more secure Union'. Biopolitics is also at the core of European efforts to counter the threat of terrorism and organized crime. Coupled with an increased presence of geopolitics, seen particularly in European efforts at co-opting neighbouring states for purposes of security and stability (Kaunert, Léonard and Wertman 2020), the field of European counter-terrorism and counter-organized crime makes for a dynamic and multifaceted area of study.

This chapter will discuss developments in the areas of terrorism, organized crime and their counter-strategies in Europe. In doing so, we account in broad strokes for national differences that exist within Europe. Nevertheless, even when fractured at different levels of decision-making, we claim that counter-terrorism and counter-organized crime strategies are tied together in what can be deemed a 'European model'. This is often distinct from a US model, and is also gradually visible in the proliferation and expansion of European-level response mechanisms. The chapter will first provide some background on counter-terrorism and organized crime in Europe. Then, it will discuss European strategies over the last decade to tackle counter-terrorism and organized crime, both at state and EU level. The chapter will pay particular attention to the constant evolution and tension between the national and the supranational that continue to shape this issue area in European politics.

# Terrorism

Terrorism has been a regular feature of European security since the 1970s, when left-wing and separatist terrorism targeted European states. Left-wing terrorism in particular targeted Italy and (West) Germany, while Spain and the UK faced terrorist tactics from the separatist group Basque Homeland and Liberty (ETA) and the Irish Republican Army (IRA), respectively. Given the specific nature of terrorist threats throughout the 1970s and 1980s, terrorism was considered a domestic issue to be tackled 'at home'. This prompted large differences and also conflict over their treatment of the issue: where France would negotiate, the UK would use policing and internment, and where ETA was prosecuted in Spain, they were given a safe haven in neighbouring France (Kaunert and Léonard 2019: 262). While early counter-terror mechanisms such as the TREVI group would initiate both diplomatic and policing coordination, the period up until 2001 was characterized by strong norms of state sovereignty over the matter, with different legal frameworks, priorities and understanding of the issue.

Even with a general growth in relevance across the continent since 2001, European states differ in their priorities and approaches to terrorism. A comparative study of nine member states grappled with the divergences and similarities across four policy dimensions – prevent, protect, pursue, respond (van Dongen 2010). The study found that Prevent and Pursue are policy dimensions built on primarily interpreting terrorism as undertaken by human beings. In contrast, Protect and Respond are more emergency-oriented policy dimensions. The study also identified the Czech Republic, Denmark, the UK and Germany as belonging to a 'maximalist approach', in which all four dimensions are equally prioritized. The Netherlands and Italy were categorized as pertaining to a 'Human Agent approach', primarily interpreting terrorism as undertaken by human beings, and thus prioritizing Prevent and Pursue policies. Finally, France and Portugal were categorized as belonging to a 'Confrontational approach', prioritizing measures in the Pursue strand, where a direct-action approach to *fight* terrorism is preferred (van Dongen 2010). This categorization underscores the point that there are significant and salient differences across European counter-terrorism practices. Focused comparisons of specific reactions to terrorist attacks have, moreover, emphasized how such events actually deepen differences rather than harmonize counter-terror approaches.

To see these national strategies in action, consider the 2015 attacks (*Charlie Hebdo* and the Jewish supermarket attacks in January, and the Paris attacks in November) in France and the 2016 Berlin Christmas market attack. France and Germany displayed remarkably different responses across public discourse, political framing and security response mechanisms (Samaan and Jacobs 2020). Notably, whereas France deployed the armed forces and issued a state of emergency in the wake of the first wave of attacks, Germany resorted to a regulatory approach where strengthened police and intelligence capacities took centre stage (Samaan and Jacobs 2020: 407–8). This was partly due to the German Constitution prohibiting the use of the armed forces for such a purpose.

We can also detect a difference in how politicians and decision-makers frame the problems met. France identified the 2015 attacks as threats to its very existence, and public intellectuals concerned with Jihadism and Islam in Society were influential in this framing. In addition, anchoring the issue in a global struggle allowed the identification of sources of radicalization as located beyond French borders. This legitimized French involvement in counter-terror operations in the Middle East and the Sahel. In Germany, the contrary reaction took place. The Berlin Christmas market attack and related smaller terror incidents were perpetrated by immigrants. Coupled with a general lack of awareness of the role of global Jihad, this led to a legal and domestic framing of the issue, linking it to social challenges of migration rather than a global and existential dimension.

These differences, the study finds, are likely to provide obstacles and disappointment both at the European- and bilateral-level cooperation on counter-terrorism (Samaan and Jacobs 2020). This is supported by the divisive issue of linking terrorism in Europe to Islam, which saw renewed debate in the wake of the deadly 2020 attacks in Paris, Nice and Vienna. Several governments including the Netherlands, Sweden, Spain, Italy and Luxembourg were seen to oppose an EU Council common position, backed by France, Germany and Austria, that would have linked counter-terror policy directly with migration, including a proposed EU Imam training centre (*Financial Times* 2020).

In addition to different political contexts and national security cultures, European states have differing laws to deal with terrorist offences. This makes it difficult to provide a holistic picture of European trends. EU Directive 2017/541 defines terrorism as intentional acts that 'seriously intimidate a population, to unduly compel a government or an international organisation to perform or abstain from performing any act, or to seriously destabilize or destroy the fundamental political, constitutional, economic or social structures of a country or an international organisation' (Council of the EU 2017: para. 8). Yet European states retain the right to flexibility in national legislation within the limits of this definition. This can also be seen also in differences in prosecution across Europe. Germany, for example, prosecutes terrorism only in those cases where the perpetrator is a member of recognized terrorist organizations. This effectively excludes 'lone wolf' terrorism, which in other states can be prosecuted on terrorism charges (Europol 2020: 10).

# Organized crime

Organized crime was largely imported into European securitization discourses from the United States in the 1980s. In Europe, it gradually turned into a vehicle for framing internal security policy and mobilize collective responses according to a European framework (Carrapico 2014). In the 1980s and 1990s, Italy and Germany became early adopters of securitizing OC, and the protagonists of Europeanization in the area of Justice and Home Affairs. Germany was especially concerned with the issue that led to the first mentioning of OC and the setting up of specific European mechanisms to counter OC in a Schengen context (Fijnaut 1993). The killing of Italian judges Giovanni Falcone e Paolo Borsellino in 1992, together with that of Irish journalist Veronica Guerin in 1996, led to national governments calling for intensified European cooperation to counter organized crime in Europe (Fijnaut and Paoli 2004).

The EU Council's Framework Decision 2008/841/JHA applies the UN Office on Drugs and Crime's (UNODC) definition of an Organised Crime Group (OCG). An OCG is 'a group of three or more persons existing over a period of time acting in concert with the aim of committing crimes for financial or material benefit' (Europol 2017: 14). However, modern organized crime is both more complex and more flexible than this definition indicates. Moreover, the EU definition remains vague, leading some observers to claim it risks being dysfunctional, and an empty signifier that 'opens the door to the inclusion of phenomena as different as the Italian 'Ndrangheta, a group of hooligans or a teenage street gang' (Carrapico 2014: 611).

Having presented a snapshot of the emergence of threats posed by terrorism and organized crime in Europe, the next section will provide an overview of the Europe-level and bilateral responses, strategies and agencies developed to tackle these threats.

# European responses: European-level and bilateral coordination

The EU has consistently sought to tackle terrorism and organized crime through a criminal justice approach, rather than a militarized or foreign-policy-oriented approach often associated with other Western states such as the US (Costi 2019: 167). Member states have been hesitant to concede sovereignty over security and defence matters, but they have been more willing to cooperate in terms of fighting criminality across Europe (Davis-Cross 2007; Costi 2019). The EU has focused on mechanisms that facilitate greater judicial and police cooperation, intelligence sharing and harmonization of substantive criminal law (Monar 2014: 202–3). This depoliticized criminal-justice-oriented paradigm aims to secure the Area of Security, Freedom and Justice across Europe. Despite the hesitancy of member states, the security threats faced by Europe in the last decade and the proliferation of EU-level mechanisms to deal with those has resulted in the EU becoming a more independent and self-reliant security actor (Kaunert and Léonard 2019). At the same time, some member states are also increasingly mobilized to counter this posture, notably the Visegrad group of four (Poland, Hungary, Czech Republic and Slovakia) in the area of border control.

## European level

Europol, Eurojust, the European Arrest Warrant and The Security Union are among some of the key EU-level mechanisms at the heart of the fight against terrorism and OC. Europol, the law enforcement agency of the European Union, was created in 1998 to facilitate police cooperation between and support member states. Although it can only act at the request of the member states, it can demand investigations by competent authorities. Europol has made considerable steps in terms of police cooperation and information sharing between member states. However, Europol's exceptionally close collaboration with third party states, particularly the United States, is criticized for lacking accountability and transparency (Jannson 2018: 436). In addition, growing levels of bureaucratic powers transferred to Europol raise fundamental questions about a lack of oversight and democratic control of Europol's investigations and activities by both EU institutions and those of member states (Gruszczak 2016: 15–6).

The European Union Agency for Criminal Justice Cooperation (Eurojust) was established in 2002 to coordinate national investigations and prosecute authorities where more than one member state is involved. Its facilitation of judicial cooperation has been an integral part of EU attempts to better coordinate OC and counter-terrorism policy. In September 2019, Eurojust launched a counter-terrorism register to enable prosecutors across the EU to work together to strengthen and speed up investigations. During 2019, Eurojust's judicial support ensured more than two billion euros of criminal assets were frozen and 2,800 suspects were arrested and handed over to the relevant member state authorities. The number of cases coordinated through national desks at Eurojust that year was double that of 2014 (Eurojust 2020).

The European Arrest Warrant (EAW), introduced in January 2004, represents a deeper level of judicial cooperation than traditional extradition (Rusu 2012: 1). An EAW issued by the judicial authority of an EU member state is automatically valid in every other member state. Decisions on EAWs are made by judicial authorities without any political interference, speeding up the process of bringing an individual back to another member state (Council of the EU 2002). The European Court of Justice (ECJ) is responsible for resolving EAW disputes, which seems at odds with the initial motivation to avoid political disagreements and speed up extradition of suspected terrorists and those involved in OC (Mortera-Martinez 2019a).

The need for the ECJ to step in and arbitrate in such disputes is called for by member states' preference to maintain national primacy when dealing with terrorism and OC. Furthermore, disputes over EAWs have revealed some of the complexities that arise from judicial and police cooperation between states in vastly different legal traditions and cultures of policing. In 2018, for instance, the Irish High Court refused to automatically grant the surrender of a man wanted on drug trafficking charges in Poland. This was due to a set of Polish laws deemed by High Court Justice Aileen Donnelly to undermine the independence of the Polish judiciary (Barrett 2018). The ECJ subsequently ruled that member states had the right to refuse or postpone EAWs issued by Poland because of concerns about breaches of human rights (ECJ 2018).

In 2016, the European Commission launched the Security Union after a wave of terrorist attacks across Europe and the so-called migrant crisis had exposed 'cracks' in the European security structures. It is tasked with improving coordination between EU frameworks and member states in five key policy areas including terrorism and OC (EU Commission 2019; Mortera-Martinez 2019b). The Security Union is perceived to have achieved tangible progress in policy areas often marred by fragmentation such as coordinating databases, information sharing and, significantly, counter-terrorism (Mortera-Martinez 2019b; Volpicelli 2019). The Security Union ensured almost all member states implemented the Passenger Name Record (PNR) Directive, which identifies and tracks dangerous individuals, including terror suspects, flying around and into Europe (Volpicelli 2019).

By November 2019, sixteen of the twenty-two legislative initiatives supported by the Security Union put to the European Parliament and the Council of the European Union had been accepted (European Commission 2019: 1).

Despite the growing number of European-level organizations and frameworks to tackle organized crime and terrorism, there has been resistance to the Europeanization of these policy areas over the last decade. For example, evidence of the resistance of some member states to incremental Europeanization of counter-terrorism and OC policies can be seen in their response to the creation of The European Public Prosecutor's Office (EPPO). The EPPO, which commenced operations in June 2021, is 'an independent and decentralised prosecution office of the European Union, with the competence to investigate, prosecute and bring to judgment crimes against the EU budget, such as fraud, corruption or serious cross-border VAT fraud' (EPPO 2022).

Citing reasons such as a desire to maintain sovereign control of such affairs and the principle of subsidiarity, several member states have opted out of the EPPO, including Ireland, Denmark, Poland and Hungary (Ljubas 2020). Sweden has asserted that its national systems are robust enough without the EPPO. This substantiates claims of a trend towards a multi-speed Europe or differentiated integration in the realm of security (Wolfstadter and Kreilinger 2017). However, Malta and the Netherlands, who originally opted out, subsequently decided to join the EPPO in 2018. This demonstrates that while member states may be opposed to the growing security personality of the EU in principle, they are also lured by the potential benefits of intergovernmental security cooperation.

EU-level mechanisms represent increasing importance in the European fight against terrorism and organized crime. Still, security remains an intergovernmental competence area. In many policy areas associated with EU internal security, EU-level mechanisms continue to coordinate and supplement rather than replace existing national and bilateral mechanisms.

## Bilateral cooperation

Bilateral cooperation in intelligence sharing and police cooperation is considered vital to any efforts to tackle terrorism and organized crime in Europe. These strategies of cooperation have existed informally at least since the 1970s. Case studies suggest that, in terms of police cooperation,

European states prefer to work bilaterally rather than through EU-level mechanisms and have developed long-term cooperation practices at this level (Boer, Hillebrand and Nölke 2008; Jaffel 2019). Given that European-level police cooperation is a relatively new practice, it has been claimed that such preferences to work bilaterally are simply due to habit. However, various studies have found that the preference to work with certain trusted partners is linked to notions of common threats, cultural similarity as well as shared values (Anderson 2002). Indeed, despite European enlargement and deepening integration, this preference of working with a small number of trusted partners persists.

Interviews with police forces in France, Germany, the UK and Spain suggest that many forms of bilateral police cooperation take place informally between trusted established contacts on an individual case-by-case basis rather than through formalized mechanisms (Guille 2010: 27). A key advantage of bilateral police cooperation is the speed with which forces can communicate and work together. EU-level mechanisms, in contrast, can be more cumbersome, bureaucratic and lengthy (Guille 2010). However, challenges to effective cooperation arise because informal bilateral police cooperation practices are not institutionalized. Bilateral cooperation, often, relies on personal contacts, the willingness of individuals to cooperate as well as a sense of mutual benefit arising from potential cooperation (Sheptycki 2002).

Before 9/11, bilateral practices were often considered by policymakers to be the most effective form of intelligence sharing in counter-terrorism (Lefebvre 2003: 529). The need to protect intelligence sources and methods is the principal reason for the preference of bilateral liaisons in counter-terrorism intelligence sharing (Lefebvre 2003: 529). Despite an increasing number of EU-level intelligence-sharing mechanisms, member states maintain the fear that widening the intelligence circle increases the threat of unauthorized disclosure and privilege certain partnerships and counter-terrorism networks over others (Boer, Hillebrand and Nölke, 2008).

Franco-British intelligence-sharing practices are among the most developed in Europe and considered especially valuable since the UK, even before leaving the EU, opted out from many aspects of the EU Justice and Home Affairs (JHA) cooperation (Jaffel 2019). While much bilateral intelligence sharing between the two nations is informal and shrouded in secrecy, intelligence sharing, particularly in the realm of counter-terrorism, is enshrined in the Lancaster Treaties signed between the two nations in 2010 (Burguburu et al. 2018).

These bilateral intelligence-sharing mechanisms became even more important in maintaining the European defence against terrorism and OC in the context of Brexit. Despite the Brexit agreement being reached in December 2020, the future of European security cooperation with the UK following the Brexit transition period remains somewhat ambiguous. This is because the EU–UK Trade and Cooperation Agreement (TCA) of 24 December 2020 does not cover security or defence matters (CFSP), while it does cover Justice and Home Affairs (JHA) (HM Government 2020). The UK has also withdrawn from several EU-level mechanisms, including the EAW, while it has pledged to new extradition arrangements which follow those under the EAW in everything but name (HM Government 2020). This seems somewhat characteristic of the British desire to continue to engage in certain intelligence sharing and security cooperation practices whilst declaring the supposed 'restitution of sovereignty' (Sweeney and Winn 2021).

Another significant challenge facing European cooperation in tackling organized crime and terrorism in the coming years is a growing sense of divergence between the cultures and practices of police and security services across the continent. European Union member states are formally defined by their commitment to democratic values, human rights and the rule of law. This places certain expectations and limits on the activities of security agencies. However, where rule of law is challenged, concerns about respecting these limits follow.

For example, when Romania and Bulgaria joined the European Union in 2007, EU officials and existing member states were concerned with corruption and links to organized crime, perceived to be endemic to these societies. The EU conditioned enlargement by the acceptance of a Cooperation and Verification Mechanism (CVM). The CVM is designed to monitor Bulgaria and Romania's progress in tackling corruption and building an independent judiciary. Such situations of differentiated integration reinforce member states' reluctances to work multilaterally. Moreover, in Hungary, Prime Minister Viktor Orbán relies heavily on the securitization of threats such as terrorism and organized crime to justify illiberal and authoritarian police practices that represent an erosion of democratic values necessary for EU membership (Harper 2016). These examples further illustrate the dilemmas member states face in enhancing multilateral police cooperation on terrorism and organized crime and why the preference to work bilaterally with trusted partners continues to prevail.

# Preventing violent extremism (PVE) in Europe: new policies, new divergences

The increase in the number of new policies to prevent radicalization is a significant development over the last decade. In fact, preventing violent extremism (PVE) is emerging as a global norm in counter-terrorism policy (cf. Stephens, Sieckelinck and Boutellier 2019 for a review). In 2015, the UN Secretary-General stated all nations should consider developing a national PVE strategy (UN General Assembly 2015).

PVE is not uncontroversial, however, and exposes the securitization of public policy more generally. For example, the UK's flagship PVE strategy, 'Prevent', is often criticized by faith groups, community organizations and researchers for profiling and stigmatizing British Muslims, potentially deepening social exclusion and resentment, both of which have been directly linked to radicalization (Fenwick 2019: 22). 'Prevent' has been particularly criticized for the way in which 'educational institutions are securitised through such a policy and tasked to act as the arm of the counter-terror strategy' (Davis and Limbada 2019: 2).

In contrast, German PVE models have long been held up as examples of best practice (Lavut 2016). Arguably, Germany's long-established mechanisms to prevent far-right extremism provided a strong basis to develop PVE models to tackle other forms of radicalization (Lavut 2016). Compared to the very centralized structure of many European models, Germany's PVE efforts operate predominately at local and federal level with a national working group disseminating examples of best practice (Said and Fouad 2018: 3–4).

Article 8 of the EU Counter-Terrorism Strategy (Council of the European Union 2005) states that 'the challenge of combating radicalisation and terrorist recruitment lies primarily with Member States', with the EU providing coordination of national policies, information sharing and determining good practice. National PVE frameworks maintain primacy over EU-level mechanisms, and there are divergences between member states' national frameworks to tackle radicalization. However, member states' commitment to the EU's norms and values have shaped their PVE policy frameworks. Similarly, member states' national PVE policies have been developed in junction with EU frameworks and therefore shaped by them.

The differences between the German and British approaches above demonstrate that it is an over-generalization to speak of a single European model of PVE. However, research suggests European counter-radicalization models, in general, tend to differ radically from the American strategy. The US focuses on ensuring radical beliefs do not translate into terrorist activities while not really engaging on preventing the development of these radical beliefs in the first place (Neumann 2013). By contrast, European nations seek to prevent individuals from developing these extremist views and beliefs in the first instance (Neumann 2013). It is argued that the European model seeks to reduce social divisions that contribute to radicalization by engaging the broader community such as universities, youth groups, healthcare providers, specific communities and faith groups in the fight against radicalization (Ou 2016: 1).

However, the EU's predominately criminal justice approach to counter-terrorism coupled with member states' reluctance to engage multilaterally on issues such as PVE has meant EU-level mechanisms to counter radicalization are relatively underdeveloped and impotent. Yet, since 2015 the EU has developed various PVE focused mechanisms such as the EU Radicalisation Network, a pan-European Network to tackle radicalization (European Commission 2017: 3). As with other elements of security policy, member states have been more willing to cooperate in EU-level intergovernmental information sharing rather than pursuing the Europeanization of competencies.

# Conclusion

The last decade has witnessed a rapid expansion of European-level counter-terrorism and organized crime practices. European counter-terror and counter-organized crime efforts are increasingly concerted. In part, collaboration in this area *drives* efforts towards deeper European integration, cutting through the external–internal security distinction, and creating harmonization in policy areas traditionally defined by national sovereignty. European states developed an onslaught of measures to combat and prevent terrorism and organized crime from emerging in the first place. Where such challenges do emerge, EU member states try to develop criminal justice approaches to manage them.

Yet, despite the discourse of a truly European effort, national differences continue to characterize counter-terrorism and organized crime because of bilateral intelligence-sharing practices, regional varieties and priorities, and uneven Europeanization of even basic legislation. Research has shown that similar threats do not necessarily produce similar responses in different national contexts. Recognizing that European security politics is an extremely fragmented field, this is unlikely to change in the next decade.

# Questions for discussion

1   How are the two policy areas terrorism and organized crime linked, and how are they distinct?
2   What are the main reasons that security cooperation in Europe operates on a bilateral and often informal level?
3   Why do different European states react and respond differently to terrorist attacks?
4   What are the significant developments in European-level security cooperation in the last twenty years, and to what extent do they drive wider European integration?

# Recommended for Further Reading

Allum, F. and Gilmour, S., eds (2022) *Routledge Handbook of Transnational Organized Crime*, 2nd edn. London: Routledge.

Europol (2021) *European Union Terrorism Situation and Trend Report (TESAT)*, Publications Office of the European Union, Luxembourg. Available at European Union Terrorism Situation and Trend report 2021 (TESAT) | Europol (europa.eu).

Fijnaut, C., Paoli, L. and Wouters, J. (2022) *The Nexus between Organized Crime and Terrorism: Types and Responses*. Cheltenham: Edward Elgar Publishing.

Silke, A. (2019) *Routledge Handbook of Terrorism and Counterterrorism*. London: Routledge.

van Duyne, P., Siegel, D., Antonopoulos, G., Harvey, J. and von Lampe, K., eds (2020) *Criminal Defiance in Europe and Beyond: From Organised Crime to Crime-Terror Nexus*. Den Haag: Boomuitgevers.

# 14

# European Foreign Policy

## *Sonia Lucarelli*

The first two decades of the twenty-first century have made clear once more the dilemma that characterizes European foreign policy (EFP): the more necessary a high degree of coordination, the less it is provided. Transnational terrorism, pandemics, huge and sudden flows of irregular migrants, cyber insecurities, economic insecurity, a more assertive role of illiberal powers, instability in the Middle East and North Africa, the general crisis of the liberal order are among the challenges that would deserve a more coherent, coordinated – when not unitary – EFP. Yet, these and others are also the issues on which European states are most divided. Russia's invasion of Ukraine elevated the need for coherent action even further. The lack of a coherent foreign policy will have significant consequences for Europeans' security and well-being.

This chapter explores the structural constraints and contingent challenges that have shaped the recent developments in European foreign policy as a European system of governance in the domain of foreign policymaking; it widens out to include European states' policies in and towards the EU and NATO; it expands further to look at Europe's relations with its immediate neighbourhood; and it stretches finally to the international and global levels. The conclusion is that the greatest enemy of an efficient European foreign policy is inside Europe: its fragmentation.

# The nature of the beast: European foreign policy as a system of governance

'European foreign policy' is a polysemic phrase that has been used to refer alternatively to the Common foreign and security policy (CFSP) of the EU, to the foreign policies of the member states, and to the external relations of the EU that do not fall within the CFSP. In reality, foreign policy dynamics in Europe result from the interplay between all these dimensions in what has been labelled a 'symbiotic but uneasy relationship' (Hadfield, Manners and Whitman 2017: 1) approximating a *system of governance* in which national governments, international institutions and private actors interact among themselves according to variable geometries depending on the issue at stake. A large part of interactions occurs between European states, particularly within international organizations. Moreover, the system is such that the recurrence of interaction and consultation among states within and with international organizations (the EU, and NATO in particular) have produced forms of socialization ('downloading', to use the term of the Europeanization literature; Featherstone and Radaelli 2003; Wong and Hill 2011; Tonra 2015), and mutual learning ('cross-loading'; Wong and Hill 2011). These processes changed national foreign policy practices and institutions.

At the same time, the foreign policy of the institutions to which European states participate – particularly the EU and NATO – is the result of the combination between institutional priorities and the attempt of the member states to channel national preferences through these international organizations so to make an enhanced foreign policy action (what the literature on Europeanization refers to as bottom-up Europeanization or 'uploading'; Tonra 2015). This leads us to imagine two criteria to evaluate European foreign policy as a system of governance dominated by its member states:

- the cohesiveness of the positions of the states inside the system (which is also the condition to enable the EU and NATO to make decisions and implement them), and well as
- the coherence and effectiveness of the actions of the system of governance (member states and institutions alike).

These criteria apply within Europe, towards its neighbourhood, and with respect to wider or global challenges. This chapter introduces each of the three levels (internal, towards the neighbourhood and at the global level) in turn.

# Dynamics within the European system of foreign policy governance: attitudes towards the EU

The main obstacle to a cohesive and efficient EFP continues to be the diverging interests of different European states on various dossiers. The cleavages are well known and already largely explored (Whitman and Stewart 2011; Hadfield, Manners and Whitman 2017): large and small, Northern and Eastern, Western and Eastern, old and new members of the EU and NATO, with or without a colonial past, European states' priorities traditionally diverge along different dividing lines. Such traditional diving lines have been enhanced in the wake of the financial, economic, migratory and health crises of the early twenty-first century.

The traditional cleavages have also deepened alongside the rise of right-wing populism and rediscovered nationalism in several European countries. Particularly since the economic crisis of 2008, the rise of populism, renewed nationalism and a diffused sense of insecurity in European societies, triggered and exploited by populist sovereigntist leaders, have added new obstacles to the definition of a truly cohesive European foreign policy and have sometimes transformed the countries' attitude towards the EU. At the same time, however, a renovated agreement among some leading countries has fostered enhanced cooperation in the defence sector, as we shall see below.

'Europe policy' has been a long-term pillar of the foreign policy of countries like Belgium, Germany, Italy, but also – though in a more articulated way – France. Since the late 2000s, all European countries have acknowledged a rise in Eurosceptical attitudes, and some have also changed their attitude towards the EU and intra-EU relations.

The case of the UK is particularly striking. Though never being a euro-enthusiast and having been little affected by any form of Europeanization of foreign policy (if not in terms of 'up-loading' at the EU level issues of national concern) (Whitman and Tonra 2017), the UK had been an important member of the EU. It co-authored the very launch of the European security and defence policy (CSDP) – with the signature, with France, of the famous St Malò declaration (1998). Later, the UK contributed to several European policies and contributed personnel, expertise and equipment to EU missions, particularly in the anti-piracy missions in the Horn of Africa and the anti-smuggling operations in the Mediterranean. The withdrawal of the UK from the EU is therefore the single most important foreign policy decision of the country in decades, and it is likely to have a significant impact on its foreign policy in the future and possibly also on intra-European relations within NATO (see also the contribution by Maryon and Tholens in this volume).

The other case of a significantly transformed EU policy is that of the new member states of Eastern Europe and particularly the so-called Visegrad 4 (V4 – Czech Republic, Hungary, Poland and Slovakia), which has evolved from being a bloc aimed at pulling strength to enter the EU and NATO into a watchdog for national sovereignty in the EU. Following the migration crisis and the strengthening of right-wing forces in Slovenia (March 2020) and in Austria (2017, 2020), these two countries have come closer to the V4's view of an intergovernmental Europe, with limited supranational powers and limited internal mechanisms of solidarity in terms of redistribution – not so much of resources but – of efforts (as in the schemes to redistribute migrants from Southern Europe to other parts of the Union). The Netherlands is another country that has shifted to favour a limited, more intergovernmental EU. Indeed, a firm intergovernmental position in the Netherlands became more evident since the UK departure.

In this cloudy scenario as far as member states' European policy is concerned, France and Germany are of notable interest. These two countries initially disagreed over the management of the economic crisis. Nevertheless, under the pressure of an unfriendly Trump Administration, strong domestic right-wing populism, and Brexit negotiations, they chose to reinforce their partnership in support of both world multilateralism and a relaunched EU. In January 2018, at the 55th anniversary of the Élysée Treaty, French President Emmanuel Macron and German Chancellor Angela Merkel renewed their cooperation to face common challenges; in April 2019, the two leaders launched the 'Alliance for multilateralism', and in May 2020 they supported the European Commission's courageous proposal of a €500bn European recovery fund for the EU countries most affected by Covid-19. This proposal was the basis for the Next Generation EU Recovery Plan approved by the

European Council in July 2020 (European Council 2020). Although initially sceptical, Germany followed France in supporting an unprecedented plan to provide economic support with the emission of euro bonds and euro bills.

Interestingly, though, the area in which there has been more progress in intra-European cooperation in the past few years, has been that of defence. In this case too, the attitude of France (a traditional supporter of Europe's strategic autonomy) and Germany (a supporter of transatlantic relations that has at points supported a greater European strategic autonomy) has been crucial. The main triggering factors have been the economic crisis, Brexit and the transatlantic drift: steps ahead in the direction of enhanced cooperation in the defence sector had become an economic imperative to cut on spending, but also a political necessity to strengthen European capabilities in a union that was losing a strong member – the UK – and could not take for granted anymore a fundamental strategic partner as the US.

To make progress in defence cooperation, France and Germany (supported by Italy and Spain) took the lead in pushing for the implementation of the Permanent Structured Cooperation (PESCO). Foreseen by the Lisbon Treaty, relaunched in the 2016 Global Strategy and adopted by the December 2017 European Council, PESCO is a framework in which capable and willing EU member states can subscribe to more binding commitments to invest, develop and use defence capabilities together. The Council has presented it as 'a crucial step towards strengthening the common defence policy [...] an element of a possible development towards a common defence' (European Council 2017).

Three things are particularly relevant of PESCO: it is states-driven, the agreements are binding, the aim is to jointly develop a full spectrum of defence capabilities available to member states not only for missions in the EU context but also for national and multinational (EU, NATO, UN,...) missions. Furthermore, in January 2021 the Council decided to establish a European Peace Facility (EPF), as an off-budget instrument that will cover for EU military operations common costs and, most notably, enables the Union to deliver lethal equipment and combat training to third states, ad hoc coalitions and other international organizations. Although not risk-free, the EPF marks a significant shift in the EU's external military engagement and increases its defence projection capacity in a domain that has so far remained firmly in the hand of individual member states.

It is interesting to note that different European leaders have attached a different meaning to PESCO. If Macron has regarded it as one of the instruments to create a real European strategic autonomy in the defence sector, this is not the case with Germany, whose Defence Minister has defined strategic autonomy an illusion (Tocci 2021).

To enhance defence cooperation, a dialogue towards the definition of a 'Strategic Compass' for the EU was launched in 2020.This led to the presentation, in November 2021, of a first draft of a strategic document drafted by the High Representative of the Union for Foreign Affairs and Security Policy Josep Borrell. The final version was approved in March 2022 as Russia invaded Ukraine. The document aims at boosting the EU's operational capacity in different strategic domains, also by providing the EU with a rapid reaction force of five thousand troops (Fiott and Lindstrom 2021). The document's faith will depend on the member states' willingness to implement it and to actually use the instruments envisioned by the document.

In reality, the prospect of a European strategic autonomy in the defence sector has several opponents (particularly those fearing a disentanglement from the US) and many sceptical observers (who regard it as unrealistic). If on the one side a more strategically autonomous Europe would also respond to a long-term request by the US for a greater European contribution to NATO, on the other side a greater independence from the US would need to be handled with great diplomatic attention to safeguard a (transatlantic) relation that Europe cannot fully replace. Moreover, the economic crisis and redefined priorities due to Covid-19 risk also to diminish the resources at disposal of PESCO, jeopardizing the completion of several defence projects agreed upon (Deen and Kruijever 2020; Erlanger 2020). But what is most important, greater strategic autonomy in the defence sector cannot be achieved by mere capabilities in the absence of a unitary strategic approach, an approach which is still lacking, as Europe's relations in the neighbourhood show (see section 3).

# EFP and its wider neighbourhood

Relations between the actors of the European system of foreign policy and its neighbourhood are marked by divergences among European foreign policies. Consider Russia. Despite the fact that a large part of the Russian territory extending from Poland to the Urals is geographically placed in Europe, Russia is not a member of the EU or NATO. More important, Russia defines its identity, interests and foreign policy strategies in independent and frequently oppositional terms with respect to Europe (Roberts 2017). With Russian President Vladimir Putin's consolidation of power, the enlargement of the EU and NATO to countries of the former Soviet bloc, and the plan to enlarge further to countries in what Russia considers its traditional sphere of influence (Ukraine, Georgia), Russia and Europe have come to represent each other's 'Other'. In the Russo-Georgian War (2008), Russia's annexation of Crimea (2014) and subsequent military action in Southeastern Ukraine, have been important pressure points in the troubled relationship between Russia and the rest of Europe. The invasion of Ukraine in early 2022 escalated this conflict in ways we are still to understand. The European response to the Russo-Georgian War was hesitant and divided, while the reaction to the illegal annexation of Crimea was more vocal and quickly led to the imposition of EU sanctions against Russia. The reaction to Russia's invasion of Ukraine was much swifter and more determined.

The role of Germany was crucial in making the transition. Despite its many-layered relationship with Russia, and a traditional reluctance to take a leadership role in EU foreign and security policy (Aggestam and Hyde-Price 2020), Merkel took the lead in Europe's response to Russia's annexation of Crimea. Germany's leadership was also crucial in the diplomatic work that led to the negotiation of the Minsk I and II agreements, using its weight and diplomatic skills both within the EU and NATO. Germany's 'cross-loading with leadership' has been strong enough to keep the European front together in the face of pressure to abandon the sanctions regime imposed after 2014.

However, despite the European concerted response to Russia's increasing aggression, some European governments have continued to cultivate close ties with the Kremlin; Mitchell Orenstein and R. Daniel Kelemen call them Putin's 'Trojan horses'. Cyprus' agreement with Russia for the use of its ports is one example; Hungary's agreement to have Russia be its sole supplier of nuclear fuel is another; Greece's agreement for the construction of a gas pipeline that links back to Russia is a third (Orenstein and Kelemen 2017). Moreover, it wasn't until the full-scale attack of Ukraine that Germany decided to suspend the completion of the gas pipeline North Stream 2. Previously, Germany had resisted criticism – particularly from the US and France – that building Nord Stream 2 would perpetuate if not enhance Europe's energy dependency on Russia.

Russia also succeeded in establishing close relations with MEPs of the Europe of Freedom and Nations (ENF) group in the European Parliament – a transnational radical right populist group – and individual far-right parties in European countries (Simon 2017). An *EUobserver* article spoke of

Russia's power to infiltrate the European Parliament through far-right MEPs (Schekhovtsov 2021). As a result, while European states stood together behind sanctions against Russia, that unity was only superficial. Some of them circumvented the sanctions and went ahead with agreements with Russia (particularly in the energy sector) and many experienced the rise of a pro-Russian narrative and political stance by far-right forces in their political systems. In other words, the invasion of Ukraine was preceded by a less than successful European foreign policy to contain Russian aggression.

The relationship with Turkey has also been difficult. A long-term candidate to the EU and a member of NATO, Turkey has taken a slippery authoritarian and interventionist slope which has eliminated the possibility for it to become an EU member state. Not only have human rights and democratic institutions been compromised under the leadership of Recep Tayyip Erdoğan, but the country has transformed its foreign policy with the aim of gaining military autonomy and re-establishing the posture and recognition of a great power in a multipolar world (Haugom 2019; Kaliber and Kaliber 2019).

Over the past few years, Turkey has opened bases in Qatar and Somalia, deployed troops to Libya, provided training in Sudan, supported Sunni militia groups in Syria and Azebaijani forces in the 2020 revamped Nagorno Karabach conflict, and – along among NATO countries – recognized the election of Belarus' president Lukashenko in August 2020. Turkey is also in a standoff with Greece and Cyprus over Turkey's exploratory drilling in the Eastern Mediterranean. Turkey's illiberal drift and aggressive foreign policy are compromising relations with the EU and creating tensions within NATO.

Several EU countries have become rather cold on the perspective of an EU enlargement to Turkey (France, Germany and Austria, for example) and in March 2019, in a non-binding vote, the EU Parliament called for the suspension of EU accession talks with Turkey. The fact that Turkey has become the bulwark against illegal immigration transiting from Syria to Europe (as foreseen by the 2016 Turkey Statement) has given it an important leverage on European countries, diminishing their ability to exercise pressure on Turkey's (domestic and foreign) policy.

As for the Western Balkans, Germany is among the most firmly convinced EU members towards enlargement (cf. the Berlin Process launched in 2014). Italy, Austria, the V4, Malta, Poland, the Baltics are also supportive; Spain, France and the Netherlands have become much more cautious. In late 2019, France won the support of the Netherlands and Denmark in opposing the start of EU entry talks with Albania and

North Macedonia (which was labelled an 'historic error' by EU institutions representatives; Emmott et al. 2019).

Significant challenges come from the Southern shore: from Libya to Syria, from Yemen to Iraq, the southern neighbourhood of Europe is one of the most dangerous, destabilized and conflictual areas of the world. It is also one of the areas where regional and world powers have taken different sides In Syria, for example, the US, France, the UK, Turkey, Saudi Arabia and Qatar support rebel forces, while Iran, and Russia support the government. Europe's position has been critical of the Assad government, against which it has issued sanctions, yet little effective in influencing the dynamics on the ground. Moreover, if the UK, Germany and France have remained loyal to the jointly agreed position, other European states, like Italy, Austria, Hungary and Poland, re-established relations with Assad's close circles or discussed reopening their embassies once it became clear that the Assad government was winning the war. The EU has not played a prominent role in the Syrian crisis, the only exception being its significant financial support to contain the humanitarian fallout of the conflict. Given these premises, it is likely that Europe will be divided also in the reconstruction phase.

Europe's performance has not been any better in Libya, where European foreign policy has been both incoherent and divisive. In the case of Libya, European states have undertaken policies dictated mainly by their concern for irregular migration and their interests in the post-reconstruction phase. This has led to incoherent policies, with several implications with respect to protection of human rights. Already at the time of the international intervention to remove Libyan leader Muammar Gaddafi, European states had been divided, with France, the UK and the US taking the initiative first (followed by other nine countries among which six European – Italy, Denmark, Belgium, Greece, Norway, Spain – under NATO lead), while Germany stayed out of the conflict. Divisions manifested clearly during the subsequent Libyan civil war, when France stood on the side of the rebel forces led by General Khalifa Haftar, and Italy backed the internationally recognized government in Tripoli, led by Fayez al-Serraj.

Agreement among European countries was gained only with respect to their anti-immigration agenda. In the effort to stop would-be-migrants leaving the Libyan coast, the EU member states backed the reactivation of the EU border assistance mission (EUBAM) in 2016, then the Italy–Libya agreement of 2017 and agreed on an EU's training of the Libyan coast guard through Operation Sophia (then with operation Irini). The case of Libya showed the persistence of separate foreign policies of European countries in the region and their convergence only around a common concern for irregular migration.

The lack of strategic coherence among the most engaged member states has harmed the potential role the EU could have played in Libya as a lead mediator and broker. As a result, Brussels put its weight behind UN-led efforts, despite its frustration with faltering progress by its support mission to Libya (UNSMIL). The result has been a myopic and ineffective European policy: it did not help the stabilization of Libya, and it did not address the challenge of migration through a broad European strategy.

A similar trend has been visible in the Sahel, which in recent years has become part of Europe's broader neighbourhood. The Sahel is an area of concern for the external dimension of the fight against both terrorism and irregular migration. As a result, European foreign policy is very active in the region in terms of the presence of military operations and civilian missions (EUTM Mali, EUCAP Sahel Niger, EUCAP Sahel Mali, Regional advisory and Coordination cell) and economic support (EU Trust Fund). These interventions have been guided by the specific and different priorities of the member states.

The Sahel has not become more secure as a result of European incoherence. For example, if the leading European country in the area, France, is driven by a counter-terrorism agenda, Italy has an anti-immigration priority and this created inefficiencies on the ground which were easily exploitable by local stakeholders. At the same time, although Germany took the lead to advance the cause of a more coordinated engagement in the delivery of international aid and prevented a closer engagement of EUTM in combat operation, it failed to produce an alternative strategy to offset the French-driven agenda. At the juxtaposition of these efforts, 'Jihadist attacks have increased fivefold since 2016 and inter-ethnic violence has ballooned' (ICG 2021).

# EFP and the world

An area in which Europe (and particularly the EU) is more cohesive is its support of multilateralism. The EU and its member states have always been supporters and promoters of multilateralism. Even there, however, problems have emerged in recent years. Internal divisions among the EU member states risk jeopardizing the EU's support to several multilateral regimes. Consider the situation with respect to climate change, which is one of the areas in which Europe (and particularly the EU) has taken the lead in global governance. Europe's plans to implement the Paris Agreement and the ambitious New Green Deal put forward by Ursula von der Leyen Commission are both suffering from a division between Eastern and Western countries. As a result, the European may fail to achieve climate-neutrality by 2050, and so lose much of its international credibility.

Another very important area of multilateral engagement for European foreign policy has been the negotiation of the 2015 multilateral agreement on Iran's nuclear programme. That was an issue where 'the EU in the shape of the UK, Germany and France had pursued a strongly multilateral approach' (Smith 2018: 548) since the early 2000s. In 2003, negotiations were started by the three European countries, then joined by China, Russia and the US three years later. The final agreement had a multilateral endorsement through the 'P5 + 1' negotiations format (5 permanent UN Security Council members plus Germany – hence 3 European and 3 non-European countries – E3+3).

Europe has also been united in keeping the Iran nuclear agreement even after the Trump Administration's withdrawal from the Joint Comprehensive Plan of Action (JCPOA) and following the imposition of several rounds of sanctions on Iran by the United States. The EU responded by adopting measures designed to mitigate the impact of sanctions on European economic operators trading with Iran, although they provided little incentives against the risk of losing access to the US market). President Joe Biden's position for renewed negotiations with Iran brought the United States and Europe closer on this issue. In fact, it would have always been close to impossible for the EU and European states to save the deal without the US onboard (Cronberg 2017: 1).

The European states have taken different positions in the area of migration, where it is hard to find the expression of a common (EU) voice (see also the chapter by Paul in this volume). The signature of the Global Compact for Safe, Orderly and Regular Migration, in December 2018 could be the first step in the direction of a more multilateral management of migration as a global phenomenon. Yet, on this occasion European states have failed to act in a coordinated manner and to support multilateral governance: of the five countries who voted against the final text, three were European (the Czech Republic, Hungary and Poland). Of the twelve countries around the globe that abstained, seven were European (Austria, Bulgaria, Italy, Latvia, Romania, Switzerland and Lichtenstein). A significant portion of such a debacle of European multilateralism was due to the rise of nationalism in European politics and to the politicization of migration in public debates since the 2015–16 migration crisis.

Relations with China and the US are also important for European foreign policy. European states have been divided recently with respect to their participation in the Belt and Road initiative and the adoption of Chinese manufactured 5G technology (on which China is a leader). The 17+1 format launched by China to discuss with seventeen Central and Eastern European countries about possible Chinese investments, is a striking example of an attempt by China to 'divide and conquer' Europe. However, there has been a rising consensus among European countries that China is not a cost-free trade partner. Not only does China fail to reciprocate market openings, but it keeps acquiring strategic assets in Europe.

At the same time, opposition is rising in European countries against China's policy in Hong Kong, in Tibet and in the Xinjiang, where China's persecution of Uyghurs is relentless. Again, France started off a symbolic European turn in its foreign policy towards China, by inviting Merkel and then EU Commission President Jean-Claude Junker to join French President Emanuel Macron and present a united European front in March 2019, on Chinese President Xi Jinping's visit to France. Already at that point, in the revision of the EU's 2016 strategy on China, the balance between challenges and opportunities presented by the latter had shifted in favour of it representing a systemic rival. China's subsequent crackdown on Hong Kong in 2019 and the country's less than transparent handling of the Covid-19 outbreak on its territory have fuelled scepticism and possibly created the conditions for a more cautious and coordinated approach. These changes might be seen in relation to China's investments in Europe through the Belt & Road initiative, or in relation to political responses to human rights violations in China.

As for transatlantic relations, they were probably at their lowest point in history during the Trump administration. Never have the two sides of the Atlantic appeared so distant. Trump not only accelerated and significantly deepened a shift of US foreign policy away from Europe but also delegitimized and dismissed the Transatlantic Alliance and undertook a systematic deconstruction of multilateral platforms dear to the Europeans. The election of Joe Biden to the US presidency has created the conditions for a relaunch of transatlantic relations but it has not eliminated the tensions across the Atlantic on several dossiers (China, in the first place, but also – at least potentially – the search for a European strategic autonomy). While the invasion of Ukraine has led to the strengthening of the transatlantic relationship, structural tensions remain in the background.

A foreign policy centred on reconstructing the transatlantic bond and relaunching multilateralism, in the aftermath of Covid-19 Biden's political agenda will inevitably focus on domestic politics and economics. Such attention will demand not only a lot of energy and resources spent domestically, but it will also require an approach to globalization and global trade aimed at diminishing the US's external dependence and delocalization. Reshoring and shortening of supply chains are topics on the agenda of the US administration that will have consequences on the global economy, and hence on Europe, which need to be faced cohesively by Europe. Again, in a post-pandemic world, intra-European cohesion will be crucial.

# Conclusion

European foreign policy is in many respects a deficient enterprise. This will raise important challenges as Russia's invasion of Ukraine demands fast-moving and efficient decision-making. An efficient foreign policy would need a clear grand strategy, clear aims, shorter-term strategic and tactical choices, and means to evaluate impact on the ground. The foreign policy of European states and institutions, on the contrary, is the result of a system of governance that is institutionally and politically fragmented, with different (if not contrasting) foreign policy aims, priorities and strategic views of the different stakeholders (mostly states). This peculiar foreign policy system is more capable of speaking with one voice on issues of global governance (climate change, Iran nuclear deal) than it is on issues related to intra-European cooperation and policies towards the neighbourhood.

In the past decade, particularly as a result of a strengthened Franco-German partnership, we have seen progress toward the definition of a global strategy for the EU and of cooperation in the defence sector. However, none of the initiatives taken so far provides what European foreign policy needs most: a shared view of the objectives, priorities and strategic means to deal with challenges in current world politics. Without such a shared grand strategy, no efficient European foreign policy can ever develop.

# Questions for discussion

1  What is the European system of foreign policy?
2  What are the internal dynamics of the European system of foreign policy?
3  What are the areas of disagreement among European states regarding Europe's relations with its wider neighbourhood?
4  What are the areas of disagreement among European states regarding Europe's global role?

# Recommended for Further Reading

Fiott, D. and Lindstrom, G., eds (2021) *Strategic Compass: New Bearings for EU Security and Defense?*. EUISS, Challiot Paper 171.

Hadfield, A., Manners, I. and Whitman, R. G., eds (2017) *Foreign Policies of EU Member States Continuity and Europeanisation*. London: Routledge.

Keukeleire, S. and Delreux, T. (2014) *The Foreign Policy of the European Union*, 3rd edn. London: Bloomsbury Academic.

Müller P., Pomorska, K. and Tonra, B. (2021) 'The Domestic Challenge to EU Foreign Policy-Making: From Europeanisation to de-Europeanisation?', *Journal of European Integration* 43 (5): 519–34. doi:10.1080/07036337.2021.1927015.

Thomas, D. C. (2021) 'The Return of Intergovernmentalism? De-Europeanisation and EU Foreign Policy Decision-making', *Journal of European Integration* 43 (5): 619–35. doi:10.1080/07036337.2021.1927013.

# Conclusion

## Veronica Anghel and Erik Jones

The introduction to this volume looks back at the changes that have taken place in Europe over the past decade to set the stage for the contributions to follow. The picture it paints is sombre. The danger of complacency and contentment has never been greater. We identify numerous internal and external challenges that question the viability of further European integration, not least a lack of ambition in building European unity further. Nevertheless, Europe managed to pull itself together during the Covid-19 pandemic. It also appears to find more room for unity in the immediate aftermath of Russia's invasion of Ukraine.

The European Council's agreement on Next Generation EU represents a culmination of renewed solidarity both for the European Union and for European citizens. That kind of compromise is an act of strength and not weakness. While the withdrawal within physical borders appeared a necessary first response to limit the spread of the virus, policy dividing lines among different European governing systems proved detrimental to dealing with a borderless challenge. A much greater challenge awaits Europe following Russia's invasion of Ukraine in February 2022.

The European project came out of the pandemic looking better than going into it (Jones 2021). Europeans came together in response to Russian aggression as well. One of the puzzles underlying this collection is to understand how that took place. We did not ask our contributors to answer that question directly; events were unfolding as this volume came together. That puzzle was less an analytical challenge than a shared experience. Our contributors had to wrestle with the pandemic – both personally and intellectually – as they completed their work. If the scholars featured in the volume end on a more optimistic note, that is a reflection of resilience amidst widespread tragedy. The question that remains is how things will develop in the future.

This conclusion anticipates the challenges that Europeans will face. The list is easy to imagine. Public health, economic performance, war, and climate change tend to capture most headlines, but rule of law, social equality and political representation are not far behind. None of these challenges are unique to Europe. People everywhere face them. What is unique is the context that Europe represents. We call this collection *Developments in European Politics* not because we want to suggest that Europeans face something exceptional, but rather to highlight the characteristics of the European context.

# Unity and diversity

That notion of context is the most salient theme that unites the various chapters in this collection. When our contributors point to national differences in terms of how Europeans perceive democratic institutions, how they participate in the democratic process or how they interact with political authority, the issue is never that 'Europeans' are somehow different from one another or from those who live in the rest of the world. The variations come from social institutions, not from the people themselves. Moreover, those institutions do not have to be written to order individuals' lives. Informal institutions can also shape perceptions and behaviour in ways that make a difference in how the people who live within them (and so take them as given) respond to problems that are otherwise ubiquitous.

Context explains why political mobilization and social movements differ from one place to the next even when they link up across national boundaries. Context also explains why the debate about climate change lacks a global frame, why we talk about varieties of capitalism, how welfare can mean something different depending upon the welfare state, and why the struggle for something as universal as gender equality is not everywhere the same. Knowing why different countries respond differently to migration, why they have so much difficulty embracing interdependence, why they fail to cooperate in the fight against terrorism and organized crime, and why they lack a common strategy for dealing with the outside world requires an understanding of variation in context.

By underscoring the importance of context, we reveal an analytical bias toward structural explanations (Ostrom 2005). The investigation of formal and informal institutions, geography, the implications of size, location and distance helps us to make well-informed estimates about how people are likely to behave. We do not deny human agency or obscure individual or collective responsibility. Rather we aim to highlight humans – everywhere – are boundedly rational.

The challenge lies in using detailed contextual analysis to inform solid predictions. Making that leap depends on knowing in advance both which contextual differences are likely to be important for any given issue, and what impact they are likely to have. It also depends on knowing how resilient any differences are likely to be. That kind of knowledge is hard to obtain, particularly for anyone hoping to make broad generalizations based on the law of large numbers (Cartwright and Hardie 2012). The difficulty to arrive at and maintain a uniform understanding of core European values explains why European integration remains a work in progress. Europeans may not be so different to impede unity, but that goal is consistently challenged by persistent structural diversity at the national, regional and local level.

Here, the tragedy of the Western Balkans reveals the magnitude of the difficulty. That is a region united by language, food, music, art and literature. Nevertheless, it is divided by institutions, resources and power politics. For every new peace initiative, there are any number of political entrepreneurs looking to exploit the tyranny of small differences and to capitalize on the fear that no matter how bad things are at any given point in time, they can always get worse. We highlight this case not as an indictment of the Western Balkans as a region, but as a warning that the people who live there are far from unique. The same dynamics could take root in other parts of Europe, the United States or elsewhere.

The lesson from the Western Balkans is that mapping Europe's future is more about identifying points of tension than any coherent story of convergence or divergence. These points of tension will never be unique to Europe. What matters is how Europeans respond to them and where they are likely to strike the balance. By identifying these points of tension, we hope to focus attention more than to engage in scenario planning. Three such points of tension warrant close consideration – between democracy and solidarity, consensus and adjustment, and leadership and the rule of law.

# Democracy and solidarity

The two great structures that shape political life are constitutional arrangements and social cleavages. Constitutional arrangements tell us how decisions are made and by whom; social cleavages tell us how society is organized into groups and what is the power between them. Importantly, you can find these structures at any level of aggregation.

Democracy describes a particular constitutional arrangement through which the people make collective decisions. Solidarity describes how different groups relate to one another. These things are in tension because not all groups have the same access to or influence over democratic procedures. Those that find themselves in a privileged position are likely to ignore the needs or aspirations of the rest. Hence the challenge is to avoid the prospect that any one group will abuse a position of privilege in order to dominate the constitutional arrangement. This challenge exists in every political context.

The problem for Europe is that democracy is uniquely vulnerable to the dominance of large groups – both real and imagined. Again, this is true at all levels of aggregation. Just think about the fate of the Roma living in the Swedish municipalities that Jennifer Fitzgerald mentions. By contrast, the promise of democracy is meant to be inclusive. This is why the dominance of large groups is important even if only imagined. Such perceptions chip away at the perceived legitimacy of the arrangement even when such dominance does not exist. And when smaller groups feel they are being ignored or mistreated within a democracy, they have a strong tendency to turn against the system – by withdrawing their active support, by seeking to change the constitutional arrangement or by striving to exit and create a more suitable constitutional arrangement.

The populist groups Léonie de Jonge describes tend to support the anti-European causes Nicole Lindstrom introduces in the name of democracy, bringing power to the people. They also tend to push back against migration (and to limit the rights of migrants) for the same reason. Such groups do not deny the importance of the welfare state; they just want to set clear boundaries for solidarity. This does not make them anti-European. If anything, this combination of attitudes is only likely to be found in Europe.

Moreover, as de Jonge underscores, such populists are not necessarily extremist or exclusive. They can arise in the political mainstream, particularly in Central and Eastern Europe, and they can represent groups that struggle to be heard in expressing their concern for the environment, for gender or the impact of globalized trade and finance. Imagining a constitutional arrangement where all such voices can be effectively represented is no easy task. Imagining such an arrangement that can accommodate the variety of political parties, trade unions, employers' associations and social movements is even harder – and that is before we consider the fact that these groups do not speak a common language and that linguistic minorities are acutely sensitive to the threat of exclusion.

Constitutional arrangements and social cleavages can also change. Simona Piattoni and Julia Schulte-Cloos highlight these evolutions in their contributions. In her analysis of informal institutions as dynamic structures, Veronica Anghel focuses on another layer of governing complexity that is even less visible or available for study. These elements converge towards a point of tension between democracy and solidarity. No balance struck between them is likely to be permanent. Democracy is a work in progress in that sense. As Steven Levitsky and Daniel Ziblatt (2018) argue, the failure to manage that tension between democracy and solidarity is how democracies die. We argue that the contract among Europeans that makes the European Union also relies on constant effort to keep democracy and solidarity in balance.

# Consensus and adjustment

That Europe has held together as well as it has – both as a collection of more or less like-minded states and as a political project – is impressive. Given the events of that last century, that achievement should not be taken for granted (Jones and Menon 2019). The relative success of the past century is all the more reason to study Europe! Doing so reveals a second point of tension – between the interest of Europeans to embrace Europe as a project, and the costs of maintaining that project in the face of global challenges. This is the tension between consensus and adjustment.

The consensus does not have to be enthusiastic to be effective. Indeed, most theorists of European integration believe that whatever consensus did exist around European integration was limited to the fact that it is an elite project with few meaningful popular implications. This is the kind of consensus that Liesbet Hooghe and Gary Marks (2009) imagine. It reflects the limited popular reach of Europe described by Neil Fligstein (2009). Unsurprisingly, the reason is context. Fligstein shows that most Europeans live very local lives, in local languages, with local friends and local economic opportunities. They live in Europe, but they identify more with their local context than with any broader European construct or identity. Europeans are very much like people everywhere else in the world in that respect. Their sense of community is personal rather than political. It comes from lived experience and not political ideology.

The problem arises when outside forces start to impose costs on this lived experience. This problem is hardly unique to Europe. On the contrary, Europe often imposed huge costs on the outside world through the colonial experience. Such costs have hardly been acknowledged, let alone repaid (Bhambra 2022). Initiatives to decolonise our academic understanding of world politics are scarce. Our point is not to minimize this broader historical context. Rather it is to underscore that Europeans are as prone to react strongly to the forces that impinge upon their lives as individuals in any other part of the globe. This is the problem of adjustment. Such forces could include technological change, economic exchange, immigration, global warming, communicable diseases, and war. Citizens' connection to the European project – or to any political project – is less important than the simple fact that they force people to adapt, both as individuals and as communities. The costs associated with that adaptation are the costs of adjustment. The higher these costs, the more people begin to focus their attention on who is going to pay those costs and when.

There are any number of ways that the emergence of costs can upset consensus, particularly a weak consensus to let somebody else make all the important decisions. This dynamic is ubiquitous. Lester Thurow (1980) famously analysed this tension in terms of the zero-sum society. He argued that as soon as the costs of adjustment began to compete with the costs of achieving any other political objective, then the two issues get tangled together. Once the choice between the two projects became mutually exclusive – meaning the achievement of one meant the abandonment of the other – the result was inevitable conflict. Consensus breaks down not because people change their minds where they were previously in agreement, but because they do not share the same priorities and they would rather shift that burden of adjustment elsewhere.

This problem is only uniquely European insofar as national economies in Europe are so tightly interdependent. This interdependence means European countries tend to experience those forces for change in the same way and at the same time; in turn, that means they face many similar adjustment problems. The relative costs may nevertheless be very different and so may the ability of individual countries to shift those burdens onto others. Here it is useful to think about the cost of adapting to climate change. In this volume, Claire Saunders shows how EU's agency has been challenged by countries wanting policies tailored to their own interests. Every European country will need to move away from relying on hydrocarbons for fuel, but those countries that specialize in the production of diesel-powered transportation vehicles or rely on coal to power their economies will find making that transition more expensive than others.

Migration is another good illustration. All European countries have struggled with migration, but not all countries sit geographically on the frontiers of Europe. Those countries that do not sit on Europe's external borders find it easier to shift the burden of migration onto those that do. This has been the dilemma for Greece and Italy. It is a major challenge for the countries of the Western Balkans as well. So long as other European countries will not accept the relocation of asylum seekers – many of whom may turn out to be economic migrants – any adjustment to increased migration flows will fall disproportionately on them. Regine Paul highlights these tensions in her contribution. The superior manner in which Europeans have dealt with the flow of Ukrainian refugees highlights Europe's double standards. The invasion of Ukraine and the prioritization of the needs of those running from Russian invaders will further strain Europe's solidarity with people running from wars elsewhere.

Security challenges represent a similar concern. Rosa Maryon and Simone Tholens show that preferences for national and bilateral strategies to deal with terrorism and organized crime remain salient, despite the many EU efforts in the direction of European cooperation. European security is heavily influenced by what happens to the east and south. Some countries are more exposed to Russian threats; some to organized crime; and some to terrorism, both domestic and foreign. The costs of managing these vulnerabilities fall unequally. Fighting security threats requires an efficient European foreign policy. However, as Sonia Lucarelli shows in her contribution, internal fragmentation remains the greatest obstacle in achieving that outcome. That internal fragmentation will also limit the effectiveness of European responses to the Russian invasion of Ukraine.

These three illustrations are all interconnected. Climate change increases migration pressure and heightens security tensions. Migration exacerbates security problems as well. Both migration and security compete with efforts to combat climate change for resources and attention. It is small wonder therefore that Europeans find it so difficult to find consensus on these issues. The tragedy is that tackling these issues will be easier and more effective with European coordination. That is an essential part of the economics of interdependence (Cooper 1968). Indeed, it is one of the main reasons that the European project exists in the first place (Milward 1999). If Europeans do not reconcile the tension between consensus and adjustment, the danger is that they will squander both goodwill and valuable resources – losing consensus and failing to adjust at same time.

In the worst case, Europeans might even slide into localized conflicts. War is no longer a far-fetched scenario for Europeans. Such a phrase would have seemed out of place in previous editions of *Developments in European Politics* or… *West European Politics*. The experience of Britain's departure from the European Union now makes that outcome more plausible. The simmering violence at the border between the Republic of Ireland and Northern Ireland is one confirmation of the need for peace guarantees that the structures of a nation-state failed to offer. Since the vote for Brexit came through, Ireland has been shown unflinching solidarity from EU members and institutions. However, erasing the EU umbrella and replacing it with borders on the Irish Island recreates the conditions for violence. The renewed push for territorial independence in parts of Spain is another potential source of violent conflict; the EU has so far had a moderating influence, but as Nicole Lindstrom discusses in her chapter on European disintegration, we do not know how long that moderation can last. The Russian annexation of Crimea, the prolonged war in Ukraine, the threat of nuclear conflict and Russian cyber-attacks on European infrastructure bring the possibility of escalating conflict even closer.

# Leadership and the rule of law

Forging an effective response to such challenges requires leadership and coordination. French President Emmanuel Macron refers to this kind of coordination as 'strategic autonomy' and 'European sovereignty'. European Commission President Ursula von der Leyen uses similar language. In doing so, they restate the basic idea that the European Union could be more effective in dealing with issues ranging from security and migration to tech giants and climate change if European institutions could act decisively on behalf of EU member states.

Such assertions about autonomy and sovereignty are not that far-fetched. The European Union is both powerful and wealthy: European countries have more collective military might than any other global power apart from the United States; Europe's combined economic output makes it the world's largest marketplace. If such resources could be used strategically, Europe –

as a collective – would be capable of things no other global power apart from the United States and perhaps China could easily match.

Two things stop Europe from asserting this kind of potential. One is the absence of effective leadership; the other is the weakness of European law. These two things are tightly interconnected. European leadership is ineffective because European law is weak. The problem is not that European societies fail to generate political elites capable of strategic vision and decisive action. Europe has plenty of able leaders at all levels of government, from small municipalities to European institutions. The problem is that these leaders cannot compel others to follow them. In that sense what Europe lacks is not leaders but followers. If anything, it has too many leaders – and without powerful rules to bind them, these leaders are more likely to do what they want than to take instructions either from above or from below.

This weakness of European law is a feature of European integration, not a bug. The member states never aspired to surrender their sovereignty to a European Union. Instead, they hoped to pool just enough of that sovereignty to solve problems collectively while reserving enough leeway to demand exceptions to common activities should the need arise. The fact that Britain was able to leave the European Union is not exceptional, it is an essential part of the framework within which the member state governments chose to cooperate.

Where European law is weak, however, the rule of law at the national level tends to be strong. This national rule of law places a more direct constraint on leadership. Although leaders can expect to be followed, they face powerful institutional obstacles in the form of checks and balances, veto players and detailed official mandates. Again, this is a feature not a bug.

Too many European countries experienced the trauma of unrestrained leadership during the first half of the twentieth century in Western Europe and virtually the whole of the twentieth century in Central and Eastern Europe. As a result of that trauma, they built (or, perhaps better, sought to build) constitutional arrangements that would prevent leaders from abusing their power, trampling minorities and other vested interests or severing the link between public office and periodic competitive elections. Under such arrangements, national political leaders simply do not have the power to surrender legal authority to Europe without constitutional amendment. In some cases, like Germany, the necessary amendments may not even be possible.

This combination of factors not only explains why Europe is unable to exercise collective sovereignty but also why European politicians find it so difficult to deal with those countries where constitutional arrangements have been less successful at constraining national leadership. Europe would need .stronger law to hold national leaders to account for rewriting the constitutional rules that are meant to constrain them (Anghel 2020). It also explains why the European Union has had so little success in stabilizing the Western Balkans. The EU clearly has the resources. Nevertheless, no amount of aid can build domestic consensus; only domestic political leadership can do that.

The mistake is to assume that Europe's failures stem from the weakness of domestic political institutions. On the contrary, European law is weak because the constitutional frameworks in other countries are so strong. This is easier to illustrate in terms of macroeconomic governance, perhaps, than in terms of what has come to be called democratic backsliding. If you ask a Dutch or German politician whether Europe should have strong rules to enforce fiscal discipline in Greece, for example, they will give an unreserved yes in response. If you ask them whether the same rules should be used to discipline Dutch or German politicians, they will evade the question by saying that such interference is unnecessary because Dutch and German politicians will always govern their economies appropriately and they will point to the recent past.

This tension is most obvious when it comes to European fiscal policy. Dutch and German politicians refuse to be bound to rules for the redistribution of tax resources. The reason, they claim, is that the burdens would be disproportionate. When pushed they retreat to the importance of democratic legitimation. Here again, the tension between leadership and the rule of law becomes entangled with the tension between consensus and adjustment and the tension between democracy and solidarity.

Advocates of European fiscal union say Europe needs fiscal institutions capable of financing adjustment costs where needed as an act of solidarity; opponents say that Europe needs rules that reflect a consensus built on democratic representation. Both sides are 'right' in the sense that they make strong arguments. The question is whether the European Union can survive their continued disagreement.

# Europe's future

Europeans are hardly alone in facing these kinds of dilemmas. The fact that their problems are shared elsewhere, however, does not make this debate any less important for Europe's future. On the contrary, that debate is important.

Europeans must decide at some point how they want to legitimate their government and with whom they want to make decisions. They need to decide how to deal with opposition to the difficult choices that must be made and how to pay for inevitable adjustments to changes both at home and abroad. And they must strike a balance between the need for effective leadership and the preservation of the rule of law.

None of these decisions will be easy. The fact that Europeans were able to forge a compromise in response to the Covid-19 pandemic shows that they are able to work together. The fact that Europeans stood united in sanctioning Russia and delivered weapons to Ukraine to defend their territory shows a willingness to reconsider long-standing ambiguities in domestic and foreign policy. This collaboration is not obvious, and neither should it be taken for granted. It is hard fought. That is what makes Europe so interesting for research and why we identify an ongoing need for the detailed study of European politics. In many ways, Europeans face challenges that are everywhere familiar; in many ways, they face those challenges with unique capabilities, opportunities and obligations. Their success or failure will have a global impact.

# References

## Introduction

Anghel, V. (2020) 'Together or Apart? The European Union's East–West Divide', *Survival* 62(3): 179–202.

Anghel, V. and Jones, E. (2021) 'Failing Forward in Eastern Enlargement: Problem Solving through Problem Making', *Journal of European Public Policy*, online first. https://doi.org/10.1080/13501763.2021.1927155.

Cooper, R. (1968) *The Economics of Interdependence: Economic Policy in the Atlantic Community*. New York, NY: Columbia University Press.

Curato, N. and Fossati, D. (2020) 'Authoritarian Innovations: Crafting Support for a Less Democratic Southeast Asia', *Democratization* 27(6): 1006–20.

Drezner, D. W. (2014) *The System Worked: How the World Stopped another Great Depression*. New York, NY: Oxford University Press.

Enyedi, Z. (2020) 'Right-Wing Authoritarian Innovations in Central and Eastern Europe', *East European Politics* 36(3): 363–77.

Ganev, V. I. (2001) 'The Dorian Gray Effect: Winners as State Breakers in Postcommunism', *Communist and Post-Communist Studies* 24(1): 1–25.

Hellman, J. S. (1998) 'Winners Take All: The Politics of Partial Reform in Postcommunist Transitions', *World Politics* 50(2): 203–34.

Jones, E. (2006) 'Europe's Market Liberalization is a Bad Model for a Global Trade Agenda', *Journal of European Public Policy* 13(6): 945–59.

Jones, E. (2007) 'Populism in Europe', *SAIS Review* 27(1): 37–47.

Jones, E. (2017) 'The Rise of Populism and the Fall of Europe', *SAIS Review* 37(1): 47–57.

Lepenies, P. (2016) *The Power of a Single Number: A Political History of GDP*. New York, NY: Columbia University Press.

Luce, E. (2017) *The Retreat of Western Liberalism*. New York, NY: Atlantic Monthly Press.

Lührmann, A. and Lindberg, S. (2019) 'A Third Wave of Autocratization is Here: What is New about it?' *Democratization* 26(7): 1095–113.

Myrdal, G. (1956) *An International Economy: Problems and Prospects*. New York, NY: Harper & Brothers.

Tooze, A. (2018) *Crashed: How a Decade of Financial Crises Changed the World*. New York, NY: Viking.

Young, A. R. (2017) *The New Politics of Trade: Lessons from TTIP*. London: Agenda Publishing.

Zakaria, F. (2007) *The Future of Freedom*, rev. edn. New York, NY: W.W. Norton & Co.

# Chapter 1

Achen, C. and Bartels, L. (2017) *Democracy for Realists. Why Elections Do Not Produce Responsive Government*. Princeton, NJ: Princeton University Press.

Alonso S. and Ruiz-Rufino, R. (2020) 'The Costs of Responsibility for the Political Establishment of the Eurozone (1999–2015)', *Party Politics* 26(3): 317–33.

Bardi L., Bartolini, S. and Trechsel, A., eds (2014) 'Responsive and Responsible? The Role of Parties in Twenty-First Century Politics', *West European Politics* (special issue) 37(2): 235–455.

Bellamy, R. (2019) *A Republican Europe of States: Cosmopolitanism, Intergovernmentalism and Democracy in the EU*. Cambridge: Cambridge University Press.

Bellamy, R. and Kröger, S. (2014) 'Domesticating the Democratic Deficit? The Role of National Parliaments and Parties in the EU's System of Governance', *Parliamentary Affairs* 67(2): 437–57.

Berger, S. (1979) 'Politics and Anti-politics in Western Europe in the Seventies', *Daedalus* 108(1): 27–50.

Bogaards, M. and Helms, L., eds (2019) 'Half a Century of Consociationalism: Cases and Comparisons', *Swiss Political Science Review* (special issue) 25(4): 341–574.

Bohman, J. (1996) *Public Deliberation: Pluralism, Complexity, and Democracy*. Cambridge, MA: MIT Press.

Bovens, M. (2007) 'Analysing and Assessing Accountability: A Conceptual framework', *European Law Journal* 13(4): 447–68.

Brennan, J. (2018) *Against Democracy*. Princeton, NJ: Princeton University Press.

Cooper, I. (2012) 'A "Virtual Third Chamber" for the European Union? National parliaments after the Treaty of Lisbon', *West European Politics* 35(3): 441–65.

Crouch, C. (2004) *Post-Democracy*. London: Polity.

Crozier, M., Huntington, S. and Watanuki, J. (1975) *The Crisis of Democracy: Report on the Governability of Democracies to the Trilateral Commission*. New York, NY: New York University Press.

Crum, B. and Fossum, J.-E. (2009) 'The Multilevel Parliamentary Field: A Framework for Theorizing Representative Democracy in the EU', *European Political Science Review* 1(2): 249–71.

Csehi, R. and Zgut, E. (2021) '"We won't let Brussels dictate us": Eurosceptic populism in Hungary and Poland', *European Politics and Society* 22(1): 53–68. https://www.tandfonline.com/doi/full/10.1080/23745118.2020.1717064.

De Wilde, P. and Zürn, M. (2012) 'Can the Politicization of European Integration be Reversed?' *Journal of Common Market Studies* 50(S1): 137–53.

Fabbrini, S. (2015) *Which European Union? Europe after the Euro Crisis*. Cambridge: Cambridge University Press.

Friedman, M. (1962) *Capitalism and Freedom*. Chicago, IL: The University of Chicago Press.

Goodhart, D. (2017) *The Road to Somewhere: The New Tribes Shaping British Politics*. London: Hurst.

Hobolt, S. and Tilley, J. (2014) *Blaming Europe? Responsibility without Accountability in the European Union*. Oxford: Oxford University Press.

Hobolt, S. and de Vries, K. (2016) 'Turning against the Union? The impact of the crisis on the Eurosceptic vote in the 2014 European Parliament elections', *Electoral Studies* 44: 504–14.

Hooghe, L. and Marks, G. (2017) 'Cleavage Theory Meets Europe's Crises: Lipset, Rokkan, and the Transnational Cleavage', *Journal of European Public Policy* 25(1): 109–35.

Inglehart, R. (1977) *The Silent Revolution: Changing Values and Political Styles among Western Publics*. Princeton, NJ: Princeton University Press.

Kiewiet, R. and McCubbins, M. (1991) *The Logic of Delegation: Congressional Parties and the Appropriations Process*. Chicago, IL: The University of Chicago Press.

Kokkonen, A. and Linde, J. (2021) 'Nativist Attitudes and Opportunistic Support for Democracy', *West European Politics*. https://doi.org/10.1080/01402382.2021.2007459.

Lilla, M. (2017) *The Once and Future Liberal: After Identity Politics*. New York, NY: Harper Collins.

Lord, C. (2006) 'Democracy and the European Union: Matching means to standards', *Democratization* 13(4): 668–84.

Lord, C. (2015) 'Utopia or dystopia? Towards a normative analysis of differentiated integration', *Journal of European Public Policy* 22(6): 783–98.

Mair, P. (2013) *Ruling the Void: The Hollowing of Western Democracy*. London: Verso.

Majone, G. (2014) *Rethinking the Union of Europe Post-Crisis. Has Integration Gone Too Far?* Cambridge: Cambridge University Press.

Mounk, Y. (2018) *The People vs. Democracy. Why Our Freedom Is in Danger and How to Save It*. Cambridge, MA: Harvard University Press.

Nicolaidis, K. (2013) 'European Demoicracy and Its Crisis', *Journal of Common Market Studies* 51(2): 351–69.

Papadopoulos, Y. (2007) 'Problems of Democratic Accountability in Network and Multilevel Governance', *European Law Journal* 13(4): 469–86.

Pettit, P. (1997) *Republicanism: A Theory of Freedom and Government*. Oxford: Oxford University Press.

Pharr, S. and Putnam, R. (2000) *Disaffected Democracies: What's Troubling the Trilateral Countries?* Princeton, NJ: Princeton University Press.

Piattoni, S. (2010) *The Theory of Multilevel Governance: Empirical, Analytical and Normative Challenges*. Oxford: Oxford University Press.

Piattoni, S. (2017) 'The European Union between Intergovernmentalism and "Shared and Responsible Sovereignty": The Haptic Potential of EMU's Institutional Architecture (The Government and Opposition/Leonard Schapiro Lecture, 2016)', *Government and Opposition* 52(3): 385–411.

Piketty, T. (2014) *Capital in the Twenty-First Century*. Cambridge, MA: The Belknap Press of Harvard University Press.

Putnam, R., ed. (2004) *Democracies in Flux: The Evolution of Social Capital in Contemporary Society*. Oxford: Oxford University Press.

Rodrik, D. (2001) *The Globalization Paradox. Why Global Markets, States and Democracy Can't Coexist*. Oxford: Oxford University Press.

Sabel, C. and Zeitlin, J., eds (2007) *Experimentalist Governance in the European Union: Towards a New Architecture*. Oxford: Oxford University Press.

Scharpf, F. (1999) *Governing in Europe: Effective and Democratic?* Oxford: Oxford University Press.

Scharpf, F. (2000) 'Interdependence and Democratic Legitimacy', in S. Pharr and R. Putnam (eds), *Disaffected Democracies: What's Troubling the Trilateral Countries?*, 101–21. Princeton, NJ: Princeton University Press.

Scharpf, F. (2009) 'Legitimacy in the European multilevel polity', *European Political Science Review* 1(2): 173–204.

Stone-Sweet, A. and Thatcher, M. (2002) 'Theory and Practice of Delegation to non-majoritarian institutions', *West European Politics* 25(1): 1–22.

Strøm, K., Müller, W. and Bergman, T., eds (2003) *Delegation and Accountability in Parliamentary Democracies*. Oxford: Oxford University Press.

Weiler, J. (1995) 'Does Europe Need a Constitution? Demos, Telos and the German Maastricht Decision', *European Law Journal* 1(3): 219–58.

Zakaria, F. (2007) *The Future of Freedom: Illiberal Democracy at Home and Abroad*. New York, NY: W.W. Norton & Co.

# Chapter 2

Abou-Chadi, T. and Krause, W. (2018) 'The Causal Effect of Radical Right Success on Mainstream Parties' Policy Positions: A Regression Discontinuity Approach', *British Journal of Political Science* 50(3): 1–19.

Akkerman, A., Mudde, C. and Zaslove, A. (2014) 'How Populist are the People? Measuring Populist Attitudes in Voters', *Comparative Political Studies* 47(9): 1324–53.

Arzheimer, K. (2018) 'Explaining Electoral Support for the Radical Right', in J. Rydgren (ed.), *The Oxford Handbook of the Radical Right*, 212–38. Oxford: Oxford University Press.

Bartolini, S. and Mair, P. (1990) *Identity, Competition and Electoral Availability: The Stabilisation of European Electorates 1885–1985*. Cambridge: Cambridge University Press.

Benedetto, G., Hix, S. and Mastrorocco, N. (2020) 'The Rise and Fall of Social Democracy, 1918–2017', *American Political Science Review* 114(3): 928–39.

Bornschier, S. (2010) *Cleavage Politics and the Populist Right*. Philadelphia, PA: Temple University Press.

Bremer, B. and Schulte-Cloos, J. (2019) 'The Restructuring of British and German Party Politics in Times of Crisis', in S. Hutter and H. Kriesi, *European Party Politics in Times of Crisis*, 281–301. Cambridge: Cambridge University Press.

Caramani, D. (2017) 'Will vs. Reason: The Populist and Technocratic Forms of Political Representation and Their Critique to Party Government', *American Political Science Review* 111(1): 54–67.

Caselli, M., Fracasso, A. and Traverso, S. (2020) 'Globalization and Electoral Outcomes: Evidence from Italy', *Economics & Politics* 321: 68–103.

Colantone, I. and Stanig, P. (2018) 'Global Competition and Brexit', *American Political Science Review* 112(2): 201–18.

Deegan-Krause, K. (2007) 'New Dimensions of Political Cleavage', in R. J. Dalton and H.-D. Klingemann (eds), *The Oxford Handbook of Political Behavior*, 538–56. Oxford: Oxford University Press.

Dinas, E. and Riera, P. (2018) 'Do European Parliament Elections Impact National Party System Fragmentation?' *Comparative Political Studies* 51(4): 447–76.

Döring, H. and Manow, P. (2021) 'Parliaments and governments database (ParlGov): Information on parties, elections and cabinets in modern democracies'. Development version. https://www.parlgov.org/about/.

Eijk, C. van der, Franklin, M. and Marsh, M. (1996) 'What Voters Teach Us about Europe-wide Elections: What Europe-wide Elections Teach Us about Voters', *Electoral Studies* 15(2): 149–66.

Engler, S., Pytlas, B. and Deegan-Krause, K. (2019) 'Assessing the Diversity of Anti-establishment and Populist Politics in Central and Eastern Europe', *West European Politics* 42(6): 1310–36.

Frankland, E. G. (2016) 'Central and Eastern European Green Parties: Rise, Fall and Revival?', in E. Van Haute (ed.), *Green Parties in Europe*, 59–91. London: Routledge.

Gingrich, J. and Häusermann, S. (2015) 'The Decline of the Working-class Vote, the Reconfiguration of the Welfare Support Coalition and Consequences for the Welfare State', *Journal of European Social Policy* 25(1): 50–75.

Hernández, E. and Kriesi, H. (2016) 'The Electoral Consequences of the Financial and Economic Crisis in Europe', *European Journal of Political Research* 55(2): 203–24.

Holmes, M. and Lightfoot, S. (2016) 'To EU or not to EU? The Transnational Radical Left and the Crisis', in L. March and D. Keith (eds), *Europe's Radical Left: From Marginality to the Mainstream?*, 333–52. Lanham, MD: Rowman & Littlefield.

Hooghe, L., Marks, G. and Wilson, C. J. (2002) 'Does Left/Right Structure Party Positions on European Integration?' *Comparative Political Studies* 35(8): 965–89.

Hopkin, J. (2020) *Anti-System Politics: The Crisis of Market Liberalism in Rich Democracies*. Oxford: Oxford University Press.

Houtman, A., Achterberg, P. and Derks, A. (2008) *Farewell to the Leftist Working Class*. London and New York, NY: Routledge.

Hutter, S. and Kriesi, H. (2019) *European Party Politics in Times of Crisis*. Cambridge: Cambridge University Press.

Ignazi, P. (1992) 'The Silent Counter-revolution: Hypotheses on the Emergence of Extreme Right-wing Parties in Europe', *European Journal of Political Research* 22(1): 3–34.

Inglehart, R. (1977) *The Silent Revolution: Changing Values and Political Styles among Western Publics*. Princeton, NJ: Princeton University Press.

Jackman, R. W. and Volpert, K. (1996) 'Conditions Favouring Parties of the Extreme Right in Western Europe', *British Journal of Political Science* 26(4): 501–21.

Jordan, C. (1991) 'Greenway 1989–1990, the Foundation of the East European Green Parties', in S. Parkin (ed.), *Green Light on Europe*, 76–83. London: Heretic Books.

Kelemen, R. D. (2017) 'Europe's Other Democratic Deficit: National Authoritarianism in Europe's Democratic Union', *Government and Opposition* 52(2): 211–38.

Kitschelt, H. (1992) 'The Formation of Party Systems in East Central Europe', *Politics & Society* 20(1): 7–50.

Kitschelt, H. (1994) *The Transformation of European Social Democracy.* Cambridge: Cambridge University Press.

Kitschelt, H. (2019) *The Logics of Party Formation: Ecological Politics in Belgium and West Germany.* Ithaca, NY: Cornell University Press.

Kriesi, H. (2014) 'The Populist Challenge', *West European Politics* 37(2): 361–78.

Kriesi, H. (2016) 'The Politicization of European Integration', *Journal of Common Market Studies* 54(S1): 32.

Kriesi, H., Grande, E., Lachat, R., Dolezal, M., Bornschier, S. and Frey, T. (2008) *West European Politics in the Age of Globalization.* Cambridge: Cambridge University Press.

Kriesi, H. and Pappas, T. S. (2015) *European Populism in the Shadow of the Great Recession.* Colchester: ECPR Press.

Kriesi, H. and Schulte-Cloos, J. (2020) 'Support for Radical Parties in Western Europe: Structural Conflicts and Political Dynamics', *Electoral Studies* 65: 102138.

Lipset, S. M. and Rokkan, S. (1967) 'Cleavage Structures, Party Systems, and Voter Alignments. An Introduction', in S. M. Lipset and S. Rokkan (eds), *Party Systems and Voter Alignments: Cross-National Perspectives*, 1–64. New York: Free Press.

Lubbers, M., Gijsberts, M. and Scheepers, P. (2002) 'Extreme Right-wing Voting in Western Europe', *European Journal of Political Research* 41(3): 345–78.

Mair, P. (1997) *Party System Change: Approaches and Interpretations.* Oxford: Oxford University Press.

March, L. (2012) *Radical Left Parties in Europe.* London: Routledge.

March, L. (2016) 'Radical Left "Success" before and after the Great Recession', in L. March and D. Keith (eds), *Europe's Radical Left: From Marginality to the Mainstream?*, 27–50. Lanham, MD: Rowman & Littlefield.

Mudde, C. (2004) 'The populist zeitgeist', *Government and Opposition* 39(4): 541–63.

Mudde, C. (2007) *Populist Radical Right Parties in Europe.* Cambridge: Cambridge University Press.

Norris, P. and Inglehart, R. (2019) *Cultural Backlash: Trump, Brexit, and Authoritarian Populism.* Cambridge: Cambridge University Press.

Oesch, D. (2006) *Redrawing the Class Map: Stratification and Institutions in Britain, Germany, Sweden and Switzerland.* Basingstoke and New York, NY: Palgrave Macmillan.

Oesch, D. and Rennwald, L. (2018) 'Electoral Competition in Europe's New Tripolar Political Space: Class Voting for the Left, Centre-right and Radical Right', *European Journal of Political Research* 57(4): 783–807.

Pitkin, H. F. (1967) *The Concept of Representation.* Berkeley, CA: University of California Press.

Poguntke, T. (1987) 'New Politics and Party Systems: The Emergence of a New Type of Party?' *West European Politics* 10(1): 76–88.

Pytlas, B. (2020) 'Hijacking Europe: Counter-European Strategies and Radical Right Mainstreaming during the Humanitarian Crisis Debate 2015–16', *JCMS: Journal of Common Market Studies* 59(2): 335–53.

Rae, D. W. and Taylor, M. (1970) *The Analysis of Political Cleavages*. New Haven, CT: Yale University Press.

Reif, K. and Schmitt, H. (1980) 'Nine Second-Order National Elections – A Conceptual Framework for the Analysis of European Election Results', *European Journal of Political Research* 8(1): 3–44.

Rydgren, J. (2008) 'Immigration Sceptics, Xenophobes or Racists? Radical Right-Wing Voting in Six West European Countries', *European Journal of Political Research* 47(6): 737–65.

Schulte-Cloos, J. (2018) 'Do European Parliament Elections Foster Challenger Parties' Success on the National Level', *European Union Politics* 19(3): 408–26.

Schulte-Cloos, J. and Leininger, A. (2022) 'Electoral Participation, Political Disaffection, and the Rise of the Populist Radical Right', *Party Politics* 28(3): 431–443. https://doi.org/10.1177/1354068820985186.

Sikk, A. (2012) 'Newness as a Winning Formula for New Political Parties', *Party Politics* 18(4): 465–86.

Tindemans, L. (1975) 'European Union: Report to the European Council', in *European Yearbook*, 3–93. European Communities.

Zulianello, M. (2020) 'Varieties of Populist Parties and Party Systems in Europe: From State-of-the-Art to the Application of a Novel Classification Scheme to 66 Parties in 33 Countries', *Government and Opposition* 55(2): 327–47.

Zürn, M. (1998) *Regieren jenseits des nationalstaates. Globalisierung und de-nationalisierung als chance*. Frankfurt am Main: Suhrkamp.

# Chapter 3

Alesina, A. and Spolaore, E. (2003) *The Size of Nations*. Cambridge, MA: MIT Press.

Amnesty International (2018) *Sweden: Homeless Roma and other EU Migrants Face Widespread Discrimination and Dangerous Conditions*, 23 November.

Anthonj, C. et al. (2020) 'A Systematic Review of Water, Sanitation and Hygiene among Roma Communities in Europe: Situation Analysis, Cultural Context, and Obstacles to Improvement', *International Journal of Hygiene and Environmental Health* 226(1): 1–11.

Bess, K. D. et al (2002) 'Psychological Sense of Community: Theory, Research, and Application', in A. T. Fisher, C. C. Sonn and B. J. Bishop (eds), *Psychological Sense of Community*, 3–22. Boston, MA: Springer.

Bettiza, S. (2020) 'Coronavirus: The Lure of Mafia Money during the Crisis', BBC World Service, 5 May. www.bbc.com/news/world-europe-52537573.

Bhatti, Y. and Hansen, K. H. (2019) 'Voter Turnout and Municipal Amalgamations—Evidence from Denmark', *Local Government Studies* 45(5): 697–723.

Blom-Hansen, J. et al. (2014) 'Size, Democracy, and the Economic Costs of Running the Political System', *American Journal of Political Science* 58(4): 790–803.

Callois, J. M. and Aubert, F. (2007) 'Towards Indicators of Social Capital for Regional Development Issues: The Case of French Rural Areas', *Regional Studies* 41(6): 809–21.

Cattivelli, V. and Rusciano, V. (2020) 'Social Innovation and Food Provisioning during COVID-19: The Case for Urban-Rural Initiatives in the Province of Naples', *Sustainability* 12(11): 4444. https://doi.org/10.3390/su12114444.

Chou, M. (2020) 'Populism and Localism: A New Research Agenda', *Democratization* 27(6): 1102–09.

Costello, N. (2014) 'Roma Immigrants in Ireland Are Under Attack', *Vice*, 31 October. www.vice.com/en/article/7bapgg/roma-attacks-waterford-ireland-833.

Crețan, R. and O'Brien, T. (2019) 'Get out of Traian Square!: Roma Stigmatization as a Mobilizing Tool for the Far Right in Timișoara, Romania', *International Journal of Urban and Regional Research* 43(5): 833–47.

Dahl, R. A. (1967) 'The City in the Future of Democracy', *American Political Science Review* 61(4): 953–70.

Dahl, R. A. and Tufte, E. R. (1973) *Size and Democracy*. Palo Alto, CA: Stanford University Press.

DuPuis, E. M. and Goodman, D. (2005) 'Should We Go "home" to Eat?: Toward a Reflexive Politics of Localism', *Journal of Rural Studies* 21(3): 359–71.

European Commission (2020) *Roma integration in the EU. Facts and Figures on EU's Roma Population and Integration Strategies for Improving the Living Conditions of Roma in EU Countries.* https://ec.europa.eu/info/policies/justice-andfundamental-rights/combatting-discrimination/roma-and-eu/roma-integrationeu_en.

European Values Study (EVS) (2017) Integrated Dataset (EVS 2017). GESIS Data Archive, Cologne. ZA7500 Data file Version 3.0.0. doi:10.4232/1.13511.

Filčák, R. et al. (2018) 'No Water for the Poor: The Roma Ethnic Minority and Local Governance in Slovakia', *Ethnic and Racial Studies* 41(7): 1390–407.

Fitzgerald, J. (2018) *Close to Home: Local Ties and Voting Radical Right in Europe.* Cambridge: Cambridge University Press.

Fitzgerald, J. and Wolak, J. (2016) 'The Roots of Trust in Local Government in Western Europe', *International Political Science Review* 37(1): 130–46.

Gendzwill, A. (2019) 'Local Autonomy and National–Local Turnout Gap: Higher Stakes, Higher Turnout?' *Regional & Federal Studies.* doi:10.1080/13 597566.2019.1706496.

Green, A. E. and White, R. J. (2007) 'Attachment to Place, Social Networks, Mobility and Prospects of Young People', Joseph Rowntree Foundation, Warwick University, 29 October. https://www.jrf.org.uk/report/attachment-place-social-networks-mobility-and-prospects-young-people.

Guga, E. (2017) 'Local Government Modernization in Albania: Historical Background and the Territorial Reform 2015–2020', *International Journal of Public Sector Management* 31(4): 466–506.

Hirschfield, A. and Bowers, K. L. (1997) 'The Effect of Social Cohesion on Levels of Recorded Crime in Disadvantaged Areas', *Urban Studies* 34(8): 1275–95.

Horowitz, J. (2020) 'Comic Insults Aside, Mayors Act as Sentinels in Italy's coronavirus Tragedy', *The New York Times*, 26 April.

Ladner, A. and Keuffer, N. (2021) 'Creating an Index of Local Autonomy – Theoretical, Conceptual, and Empirical Issues', *Regional and Federal Studies* 31(2): 209–234. doi:10.1080/13597566.2018.1464443.

Lane, P. and Smith, D. (2021) 'Mid-term Review: UK Roma National Integration Strategy: Roma at the Intersection of Ethnic-inclusive, Post-racial and Hyper-ethnic Policies', *Journal of Contemporary European Studies* 29(1): 73–83. doi:10.1080/14782804.2019.1626226.

Matsubayashi, T. (2007) 'Population Size, Local Autonomy, and Support for the Political System', *Social Science Quarterly* 88(3): 830–49.

OECD (2018) 'Fiscal Decentralization Database, Organization for Economic Cooperation and Development'. www.oecd.org/ctp/federalism/fiscal-decentralisation-database.htm#A_Title.

Olivas Osuna, J. J., Gartzou-Katsouyanni, K. and Kiefel, M. (2021) 'Place matters: Analyzing the roots of political distrust and Brexit narratives at a local level', *Governance* 34(4): 1019–38.

Patana, P. (2021) 'Residential Constraints and the Political Geography of the Populist Radical Right: Evidence from France', *Perspectives on Politics*, 29 September. doi.org/10.1017/S153759272100219X.

Putnam, R. D. (1993) *Making Democracy Work: Civic Traditions in Modern Italy.* Princeton, NJ: Princeton University Press.

Rodríguez-Pose, A. (2020) 'The Rise of Populism and the Revenge of the Places that Don't Matter', *LSE Public Policy Review* 1 (1).

Sellers, J. and Lidström, A. (2012) 'The Localization of Territorial Identity: Citizen Attachment in an Era of Globalization'. Paper presented at American Political Science Association Annual Meeting, New Orleans, LA, 29 August–2 September.

Škobla, D. and Filčák, R. (2016) 'Infrastructure in Marginalised Roma Settlements: Towards a Typology of Unequal Outcomes of EU Funded Projects', *Sociologica* 48(6): 551–71.

Smith, D. (2018) 'Roma Migration, Anti-migrant Sentiment and Social Integration: A Case Study in South-east England', *Local Economy* 33(2): 187–206.

Steiner, R. (2003) 'The Causes, Spread, and Effects of Intermunicipal Cooperation and Municpal Mergers in Switzerland', *Public Management Review* 5(4): 551–71.

Tskhelishvili, B. et al. (2019) 'Women in politics: A CEMR study', Council of European Municipalities and Regions. www.ccre.org/img/uploads/piecesjointe/filename/CEMR_Women_in_politics_study_EN.pdf.

United Nations, Department of Economic and Social Affairs, Population Division (2019) World Population Prospects 2019, Online edn. Rev. 1. https://population.un.org/wpp/.

Uzzell, D. et al. (2002) 'Place Identification, Social Cohesion, and Environmental Sustainability', *Environment and Behavior* 34(1): 26–53.

Verba, S. et al. (1997) 'Knowing and Caring about Politics: Gender and Political Engagement', *Journal of Politics* 59(4): 1051–72.

Vitale, T. (2019) 'Why are Roma Being Attacked in France?', *The Conversation*, 4 July. https://theconversation.com/why-are-roma-people-being-attacked-in-france-115030.

vom Hove, T. et al. (2019) 'Mayors in Europe: Powers & Politics', City Mayors. www.citymayors.com/government/europe_mayors.html.

Walker, S. (2020) 'Europe's Marginalized Roma People Hit Hard by Coronavirus: Pandemic has Increased Deprivation and Stigmatization of Continent's Largest Minority', *The Guardian*, 11 May. www.theguardian.com/world/2020/may/11/europes-marginalised-roma-people-hit-hard-by-coronavirus.

Winter, M. (2003) 'Embeddedness, the New Food Economy and Defensive Localism', *Journal of Rural Studies* 19(1): 23–32.

# Chapter 4

Agh, A. (1999) 'Europeanization of Policy-making in East Central Europe: The Hungarian Approach to EU Accession', *Journal of European Public Policy* 6(5): 839–54. doi:10.1080/135017699343414.

Anderson, C. J. and Tverdova, Y. V. (2003) 'Corruption, Political Allegiances, and Attitudes toward Government in Contemporary democracies', *American Journal of Political Science* 47(1): 91–109. doi:10.1111/1540-5907.00007.

Anghel, V. (2020) 'Together or Apart? The European Union's East–West Divide', *Survival* 62(3): 179–202. doi:10.1080/00396338.2020.1763621.

Anghel, V. and Jones, E. (2021) 'Failing Forward in Eastern Enlargement: Problem Solving through Problem Making', *Journal of European Public Policy*, online first. doi:10.1080/13501763.2021.1927155.

Baji, P., Pavlova, M. Gulácsi, L. and Groot, W. (2012) 'Informal Payments for Healthcare Services and Short-term Effects of the Introduction of Visit Fee on These Payments in Hungary', *The International Journal of Health Planning and Management* 27(1):63–79. https://doi.org/10.1002/hpm.1106.

Buonanno, P., Durante, R., Prarolo, G. and Vanin, P. (2015) 'Poor Institutions, Rich Mines: Resource Curse in the Origins of the Sicilian Mafia', *The Economic Journal* 125: F175–F202. https://doi.org/10.1111/ecoj.12236.

Bošnjak, B. and Acton, T. (2013) 'Virginity and Early Marriage Customs in Relation to Children's Rights among Chergashe Roma from Serbia and Bosnia', *The International Journal of Human Rights* 17(5–6): 646–67. doi:10.1080/13642987.2013.831697.

Caffrey, S. and Mundy, G. (1997) 'Informal Systems of Justice: The Formation of Law within Gypsy Communities Gypsy Law Symposium', *American Journal of Comparative Law* 45: 251–68.

Cammaerts, B., Bruter, M., Banaji, S., Harrison, S. and Anstead, N. (2014) 'The Myth of Youth Apathy: Young Europeans' Critical Attitudes Toward Democratic Life', *American Behavioral Scientist* 58: 645–64. doi:10.1177/0002764213515992.

Casal Bértoa, F. and van Biezen, I. (2014) 'Party Regulation and Party Politics in Post-Communist Europe', *East European Politics*, 30(3): 295–314. doi:10.1080/21599165.2014.938738.

Christiansen, T. and Neuhold, C. (2013) 'Informal Politics in the EU', *Journal of Common Market Studies* 51: 1196–206. doi:10.1111/jcms.12068.

Christiansen, T. and Piattoni, S., eds (2003) *Informal Governance in the European Union*. Cheltenham: Edward Elgar.

Cianetti, L., Dawson, J. and Hanley, S. (2018) 'Rethinking "democratic backsliding" in Central and Eastern Europe – Looking beyond Hungary and Poland', *East European Politics* 34: 243–56. doi:10.1080/21599165.2018.1491401.

Colazingari, S. and Rose-Ackerman, S. (1998) 'Corruption in a Paternalistic Democracy, Lessons from Italy for Latin America', *Political Science Quarterly* 113: 447–70.

Daalder, H. (1996) *The Netherlands: Still a Consociational Democracy? IHS Political Science Series No. 33*, 1–20 [Policy Paper].

Della Porta, D. and Vannucci, A. (1999) *Corrupt Exchanges: Actors, Resources, and Mechanisms of Political Corruption*. New York, NY: Aldine de Gruyter.

Edyvane, D. (2020) 'Incivility as Dissent', *Political Studies* 68(1): 93–109.

European Anti-Fraud Office (OLAF) (2020) *Annual Report*. Brussels: European Commission. https://ec.europa.eu/anti-fraud/about-us/reports/annual-olaf-reports_en.

European Commission (2020) 'A More Credible, Dynamic, Predictable and Political EU Accession Process – Commission Lays Out its Proposals'. https://ec.europa.eu/commission/presscorner/detail/en/IP_20_181.

Fazekas, M. and Tóth, I. J. (2016) 'From Corruption to State Capture: A New Analytical Framework with Empirical Applications from Hungary', *Political Research Quarterly* 69(2): 320–34.

Fieschi, C. and Heywood, P. (2004) 'Trust, Cynicism and Populist Anti-politics', *Journal of Political Ideologies* 9 (3): 289–309. doi:10.1080/1356931042000263537.

Gordy, E. and Efendic, A. (2019) *Meaningful Reform in the Western Balkans – Between Formal Institutions and Informal Practices*. Bern: Peter Lang.

Grzymala-Busse, A. (2019) 'The Failure of Europe's Mainstream Parties', *Journal of Democracy* 30(4): 35–47.

Grzymala-Busse, A. (2010) 'The Best Laid Plans: The Impact of Informal Rules on Formal Institutions in Transitional Regimes', *Studies in Comparative International Development* 45: 311–33.

Hafez, F. and Heinisch, R. (2018) 'Breaking with Austrian Consociationalism: How the Rise of Rightwing Populism and Party Competition Have Changed Austria's Islam Politics', *Politics and Religion* 11(3): 649–78. doi:10.1017/S1755048318000172

Hale, H. (2011) 'Formal Constitutions in Informal Politics: Institutions and Democratization in Post-Soviet Eurasia', *World Politics* 63(4): 581–617.

Helmke, G. and Levitsky, S., eds (2006) *Informal Institutions and Democracy: Lessons from Latin America*. Baltimore, MD: The Johns Hopkins University Press.

Helms, L., Jenny, M. and Willumsen, D. M. (2019) 'Alpine Troubles: Trajectories of De-Consociationalisation in Austria and Switzerland Compared', *Swiss Political Science Review* 25: 381–407.

Hobolt, S. B. (2016) 'The Brexit Vote: A Divided Nation, a Divided Continent', *Journal of European Public Policy*, 23(9): 1259–77. doi:10.1080/13501763.2016.1225785.

Holmberg, S., Lindberg, S. and Svensson, R. (2017) 'Trust in Parliament', *Journal of Public Affairs* 17 (1–2), online first. https://doi.org/10.1002/pa.1647.

Hopkin, J. (2012) 'Technocrats Have Taken Over Governments in Southern Europe. This Is a Challenge to Democracy', *LSE European Politics and Policy Blog*. http://blogs.lse.ac.uk/europpblog/2012/04/24/technocrats-democracy-southern-europe/.

Jones, E. (2020) 'COVID-19 and the EU Economy: Try Again, Fail Better', *Survival* 62: 81–100. https://doi.org/10.1080/00396338.2020.1792124.

Jones, E., Kelemen, R. D. and Meunier, S. (2016) 'Failing Forward? The Euro Crisis and the Incomplete Nature of European Integration', *Comparative Political Studies* 49: 1010–34. https://doi.org/10.1177/0010414015617966.

Jutting, J. (2003) 'Institutions and Development: A Critical Review', Working Paper No. 210, OECD Development Centre.

Kelemen, R. (2017) 'Europe's Other Democratic Deficit: National authoritarianism in Europe's Democratic Union', *Government and Opposition*, 52(2): 211–38. doi:10.1017/gov.2016.41.

Kelemen, R. D. (2020) 'The European Union's Authoritarian Equilibrium', *Journal of European Public Policy* 27: 481–99. doi:10.1080/13501763.2020.1712455.

Kelley, J. (2004) *Ethnic Politics in Europe: The Power of Norms and Incentives*. Princeton, NJ: Princeton University Press

Klein, E. (2019) 'Explaining Legislative Party Switching in Advanced and New Democracies', *Party Politics*, online first. https://doi.org/10.1177/1354068819852262.

Klima, M. (2020) *Informal Politics in Post-Communist Europe: Political Parties, Clientelism and State Capture*. London: Routledge. doi:10.5817/PC2020-2-215.

Krook, M. (2006) 'Gender Quotas, Norms, and Politics', *Politics & Gender* 2(1): 110–18. doi:10.1017/S1743923X06231015.

Lauth, H. J. (2000) 'Informal Institutions and Democracy', *Democratization*, 7(4): 21–50. https://doi.org/10.1080/13510340008403683.

Ledeneva, A. (1998) *Russia's Economy of Favours: Blat, Networking, and Informal Exchange*. Cambridge: Cambridge University Press.

Ledeneva, A. (2006) *How Russia Really Works: Informal Practices in the 1990s*. Ithaca, NY: Cornell University Press.

Ledeneva, A. (2018) *The Global Encyclopaedia of Informality*. London: UCL Press.

Levitsky, S. and Ziblatt, D. (2018) *How Democracies Die*. New York, NY: Crown.

Magyar, B. (2017) *Post-Communist Mafia State: The Case of Hungary*. Budapest: CEU Press.

March, J. G. and Olsen, J. P. (2010) *Rediscovering Institutions*. New York, NY: Simon & Schuster.

Marinova, D. M. (2011) 'When Government Fails Us: Trust in Post-Socialist Civil Organizations', *Democratization* 18(1): 160–83. doi:10.1080/13510347.2011.532623.

Mayhew, D. R. (1974) *Congress: The Electoral Connection*. London: Yale University Press.

Neto, O. and Strøm, K. (2006) 'Breaking the Parliamentary Chain of Delegation: Presidents and Non-Partisan Cabinet Members in European Democracies', *British Journal of Political Science* 36(4): 619–43.

Nicoli, F. (2017) 'Hard-line Euroscepticism and the Eurocrisis: Evidence from a Panel Study of 108 Elections across Europe', *Journal of Common Market Studies* 55: 312–31. https://doi.org/10.1111/jcms.12463.

North, D. C. (1990) *Institutions, Institutional Change and Economic Performance*. Cambridge: Cambridge University Press.

O'Donnell, G. (1996) 'Illusions about Consolidation', *Journal of Democracy*, 7(2): 32–51

Petrova, B. (2021) 'Redistribution and the Quality of Government: Evidence from Central and Eastern Europe', *British Journal of Political Science* 51: 374–93. doi:10.1017/S0007123419000085.

Rawls, J. (1971) *A Theory of Justice*. Cambridge, MA: Harvard University Press.

Rodríguez-Pose, A., and Di Cataldo, M. (2015) 'Quality of Government and Innovative Performance in the Regions of Europe', *Journal of Economic Geography*, 15(4): 673–706. https://doi.org/10.1093/jeg/lbu023.

Rooduijn, M. (2018) 'What Unites the Voter Bases of Populist Parties? Comparing the Electorates of 15 Populist Parties', *European Political Science Review* 10(3): 351–68.

Sayan, P. (2019) 'Enforcement of the anti-Racism Legislation of the European Union against Antigypsyism', *Ethnic and Racial Studies* 42(5): 763–81. doi:10.1080/01419870.2018.1468568.

Sedelmeier, U. (2011) 'Europeanisation in New Member and Candidate States', *Living Reviews in European Governance* 6. DOI: 10.12942/lreg-2011-1.

Schimmelfennig, F.and Winzen, T. (2017) 'Eastern Enlargement and Differentiated Integration: Towards Normalization', *Journal of European Public Policy* 24: 239–58. https://doi.org/10.1080/13501763.2016.1264083.

Schubert, S. and Miller, C. (2008) 'At Siemens Bribery Was Just a Line Item', *The New York Times*, 20 December. https://www.nytimes.com/2008/12/21/business/worldbusiness/21siemens.html.

Skowronek, S., Dearborn, J. A. and King, D. (2021) *Phantoms of a Beleaguered Republic: The Deep State and the Unitary Executive*. New York, NY: Oxford University Press.

Smimou, K. (2020) 'Corporate Culture, Ethical Stimulus, and Managerial Momentum: Theory and Evidence', *Business Ethics: A European Review* 29(2): 360–87. https://doi.org/10.1111/beer.12258.

Stockemer, D., LaMontagne, B. and Scruggs, L. (2013) 'Bribes and Ballots: The Impact of Corruption on Voter Turnout in Democracies',

*International Political Science Review* 34(1): 74–90. https://doi.
org/10.1177/0192512111419824.

Timmerman, J. (2004) 'When Her Feet Touch the Ground: Conflict between the Roma Familistic Custom of Arranged Juvenile Marriage and Enforcement of International Human Rights Treaties', *Journal of Transnational Law and Policy* 13(2): 475–97.

Trantidis, A. and Tsagkroni, V. (2017) 'Clientelism and Corruption: Institutional Adaptation of State Capture Strategies in View of Resource Scarcity in Greece', *The British Journal of Politics and International Relations* 19(2): 263–81.

Ullman-Margalit, E. (1978) *The Emergence of Norms*. Oxford: Clarendon Press.

Vachudova, M. A. (2005) *Europe Undivided: Democracy, Leverage, and Integration after Communism, Europe Undivided*. Oxford: Oxford University Press.

Vachudova, M. A. (2020) 'Ethnopopulism and Democratic Backsliding in Central Europe', *East European Politics* 36: 318–40. doi:10.1080/21599165.2020.1787163.

van der Meer, T. (2010) 'In What We Trust? A Multi-level Study into Trust in Parliament as an Evaluation of State Characteristics', *International Review of Administrative Sciences* 76(3): 517–36. https://doi.
org/10.1177/0020852310372450.

Voigt, S. (2018) 'How to Measure Informal Institutions', *Journal of Institutional Economics* 14: 1–22. https://doi.org/10.1017/S1744137417000248.

Wachs, J., Fazekas, M. and Kertész, J. (2020) 'Corruption Risk in Contracting Markets: A Network Science Perspective', *Int Journal of Data Science and Analytics*, online first. https://doi.org/10.1007/s41060-019-00204-1.

Weeks, A. and Baldez, L. (2015) 'Quotas and Qualifications: The Impact of Gender Quota Laws on the Qualifications of Legislators in the Italian Parliament', *European Political Science Review* 7(1): 119–44. doi:10.1017/S1755773914000095.

Weingast, B. R. (1979) 'A Rational Choice Perspective on Congressional Norms', *American Journal of Political Science* 23(2): 245–62.

Wihl, G. (2018) 'Civil Disobedience in Democratic Regimes', *Israel Law Review*, 51(2): 301–20. doi:10.1017/S0021223718000043.

Wolkenstein, F. (2016) 'Norbert Hofer, the Friendly Face of Austria's Populist Right', *LSE Blogs*. https://blogs.lse.ac.uk/europpblog/2016/10/11/norbert-hofer-friendly-face-populist-right/.

# Chapter 5

Agrikoliansky, E. and Sommier, I., eds (2005) *Radiographie du mouvement altermondialiste*. Paris: La Dispute.

Ayoub, P. (2015) 'Contested Norms in New-Adopter States: International Determinants of LGBT Rights Legislation', *European Journal of International Relations* 21(2): 293–22.

Bjørgo, T. and Mareš, M., eds (2019) *Vigilantism against Migrants and Minorities*. London: Routledge.

Bogerts, L. and Fielitz, M. (2019) '"Do You Want Meme War?" Understanding the Visual Memes of the German Far Right', in M. Fielitz and N. Thurston (eds), *Post-Digital Cultures of the Far Right. Online Actions and Offline Consequences in Europe and the US*, 137–54. Bielefeld: Transcript.

Borbáth, E. and Gessler, T. (2020) 'Different Worlds of Contention? Protest in Northwestern, Southern and Eastern Europe', *European Journal of Political Research* 59(4): 910–935.

Bringer, B. and Pleyers, G., eds (2020) *Alerta global. Políticas, movimientos sociales y futuros en disputa en tiempos de pandemia*. Ciudad de Buenos Aires, Argentina: CLACSO.

Cabezas González, A. and Machado Brochner, G. P. (2019) 'The New Cycle of Women's Mobilizations between Latin America and Europe', in H. Cairo and B. Bringel (eds), *Critical Geopolitics and Regional (Re) Configurations: Interregionalism and Transnationalism Between Latin America and* Europe, 139–58. London, Routledge.

Caiani, M. and Graziano, P. (2018) 'Europeanisation and Social Movements: The Case of the Stop TTIP Campaign', *European Journal of Political Research* 57(4): 1031–55.

Caiani, M. and Weisskircher, M. (2020) 'How Many 'Europes'? Left-wing and Right-wing Social Movements and their Visions of Europe', in C. Flesher Fominaya and R. Feenstra (eds), *Routledge Handbook of Contemporary European Social Movements: Protest in Turbulent Times*, 30–45. London: Routledge.

Carvalho, T. (2019) *Contesting Austerity: A Comparative Approach to the Cycles of Protest in Portugal and Spain Under the Great Recession (2008–2015)*, PhD thesis, Department of Sociology, University of Cambridge.

Chakrabarty, D. (2008) *Provincializing Europe. Postcolonial Thought and Historical Difference*. Princeton, NJ: Princeton University Press.

Crespy, A. and Parks, P. (2017) 'The Connection between Parliamentary and Extra-parliamentary Opposition in the EU. From ACTA to the Financial Crisis', *Journal of European Integration* 39 (4): 453–67.

della Porta, D. (2013) *Can Democracy be Saved?: Participation, Deliberation and Social Movements*. Cambridge: Cambridge University Press.

della Porta, D. (2015) *Social Movements in Times of Austerity*. London: Polity Press.

della Porta, D. and Mattoni, A. (2014) *Spreading Protest: Social Movements in Times of Crisis*. Essex: ECPR Press.

della Porta, D. and Parks, L. (2018) 'Social Movements, the European Crisis, and EU Political Opportunities', *Comparative European Politics* 16: 85–102.

della Porta, D., Andretta, M., Calle, A., Combes, H., Eggert, N., Giugni, M., Hadden, J., Jimenez, M. and Marchetti, R. (2015) *Global Justice Movement: Cross-National and Transnational Perspectives*. London: Routledge.

Doerr, N. and Mattoni, A. (2014) 'Public Spaces and Alternative Media Practices in Europe. The Case of the EuroMayDay Parade against Precarity', in K. Fahlenbrach, E. E. Sivertsen and R.Werenskjold (eds), *Media And Revolt: Strategies and Performances from the 1960s to the Present*, 386–405. New York, NY: Berghahn Books.

Dolenec, D., Doolan, K. and Tomašević, T. (2017) 'Contesting Neoliberal Urbanism on the European Semi-periphery: The Right to the City Movement in Croatia', *Europe-asia studies* 69(9): 1–29.

Duke, B. (2020) 'The Effects of the COVID-19 Crisis on the Gig Economy and Zero Hour Contracts', *Interface* 12(1): 115–20115 – 20.

Džuverović, N., Rone, J. and Junes, T. (2021) 'Introduction: Contentious Politics and International Statebuilding in Southeast Europe', *East European Politics and Societies* 35(1): 182–9.

Fillieule, O. and Acornero, G. (2016) *Social Movement Studies in Europe: The State of the Art*. Oxford: Berghahn Books.

Flesher Fominaya, C. and Cox, L. (2013) *Understanding European Movements: New Social Movements, Global Justice Struggles, Anti-Austerity Protest* (Routledge Advances in Sociology). London: Routledge.

Flesher Fominaya, C. and Feenstra, R., eds (2019) *Routledge Handbook of Contemporary European Social Movements. Protest in Turbulent Times*, 1st edn. London: Routledge.

Forchtner, B., Kroneder, A. and Wetzel, D. (2018) 'Being Skeptical? Exploring Far-Right Climate-Change Communication in Germany', *Environmental Communication*, 12(5): 589–604.

Gattinara, P. C. and Pirro, A. L. P. (2019) 'The Far Right as Social Movement', *European Societies*, 21(4): 447–62.

Gerbaudo, P. (2017) *The Mask and the Flag: Populism, Citizenism and Global Protest*. Oxford: Oxford University Press.

Hutter, S. (2014) *Protesting Culture and Economics in Western Europe: New Cleavages in Left and Right Politics*. Minneapolis, MN: University of Minnesota Press.

Janoschka, M. and Mota, F. (2021) 'New Municipalism in Action or Urban Neoliberalisation Reloaded? An Analysis of Governance Change, Stability and Path Dependence in Madrid (2015–2019)', *Urban Studies* 58(13): 2814–2830. https://doi.org/10.1177/0042098020925345.

Kaiser, J. (2019) 'In the Heartland of Climate Scepticism: A Hyperlink Network Analysis of German Climate Sceptics and the US Right Wing', in B. Forchtner (ed.), *The Far Right and the Environment*, 257–74. London: Routledge.

Karl, P. (2019) 'Creating a New Normal: The Mainstreaming of Far-Right Ideas through Online and Offline Action in Hungary', in M. Fielitz and N. Thurston (eds), *Post-Digital Cultures of the Far Right: Online Actions and Offline Consequences in Europe and the* US, 67–78. Bielefeld: Transcript.

Kinniburgh, C. (2019) 'Climate Politics after the Yellow Vests', *Dissent* 66(2): 115–25.

Knüpfer, C. B., Hoffmann, M. and Voskresenskii, V. (2022) 'Hijacking MeToo: Transnational Dynamics and Networked Frame Contestation on the Far Right in the Case of the "120 decibels" Campaign', *Information, Communication & Society* 25(7): 1010–1028.

Mattoni, A. (2012) *Media Practices and Protest Politics: How Precarious Workers Mobilise.* London: Routledge.

Parti, K. and Wössner, G. (2020) *BlackLivesMatter – What Can the Current US Anti-racist Movement Teach Europe?.* Freiburg: Max Planck Institute for the Study of Crime, Security and Law.

Pirone, M. (2020) 'Paths of Critical Europeanism: From Blockupy to Neo-municipalism', in M. Baldassari, E. Castelli, M. Truffelli and G. Vezzani (eds), *Anti-Europeanism.* Springer, Cham.

Pleyers, G. (2016) 'Young Progressive Activists in Europe: Scales, Identity and Agency', in C. Feixa, C. Leccardi and P. Nilan (eds), *Youth, Space and Time,* 25–43. Amsterdam: Brill.

Portos García, M. (2016) 'Taking to the Streets in the Shadow of Austerity: A Chronology of the Cycle of Protest in Spain, 2007–2015', *PArtecipazione e COnflitto: The Open Journal of Socio-Political Studies* 9 (1): 181–210.

Rone, J. (2018) 'Contested International Agreements, Contested National Politics: How the Radical Left and the Radical Right Opposed TTIP in Four European Countries', *London Review of International Law* 6(2): 233–53.

Rone, J. (2020) *Contesting Austerity and Free Trade in the EU: Protest Diffusion in Complex Media and Political Arenas.* London: Routledge.

Sweeny, J. (2020) 'The #MeToo Movement in Comparative Perspective', *American University Journal of Gender, Social Policy & the Law* 29(1): 33–88.

Tejerina, B., Perugorría, I., Benski, T. and Langman, L. (2013) 'From Indignation to Occupation: A New Wave of Global Mobilization', *Current Sociology* 61(4): 377–92.

Weisskircher, M. and Berntzen, L. (2019) 'Remaining on the Streets: Anti-Islamic PEGIDA Mobilization and its Relationship to Far-right Party Politics', in M. Caiani and O. Císař, *Radical Right Movement Parties in Europe,* 114–30. London: Routledge.

Wolkenstein, F. (2019) *Rethinking Party Reform.* Oxford: Oxford University Press.

# Chapter 6

Boasson, E. L. and Wettestad, J. (2013) *EU Climate Policy: Industry, Policy Interaction and External Environment*. Farnham: Ashgate.

Barry, J. (2005) 'Ecological Modernisation', in J. S. Dryzek and D. Scholsberg (eds), *Debating the Earth: The Environmental Politics* Reader, 303–21. Oxford: Oxford University Press.

Bell, G. and Joseph, S. (2016) 'Climate Change Mitigation and the Role of Technologic Change: Impact on Selected Headline Targets of Europe's 2020 Climate and Energy Package'. Research Institute of Applied Economics, Working Paper 2016/12, 1–37.

Bocquillon, P. (2014) '(De-)Constructing Coherence? Strategic Entrepreneurs, Policy Frames and the Integration of Climate and Energy Policies in the European University', *Environmental Policy and Government* 28: 339–49. https://doi.org/10.1002/eet.1820.

Bomberg, E. (2012) 'Mind the (Mobilization) Gap: Comparing Climate Activism in the United States and European Union', *Review of Policy Research* 29(3): 408–30. https://doi.org/10.1111/j.1541-1338.2012.00566.x.

Bond, P. (2011) 'From Copenhagen to Cancún to Durban: Moving Deckchairs on the Climate Titanic', *Capitalism Nature Socialism* 22(2): 3–26. doi.org/10.1080/10455752.2011.569348.

Calel, R. and Dechezleprêtre, A. (2016) 'Environmental Policy and Directed Technological Change: Evidence from the European Carbon Market', *The Review of Economics and Statistics* 98(1): 173–91. https://doi.org/10.1162/REST_a_00470.

Casado-Asensio, J. and Steurer, R. (2015) '"Bookkeeping" rather than Climate Policymaking: National Mitigation Strategies in Western Europe'. Discussion Paper 3-2015, Institute of Forest, Environmental, and Natural Resource Policy, Universität für Bodenkultur Wein, Vienna.

Connelly, J., Smith, G., Benson, D. and Saunders, C. (2012) *Environmental Politics in Theory and Practice*. London: Routledge.

Doherty, B. and Saunders, C. (2021) 'Global Climate Strike Protesters and Media Coverage of the Protests in Truro and Manchester', in J. Bessant, A. M. Mesinas and S. Pickard (eds), *When Students Protest: Universities in the Global* North, 251–67. London: Rowman & Littlefield.

Doulton, H. and Brown, K. (2009) 'Ten Years to Prevent Catastrophe?: Discourses of Climate Change and International Development in the UK Press', *Global Environmental Change* 19(2): 191–202. doi.org/10.1016/j.gloenvcha.2008.10.004.

European Parliament (2020) 'Greta Thunberg Urges MEPs to Show Climate Leadership'. https://www.europarl.europa.eu/news/en/headlines/society/20200227STO73520/greta-thunberg-urges-meps-to-show-climate-leadership.

Fagan, A. (1994) 'Environment and Transition in the Czech Republic', *Environmental Politics* 3(3): 479–94. doi:10.1080/09644019408414156.

Fischer, S. (2014) *The EU's New Energy and Climate Policy Framework for 2030.* SWP Comments 55. Berlin: SWP. https://www.swp-berlin.org/fileadmin/contents/products/comments/2014C55_fis.pdf.

Haines, H. H. (2013) 'Radical Flank Effects', in D. A. Snow, D. della Porta, B. B. Klandermans and D. McAdam (eds), *The Wiley-Blackwell Encyclopaedia of Social and Political Movements*, 1048–50. Oxford: Blackwell.

Hannigan, J. (2006) *Environmental Sociology: A Social Constructionist Perspective.* London: Routledge.

Hansen, J. (2010) *Storms of My Grandchildren: The Truth about the Coming Climate Catastrophe and Our Last Chance to Save Humanity.* London and New York, NY: Bloomsbury Academic Press.

IEA (2020) 'Global Energy Review: CO2 Emissions in 2020: Understanding the Impacts of COVID-19 on Global CO2'. https://www.iea.org/articles/global-energy-review-co2-emissions-in-2020.

Jamison, A. (2010) 'Climate Change Knowledge and Social Movement Theory', *WIREs Climate Change* 1: 811–23. doi:10.1002/wcc.88.

Jordan, A., Huitema, D. van, Asselt, H., Rayner, T. and Berkhout, F., eds (2010) *Climate Change Policy in the European Union: Confronting the Dilemmas of Mitigation and Adaptation?* Cambridge: Cambridge University Press.

Jordan, A. and Tosun, J. (2012) 'Policy Implementation', in A. Jordan and C. Adelle (eds), *Environmental Policy in the EU: Actors, institutions and processes*, 240–60. London: Routledge.

North, P. (2011) 'The Politics of Climate Activism in the UK: A Social Movement Analysis', *Environment and Planning A: Economy and Space* 43 (7): 1581–98. https://doi.org/10.1068/a43534.

Orr, S. K. (2016) 'Institutional Control and Climate Change Activism at COP21 in Paris', *Global Environmental Politics* 3: 23–30. doi.org/10.1162/GLEP_a_00363.

Oztig, L. I. (2017) 'Europe's Climate Change Policies: The Paris Agreement and Beyond', *Energy Sources, Part B: Economics, Planning, and Policy* 12(10): 917–24. doi.org/10.1080/15567249.2017.1324534.

Parker, C. F. and Karlsson, C. (2010) 'Climate Change and the European Union's Leadership Moment: An Inconvenient Truth?', *JCMS: Journal of Common Market Studies* 48: 923–43. doi.org/10.1111/j.1468-5965.2010.02080.x.

Pilgrim, S. and Harvey, M. (2010) 'Battles over Biofuels in Europe: NGOs and the Politics of Markets', *Sociological Research Online* 15 (3). doi:10.5153/sro.2192.

Rayner, T. and Jordan, A. (2016) 'Climate Change Policy in the European Union', *Oxford Research Encyclopedias: Climate Science*. https://oxfordre.com/climatescience/view/10.1093/acrefore/9780190228620.001.0001/acrefore-9780190228620-e-47?rskey=H9J7ku&result=1.

Saunders, C. (2014) *Environmental Networks and Social Movement Theory*. London: Bloomsbury Academic.

Schreurs, M. A. and Tiberghien, Y. (2008) 'European Union Leadership in Climate Change: Mitigation through Multilevel Reinforcement', in K. Harrison and L. McIntosh Sundstrom (eds), *Global Commons, Domestic Decisions: The Comparative Politics of Climate Change*, 23–66. Cambridge, MA: MIT Press.

Skjærseth, J. B. (2014) 'Linking EU Climate and Energy Policies: Policy-making, Implementation and Reform', *International Environmental Agreements: Politics, Law and Economics* 16(4): 509–23. doi:10.1007/s10784-014-9262-5.

Skjærseth, J. B. and Wettestad, J. (2010) 'The EU's Emission Trade System Reviewed (Directive 2009/29/EC)', in S. Obserthür and M. Pallemaerts (eds), *The New Climate Policies of the European Union*, 65–92. Brussels: VUB Press.

Steinebach, Y. and Knill, C. (2016) 'Still an Entrepreneur? The Changing Role of the European Commission in EU Environmental Policy-making', *Journal of European Public Policy* 24 (3): 429–46. doi.org/10.1080/13501763.2016.1149207.

United Nations Framework Convention on Climate Change (UNFCCC) (2015) 'Report on the Structured Expert Dialogue on the 2013–2015 Review'. http://unfccc.int/resource/docs/2015/sb/eng/inf01.pdf.

United Nations Framework Convention on Climate Change (UNFCCC) (2019) 'United Nations Climate Change Annual Report 2019'. https://unfccc.int/documents/234048.

Vavilov, E. (2019) 'Lessons about Activism from a Swedish High School Student: A Rhetorical Analysis of Greta Thunberg's Public Speeches on Climate Change', unpublished Master's thesis, Jönköping University, Sweden.

# Chapter 7

Albert, M. (1993) *Capitalism against capitalism*. London: Whurr Publishers.

Amable, B. (2003) *The Diversity of Modern Capitalism*. Oxford: Oxford University Press.

Baccaro, L. and Pontusson, J. (2016) 'Rethinking Comparative Political Economy: The Growth Model Perspective', *Politics & Society* 44(2): 175–207.

Ban, C. (2019) 'Dependent Development at a Crossroads? Romanian Capitalism and its Contradictions', *West European Politics*, 42(5): 1041–68.

Bohle, D. (2018) 'European Integration, Capitalist Diversity and Crises Trajectories on Europe's Eastern Periphery', *New Political Economy* 23(2): 239–53.

Bohle, D. and Greskovits, B. (2012) *Capitalist Diversity on Europe's Periphery*. Ithaca, NY: Cornell University Press.

Bohle, D. and Greskovits, B. (2018) 'Politicising Embedded Neoliberalism: Continuity and Change in Hungary's Development Model', *West European Politics* 42(5): 1069–93.

Bruszt, L., Lundstedt, L. and Munkacsi, Zs. (2020) 'Collateral Benefit: The Developmental Effects of EU-Induced State Building in Central and Eastern Europe', *Review of International Political Economy* 27(5): 1170–91.

Dooley, N. (2014) 'Growing Pains? Rethinking the 'Immaturity' of the European Periphery', *Millennium* 42(3): 936–46.

Drahokoupil, J. (2009) *Globalization and the State in Central and Eastern Europe. The Politics of Foreign Direct Investment*. London: Routledge.

EBRD (2018) 'EBRD Transition Report 2017–18: Sustaining Growth, European Bank for Reconstruction and Development'. London.

Gerschenkron, A. (1962) *Economic Backwardness in Historical Perspective*. Cambridge, MA: Belknap Press.

Lavoie, M. and Stockhammer, E. (2013) *Wage-Led Growth*. London: Palgrave.

Hall, P. A. (2018) 'Varieties of Capitalism in Light of the Euro Crisis', *Journal of European Public Policy* 25(1): 7–30. doi:10.1080/13501763.2017.1310278.

Hall, P. A. and Gingerich, D. W. (2009) 'Varieties of Capitalism and Institutional Complementarities in the Political Economy', *British Journal of Political Science* 39(3): 449–82.

Hall, P. A. and Soskice, D., eds (2001) *Varieties of Capitalism: Institutional Foundations of Competitive Advantage*. Oxford: Oxford University Press.

Hancké, B. (2013) *Unions, Central Banks, and EMU: Labour Market Institutions and Monetary Integration in Europe*. Oxford: Oxford University Press.

Hancké, B., Rhodes, M. and Thatcher, M. (2007) *Beyond Varieties of Capitalism. Conflicts, Contradictions, and Complementarities in the European Economy*. Oxford: Oxford University Press.

Hassel, A. (2014) 'The Paradox of Liberalization. Understanding Dualism and Recovery of the German Political Economy', *British Journal of Industrial Relations* 52 (1): 57–81.

Hassel, A. and Palier, B., eds (2021) *Growth and Welfare in Advanced Capitalist Economies: How Growth Regimes Evolve*. Oxford: Oxford University Press.

Hollingsworth, R. and Boyer, R. (1997) *Contemporary Capitalism: The Embeddedness of Institutions*. Cambridge: Cambridge University Press.

Iversen, T. and Soskice, D. (2001) 'An Asset Theory of Social Policy Preferences', *American Political Science Review* 95: 875–93.

Iversen, T. and Soskice, D. (2009) 'Distribution and Redistribution: The Shadow from the Nineteenth Century', *World Politics* 61: 438–86.

Johnston, A. and Regan, A. (2016) 'European Monetary Integration and the Incompatibility of National Varieties of Capitalism', *JCMS: Journal of Common Market Studies* 54: 318–36.

Johnston, A. and Regan, A. (2018) 'Introduction: Is the European Union Capable of Integrating Diverse Models of Capitalism?', New Political Economy 23(2): 145–59.

Jones, E. (2021) 'The Financial Consequences of Export-led Growth in Germany and Italy', *German Politics*, published online 8 February.

Karl, T. L. (1997) *The Paradox of Plenty: Oil Booms and Petro-States*. Berkeley, CA: University of California Press.

Khan, M. and McClean, P. (2017) 'Dijsselbloem under Fire after Saying Eurozone Countries Wasted Money on "alcohol and women"', *Financial Times*, 21 March.

Molina, O. and Rhodes, M. (2007) 'The Political Economy of Adjustment in Mixed Market Economies: A Study of Spain and Italy', in B. Hancké, M. M. Rhodes and M. Thatcher (eds), *Beyond Varieties of Capitalism: Conflict, Contradictions, and Complementarities in the European Economy*, 223–52. Oxford: Oxford University Press.

Myant, M. and Drahokoupil, J. (2010) *Transition Economies: Political Economy in Russia, Eastern Europe, and Central Asia*. Hoboken, NJ: Wiley-Blackwell.

Nölke, A. and Vliegenthart, A. (2009) 'Enlarging the Varieties of Capitalism: The Emergence of Dependent Market Economies in East Central Europe', *World Politics* 61(4): 670–702.

Perez, S. A. and Matsaganis, M. (2018) 'The Political Economy of Austerity in Southern Europe', *New Political Economy* 23 (2): 192–207.

Scepanovic, V. and Bohle, D. (2018) 'The Institutional Embeddedness of Transnational Corporations: Dependent Capitalism in Central and Eastern Europe', in A. Nölke and C. May (eds), *Handbook of the International Political Economy of the Corporation*, 152–66. Cheltenham: Edward Elgar Publishing.

Scheiring, G. (2020) *The Retreat of Liberal Democracy: Authoritarian Capitalism and the Accumulative State in Hungary*. London: Palgrave.

Streeck, W. (1991) 'On the Institutional Conditions for Diversified Quality Production', in E. Matzner and W. Streeck (eds), *Beyond Keynesianism*, 21–61. Aldershot: Elgar.

Thelen, K. (2004) *How Institutions Evolve: The Political Economy of Skills in Germany, Britain, the United States, and Japan*. New York, NY: Cambridge University Press.

Thelen, K. (2021) 'Transitions to the Knowledge Economy in Germany, Sweden, and the Netherlands', in A. Hassel and B. Palier (eds), *Growth and Welfare in Advanced Capitalist Economies: How Growth Regimes Evolve*, 203–26. Oxford: Oxford University Press.

Ther, P. (2016) *Europe since 1989: A History*. Princeton, NJ: Princeton University Press.

Verdun, A. and Zeitlin, J. (2018) 'Introduction: The European Semester as a New Architecture of EU Socioeconomic Governance in Theory and Practice', *Journal of European Public Policy* 25(2)137–48.

Verdun A. C. and Wylie, L. (2002) 'Conclusion: Lessons from Economic and Monetary Union for Theorising European Integration', in A. C. Verdun (ed.), *The Euro: European Integration Theory and Economic and Monetary Union*, 243–49. Boulder: Rowman & Littlefield.

Zeitlin, J., Nicoli, F. and Laffan, B. (2019) 'Introduction: The European Union beyond the Polycrisis? Integration and Politicization in an Age of Shifting Cleavages', *Journal of European Public Policy* 26(7): 963–76.

# Chapter 8

Appel, H. and Orenstein, M. (2016) 'Why did Neoliberalism Triumph and Endure in the Post-Communist World?' *Comparative Politics* 48(3): 313–31.

Baldwin, P. (1990) *The Politics of Social Solidarity: Class Bases of the European Welfare State 1875–1975*. Cambridge: Cambridge University Press.

Cook, L. J. and Inglot, T. (2021) 'The Transformed Eastern European Countries', in D. Béland, S. Leibfried, K. J. Morgan, H. Obinger and C. Pierson (eds), *The Oxford Handbook of the Welfare State*, 2nd edn, 881–900. Oxford: Oxford University Press: 881

Da Roit, B. and Le Bihan, B. (2010) 'Similar and Yet So Different: Cash-for-Care in Six European Countries' Long-Term Care Policies', *Milbank Quarterly* 88(3): 286–309.

Emmenegger, P., Häusermann, S., Palier, B. and Seeleib-Kaiser, M., eds (2012) *The Age of Dualization: The Changing Face of Inequality in Deindustrializing Societies*. Oxford: Oxford University Press.

Esping-Andersen, G. (1990) *Three Worlds of Welfare Capitalism*. Princeton, NJ: Princeton University Press.

Eurostat (2019) 'Europe 2020 Indicators: Poverty and Social Exclusion'. https://ec.europa.eu/eurostat/statistics-explained/index.php?title=Archive:Europe_2020_indicators_-_poverty_and_social_exclusion&oldid=394836.

Eurostat (2020) 'Population Structure and Ageing'. https://ec.europa.eu/
     eurostat/statistics-explained/index.php/Population_structure_and_ageing.
Ferrera, M. (1996) 'The "Southern Model" of Welfare in Social Europe', *Journal
     of European Social Policy* 6(1): 17–37.
Gingrich, J. (2011) *Marking Markets in the Welfare State: The Politics of Varying
     Market Reforms.* Cambridge: Cambridge University Press.
Green-Pedersen, C. and Jensen, C. (2019) 'Electoral Competition and the
     Welfare State', *West European Politics* 42(4): 803–23. doi:10.1080/
     01402382.2019.1565736.
Huber, E. and Stephens, J. (2001) *Development and Crisis of the Welfare
     State: Parties and Politics in Global Markets.* Chicago, IL and London: The
     University of Chicago Press.
Iversen, T. and Soskice, D. (2006) 'Electoral Institutions and the Politics
     of Coalitions: Why Some Democracies Redistribute More than Others',
     *American Political Science Review* 100(2): 165–81.
Lewis, J. (1992) 'Gender and the Development of Welfare Regimes', *Journal of
     European Social Policy* 2(3): 159–73.
Morel, N., Palier, B. and Palme, J., eds (2012) *Towards A Social Investment
     States? Ideas, Policies and Challenges.* Bristol: Policy Press.
Morgan, K. J. (2013) 'Path Shifting of the Welfare State: Electoral Competition
     and the Expansion of Work-family Policies in Western Europe', *World
     Politics* 65(1): 73–115.
Palier, B. (2019) 'Work, Social Protection and the Middle Classes: What Future
     in the Digital Age?' *International Social Security Review* 72(3): 113–33.
Pierson, P. (1996) 'The New Politics of the Welfare State', *World Politics* 48(2):
     143–79.
Taylor-Gooby, P., Leruth, B. and Heejung, C. (2017) *After Austerity: Welfare
     State Transformation in Europe after the Great Recession.* Oxford: Oxford
     University Press.
Van Kersbergen, K. and Manow, P., eds (2009) *Religion, Class Coalitions, and
     Welfare States,* Cambridge; New York, NY: Cambridge University Press.

# Chapter 9

Art, D. (2018) 'The Radical Right's Gains in the Heart of Europe', *Current
     History* 117(794): 114–17.
Bjørnholt, M. and McKay, A., eds (2014) *Counting on Marilyn Waring.*
     Bradford, ON: Demeter Press.

Chiva, C. (2018) *Gender, Institutions and Political Representation: Reproducing Male Dominance in Europe's New Democracies*. New York, NY: Palgrave Macmillan.

Crenshaw, K. (1991) 'Mapping the Margins: Intersectionality, Identity Politics, and Violence against Women of Color', *Stanford Law Review* 43(6): 1241–99. www.jstor.org/stable/1229039.

Einhorn, B. (1993) *Cinderella Goes to Market: Citizenship, Gender and Women's Movements in East Central Europe*. New York, NY: Verso.

Enloe, C. (2016) *Globalization and Militarism: Feminists Make the Link*, 2nd edn. Lanham, MD: Rowman & Littlefield.

European Commission (2017) 'Summary: Gender Equality 2017: Gender Equality, Stereotypes, and Women in Politics', *Special Eurobarometer* 465, Brussels: Directorate-General for Justice and Consumers, November. https://www.globalwps.org/data/HRV/files/Eurobarometer%20in%202017.pdf.

European Commission (2020) 'A Union of Equality: Gender Equality Strategy 2020–2025'. https://ec.europa.eu/info/sites/info/files/aid_development_cooperation_fundamental_rights/gender-equality-strategy-2020-2025_en.pdf.

European Institute for Gender Equality (EIGE) (2019) 'Gender Equality Index'. https://eige.europa.eu/gender-equality-index/2019.

Grant, J. (1993) *Fundamental Feminism: Contesting the Core Concepts of Feminist Theory*. New York, NY: Routledge.

Hudson, V. et al. (2020) *The First Political Order: How Sex Shapes Governance and National Security Worldwide*. New York, NY: Columbia University Press.

Hughes, M. M. and Paxton, P. M. (2017) *Women, Politics, and Power: A Global Perspective*, 3rd edn. Washington: CQ/SAGE.

International Institute for Democracy and Electoral Assistance (IDEA) (n.d.) Quota Database. https://www.idea.int/data-tools/data/gender-quotas/database.

Interparliamentary Union (IPU) (n.d.a) 'Women in National Parliaments: 50 Years of History at a Glance'. http://archive.ipu.org/wmn-e/history.htm.

Interparliamentary Union (IPU) (2020) 'Monthly Rank of Women in National Parliaments'. https://data.ipu.org/women-ranking?month=3&year=2020.

Interparliamentary Union (IPU) (2019a) 'Women in National Parliaments: World and Regional Averages', IPU Archive. http://archive.ipu.org/wmn-e/arc/world011019.htm.

Interparliamentary Union (IPU) (2019b) 'Women in Politics: 2019'. https://www.ipu.org/resources/publications/infographics/2019-03/women-in-politics-2019.

Kantola, J. and Lombardo, E. (2017) 'Gender and the Politics of Economic Crisis in Europe', in J. Kantola and E. Lombardo (eds), *Gender and the Economic Crisis in Europe: Politics, Institutions and Intersectionality*, 1–25. New York, NY: Palgrave Macmillan.

Malgesini, G. et al. (2017) 'Poverty in Europe. European Anti-Poverty Network (EAPN)'. www.eapn.eu/wp-content/uploads/2018/03/EAPN-2017-EAPN-Briefing-Gender-and-Poverty-final.pdf.

Moscovenko, L. R. (2020) 'Gender Equality: How Post-Covid Economic Recovery Programmes Took a Step Back'. Translated by Daniel Eck. EuroActiv. 24 September. www.euractiv.com/section/non-discrimination/news/gender-equality-how-post-covid-economic-recovery-programmes-took-a-step-back/.

Mushaben, J. M. (2019) 'Women Leaders in Troubled Times: The Leadership Styles of Angela Merkel and Hillary Clinton', in E. Krimmer and P. A. Simpson (eds), *Realities and Fantasies of German Female Leadership: From Maria Antonia of Saxony to Angela Merkel*, 318–34. Rochester. NY: Camden House.

Norris, P. and Lovenduski, J. (1995) *Political Recruitment: Gender, Race, and Class in the British Parliament*. New York, NY: Cambridge University Press.

Okin, S. M. (1998) 'Feminism, Women's Human Rights and Cultural Differences', *Hypatia* 13(2): 32–52. www.jstor.org/stable/3810636.

Owens, P. (2016) *Economies of Force: Counterinsurgency and the Historical Rise of the Social*. New York, NY: Cambridge University Press.

Pateman, C. (1988) *The Sexual Contract*. Stanford, CA: Stanford University Press.

Rankin, J. (2020) 'E.U. Revives Plans for Mandatory Quotas on Company Boards', *The Guardian*, 3 March. https://www.theguardian.com/world/2020/mar/05/eu-revives-plans-for-mandatory-quotas-of-women-on-company-boards.

Sanandaji, N. (2018) 'The Nordic Glass Ceiling. Cato Institute, Policy Analysis 835'. www.cato.org/publications/policy-analysis/nordic-glass-ceiling.

Simpson, P. A. (2019) '"Mama Merkel" and "Mutti-Multikulti": The Perils of Governing while Female', in E. Krimmer and P. A. Simpson (eds), *Realities and Fantasies of German Female Leadership: From Maria Antonia of Saxony to Angela Merkel*, 301–17. Rochester, NY: Camden House.

Taub, A. and Bradley, J. (2020) 'As Domestic Abuse Rises, U.K. Failings Leave Victims in Peril', *New York Times*, 2 July. https://www.nytimes.com/interactive/2020/07/02/world/europe/uk-coronavirus-domestic-abuse.html.

Tickner, J. A. (2014) *A Feminist Voyage through International Relations*. New York, NY: Oxford University Press.

True, J. (2003) *Gender Globalization, and Postsocialism: The Czech Republic after Communism*. New York, NY: Columbia University Press.

Turkington, R. (2017) 'Macron's Gender-Balanced Cabinet Includes Europe's Ninth Female Defense Minister', Georgetown Institute for Women, Peace, and Security. https://giwps.georgetown.edu/macrons-gender-balanced-cabinet-includes-europes-9th-female-defense-minister-2/.

United Nations (2015) 'Transforming Our World: The 2030 Agenda for Sustainable Development', A/RES/70/1, New York: United Nations. https://sustainabledevelopment.un.org/post2015/transformingourworld.

Waring, M. (1999) *Counting for Nothing: What Men Value and What Women Are Worth*, 2nd edn. Toronto: University of Toronto Press.

Wood, J. (2018) 'These 4 Nordic Countries Hold the Key to Gender Equality', World Economic Forum. www.weforum.org/agenda/2018/12/nordic-countries-women-equality-gender-pay-gap-2018/.

World Economic Forum (WEF) (2020) 'Mind the 100 Year Gap'. www.weforum.org/reports/gender-gap-2020-report-100-years-pay-equality.

# Chapter 10

Akkerman, T. (2012) 'Comparing Radical Right Parties in Government: Immigration and Integration Policies in Nine Countries (1996–2010)', *West European Politics* 35(3): 511–29.

Anderson, B. (2013) *Us and Them? The Dangerous Politics of Immigration Controls*. Oxford: Oxford University Press.

Baldwin-Edwards, M. (2007) 'Navigating between Scylla and Charybdis: Migration Policies for a Romania within the European Union', *Southeast European and Black Sea Studies* 7(1): 5–35.

Boswell, C. and Geddes, A. (2011) *Migration and Mobility in the European Union*. Basingstoke: Palgrave Macmillan.

Carmel, E. and Paul, R. (2009) 'The Struggle for Coherence in EU Migration Policy', *Italian Journal of Social Policy* 2010(1): 209–30.

Carmel, E. and Paul, R. (2013) 'Complex Stratification: Understanding European Union Governance of Migrant Rights', *Regions and Cohesion* 3(3): 56–85.

Castles, S. (1986) 'The Guest-Worker in Western Europe – An Obituary', *International Migration Review* 20(4): 761–78.

Cerna, L. (2013) 'Understanding the Diversity of EU Migration Policy in Practice: The Implementation of the Blue Card Initiative', *Policy Studies* 34(2): 180–200.

Cohen, R. (2006) *Migration and its Enemies: Global Capital, Migrant Labour and the Nation-State*. Aldershot: Ashgate.

de Haas, H., Natter, K. and Vezzoli, S. (2018) 'Growing Restrictiveness or Changing Selection? The Nature and Evolution of Migration Policies', *International Migration Review* 52(2): 324–67.

Dennison, J. and Geddes, A. (2018) 'Brexit and the Perils of 'Europeanised' Migration', *Journal of European Public Policy* 25(8): 1137–53.

D'Ignoti, S. (2019) 'Can Culture, Not Blood, Make You Italian? *Foreign Policy*'. https://foreignpolicy.com/2019/12/05/italian-citizenship-culture-blood-immigration/.

Drbohlav, D. (2012) 'Patterns of Immigration in the Czech Republic, Hungary and Poland: A Comparative Perspective', in M. Okólski (ed.), *European Immigrations*, 179–210. Amsterdam: Amsterdam University Press.

Elliesen, M., Henkel, N. and Kempe, S. (2019) 'Ziemlich beste Feinde: Fidesz und die EU. Zur Entwicklung eines ambivalenten Verhältnisses', in *Staatsprojekt* Europa, 137–58. Baden-Baden: Nomos.

Favell, A. and Hansen, R. (2002) 'Markets against Politics: Migration, EU Enlargement and the Idea of Europe', *Journal of Ethnic and Migration Studies* 28(4): 581–601.

Follis, K. (2021) 'The Politics of Conceptualizing Border/Security', in E. Carmel, K. Lenner and R. Paul (eds), *Handbook on the Governance and Politics of* Migration, 60–72. Cheltenham: Edward Elgar Publishing.

Geddes, A., Hadj-Abdou, L. and Brumat, L. (2020) *Migration and Mobility in the European Union*, 2nd edn. London: Red Globe Press.

Geddes, A. and Scholten, P. (2016) *The Politics of Migration and Immigration in Europe*, 2nd edn. London: SAGE.

Grande, E., Schwarzbözl, T. and Fatke, M. (2019) 'Politicizing Immigration in Western Europe', *Journal of European Public Policy* 26(10): 1444–63.

Guia, A. (2021) 'Nativist Politics and the Mobilization of Anti-immigrant Discourses', in E. Carmel, K. Lenner and R. Paul (eds), *Handbook on the Governance and Politics of Migration*, 404–16. Cheltenham: Edward Elgar Publishing.

Hall, P. A. and Soskice, D. W., eds (2001) *Varieties of Capitalism: The Institutional Foundations of Comparative Advantage*. Oxford: Oxford University Press.

Hancké, B., Rhodes, M. and Thatcher, M. (2007) 'Beyond Varieties of Capitalism', in B. Hancké, M. Rhodes and M. Thatcher (eds), *Debating Varieties of Capitalism*, 273–300. Oxford: Oxford University Press.

Hansen, P. (2021) *A Modern Migration Theory: An Alternative Economic Approach to Failed EU Policy*. Newcastle upon Tyne: Agenda Publishing.

Hansen, P. and Hager, S. B. (2010) *The Politics of European Citizenship: Deepening Contradictions in Social Rights and Migration Policy*. Oxford: Berghahn.

Joppke, C. (1998) 'Why Liberal States Accept Unwanted Immigration', *World Politics* 50(2): 266–93.

Lavenex, S. (1998) 'Asylum, Immigration, and Central–Eastern Europe: Challenges to EU Enlargement', *European Foreign Affairs Review* 3: 275–94.

Lutz, P. (2019) 'Variation in Policy Success: Radical Right Populism and Migration Policy', *West European Politics* 42(3): 517–44.

Menz, G. (2009) *The Political Economy of Managed Migration: Nonstate Actors, Europeanization, and the Politics of Designing Migration Policies*. Oxford: Oxford University Press.

Natter, K. (2021) 'Beyond the Dichotomy of Liberal and Illiberal Migration Governance', in E. Carmel, K. Lenner and R. Paul (eds), *Elgar Handbooks in Migration*, 110–22. Cheltenham: Edward Elgar Publishing. https://doi.org/1 0.4337/9781788117234.00015.

Papadopoulos, T. (2011) 'Immigration and the Variety of Migrant Integration Regimes in the European Union', in E. Carmel, A. Cerami and T. Papadopoulos (eds), *Migration and Welfare in the New Europ: Social Protection and the Challenges of Integration*, 23–47. Bristol: Policy Press.

Paul, R. (2012) 'Limits of the Competition State: The Cultural Political Economy of European Labour Migration Policies', *Critical Policy Studies* 6(4): 379–401.

Paul, R. (2013) 'Strategic Contextualisation: Free Movement, Labour Migration Policies and the Governance of Foreign Workers in Europe', *Policy Studies* 32(2): 122–41.

Paul, R. (2015) *The Political Economy of Border-Drawing: Arranging Legality in European Labor Migration Policies*. New York, Oxford: Berghahn Books.

Paul, R. (2016) 'Negotiating Varieties of Capitalism? Crisis and Change in Contemporary British and German Labour Migration Policies', *Journal of Ethnic and Migration Studies* 42(10): 1631–50.

Paul, R. and Roos, C. (2019) 'Towards a New Ontology of Crisis? Resilience in EU Migration Governance', *European Security* 28(4): 393–412.

Peixoto, J. et al. (2012) 'Immigrants, Markets and Policies in Southern Europe: The Making of an Immigration Model?' in M. Okólski (ed.), *European Immigrations*, 107–48. Amsterdam: Amsterdam University Press.

Recchi, E. (2015) *Mobile Europe. The Theory and Practice of Free Movement*. London: Palgrave Macmillan.

Roos, C. (2019) 'The (de-) Politicization of EU Freedom of Movement: Political Parties, Opportunities, and Policy Framing in Germany and the UK', *Comparative European Politics* 17: 631–50. https://doi.org/10.1057/ s41295-018-0118-1.

Ruhs, M. (2013) *The Price of Rights. Regulating International Labor Migration.* Princeton, NJ: Princeton University Press.

Ruhs, M. and Anderson, B. (2010) *Who Needs Migrant Workers? Labour Shortages, Immigration, and Public Policy.* Oxford: Oxford University Press.

Rusu, I. (2011) 'Migration in Hungary: Historical Legacies and Differential Integration', in E. Carmel, A.Cerami and T. Papadopoulos (eds), *Migration and Welfare in the 'new' Europe: Social Protection and the Challenges of Integration*, 159–75. Bristol: Policy Press.

*The Economist* (2016) 'Big, Bad Visegrad'. https://www.economist.com/europe/2016/01/28/big-bad-visegrad.

Torpey, J. (2000) *The Invention of the Passport: Surveillance, Citizenship and the State.* Cambridge: Cambridge University Press.

Trauner, F. (2016) 'Asylum Policy: The EU's 'Crises' and the Looming Policy Regime Failure', *Journal of European Integration* 38(3): 311–25.

van Houtum, H. and Pijpers, R. (2007) 'The European Union as a Gated Community: The Two-Faced Border and Immigration Regime of the EU', *Antipode* 39: 291–309.

Weinar, A. (2019) 'Politics of Emigration in Europe', in A. Weinar, S. Bonjour and L. Zhyznomirska (eds), *The Routledge Handbook of the Politics of European Migration*, 38–49. London: Routledge.

Wilkinson, M. and Craig, G. (2011) 'Wilful Negligence: Migration Policy, Migrants' Work and the Absence of Social Protection in the UK', in E. Carmel, A.Cerami and T. Papadopoulos (eds), *Migration and Welfare in the 'new' Europe: Social Protection and the Challenges of Integration*, 177–90. Bristol: Policy Press.

Woolfson, C. (2009) 'Labour Migration, Neoliberalism and Ethno-politics in the New Europe: The Latvian Case', *Antipode* 41(5): 952–82.

Zaun, N. (2018) 'States as Gatekeepers in EU Asylum Politics: Explaining the Non-adoption of a Refugee Quota System', *Journal of Common Market Studies* 56(1): 44–62.

# Chapter 11

Abăseacă, R. and Piotrowski, G. (2018) 'Introduction: Radical Left in Central and Eastern Europe: Constraints and Opportunities', *East European Politics* 34(1): 1–5.

Akkerman, A., Mudde, C. and Zaslove, A. (2014) 'How Populist Are the People? Measuring Populist Attitudes in Voters', *Comparative Political Studies* 47(9): 1324–53.

Anghel, V. (2020) 'Together or Apart? The European Union's East West Divide', *Survival* 62(3): 179–202.

Art, D. (2011) *Inside the Radical Right: The Development of Anti-Immigrant Parties in Western Europe*. Cambridge: Cambridge University Press

Arzheimer, K. and Carter, E. (2006) 'Political Opportunity Structures and Right-Wing Extremist Party Success', *European Journal of Political Research* 45(3): 419–43.

Aslanidis, P. (2016) 'Is Populism an Ideology? A Refutation and a New Perspective', *Political Studies* 64(1): 88–104.

Buštíková, L. (2018) 'The Radical Right in Eastern Europe', in J. Rydgren (ed.), *The Oxford Handbook of The Radical Right*, 565–81. Oxford: Oxford University Press.

Canovan, M. (1999) 'Trust the People! Populism and the Two Faces of Democracy', *Political Studies* 47(1): 2–16.

Carter, E. (2018) 'Right-Wing Extremism/Radicalism: Reconstructing the Concept', *Journal of Political Ideologies* 23(2): 157–82.

Davies, G., Wu, E. and Frank, R. (2021) 'A Witch's Brew of Grievances: The Potential Effects of COVID-19 on Radicalization to Violent Extremism', *Studies in Conflict & Terrorism*. http://doi.org/10.1080/105761 0X.2021.1923188.

Dawson, J. and Hanley, S. (2016) 'What's Wrong with East-Central Europe? The Fading Mirage of the "Liberal Consensus"', *Journal of Democracy* 27(1): 20–34.

De Cleen, B., Glynos, J. and Mondon, A. (2018) 'Critical Research on Populism: Nine Rules of Engagement', *Organization* 25(5): 649–61.

de Jonge, L. (2019) 'The Populist Radical Right and the Media in the Benelux: Friend or Foe?' *The International Journal of Press/Politics* 24(2): 189–209.

de Jonge, L. (2021a) 'The Curious Case of Belgium: Why is There no Right-Wing Populism in Wallonia?' *Government and Opposition* 56(4): 598–614. https://doi.org/10.1017/gov.2020.8.

de Jonge, L. (2021b) *The Success and Failure of Right-Wing Populist Parties in the Benelux Countries*. Abingdon: Routledge.

Duverger, M. (1954) *Political Parties: Their Organization and Activity in the Modern State*. London: Methuen.

Ellinas, A. (2010) *The Media and the Far Right in Western Europe*. Cambridge: Cambridge University Press.

Fieschi, C. (2020) *Populocracy: The Tyranny of Authenticity and the Rise of Populism*. New York, NY: Columbia University Press.

Grzymala-Busse, A. (2019) 'The Failure of Europe's Mainstream Parties', *Journal of Democracy* 30(4): 35–47.

Hallin, D. and Mancini, P. (2004) *Comparing Media Systems*. Cambridge: Cambridge University Press.

Halikiopoulou, D. and Vlandas, T. (2020) 'When Economic and Cultural Interests Align: The Anti-Immigration Voter Coalitions Driving Far Right Party Success in Europe', *European Political Science Review* 1–22. https://doi.org/10.1017/S175577392000020X.

Halikiopoulou, D. and Vasilopoulou, S. (2018) 'Breaching the Social Contract: Crises of Democratic Representation and Patterns of Extreme Right Party Support', *Government and Opposition* 53(1): 26–50.

Heinze, A. (2018) 'Strategies of Mainstream Parties towards their Right-wing Populist Challengers: Denmark, Norway, Sweden and Finland in Comparison', *West European Politics* 41(2): 287–309.

Ivarsflaten, E. (2008) 'What Unites Right-Wing Populists in Western Europe?: Re-Examining Grievance Mobilization Models in Seven Successful Cases', *Comparative Political Studies* 41(1): 3–23.

Jenne, E. and Mudde, C. (2012) 'Hungary's Illiberal Turn: Can Outsiders Help?' *Journal of Democracy* 23(3): 147–55.

Katsambekis, G. and Kioupkiolis, A. (2019) *The Populist Radical Left in Europe*. London: Routledge.

Katz, R. and Mair, P. (2009) 'The Cartel Party Thesis: A Restatement', *Perspectives on Politics* 7(4): 753–66.

Kelemen, R. (2017) 'Europe's Other Democratic Deficit: National Authoritarianism in Europe's Democratic Union', *Government and Opposition* 52(2): 211–38.

Koopmans, R. and Muis, J. (2009) 'The Rise of Right-Wing Populist Pim Fortuyn in the Netherlands: A Discursive Opportunity Approach', *European Journal of Political Research* 48(5): 642–64.

Krastev, I. (2016) 'Liberalism's Failure to Deliver', *Journal of Democracy* 27(1): 35–8.

Kriesi, H., Grande, E., Dolezal, M., Helbling, M., Höglinger, D., Hutter, S. and Wüest, B. (2012) *Political Conflict in Western Europe*. Cambridge: Cambridge University Press.

Kübler, D. and Kriesi, H. (2017) 'How Globalisation and Mediatisation Challenge our Democracies', *Swiss Political Science Review* 23(3): 231–45

Lipset, S. and Rokkan, S. (1967) *Party Systems and Voter Alignments: Cross-National Perspectives*. Toronto: The Free Press.

Mair, P. (2013) *Ruling the Void: The Hollowing out of Western Democracies*. London: Verso.

Moffitt, B. (2015) 'How to Perform Crisis: A Model for Understanding the Key Role of Crisis in Contemporary Populism', *Government and Opposition* 50(2): 189–217.

Moffitt, B. (2020) *Populism*. Cambridge: Polity Press.

Moffitt, B. and Tormey, S. (2014) 'Rethinking Populism: Politics, Mediatisation and Political Style', *Political Studies* 62: 381–97.

March, L. (2011) *Radical Left Parties in Europe*. London: Routledge

March, L. (2017) 'Left and Right Populism Compared: The British Case', *The British Journal of Politics and International Relations* 19(2): 282–303.

Meguid, B. (2005) 'Competition Between Unequals: The Role of Mainstream Party Strategy in Niche Party Success', *American Political Science Review* 99(3): 347–59.

Mouffe, C. (2018) *For a Left Populism*. London: Verso.

Mudde, C. (2004) 'The Populist Zeitgeist', *Government and Opposition* 39(3): 541–63.

Mudde, C. (2007) *Populist Radical Right Parties in Europe*. Cambridge: Cambridge University Press.

Mudde, C. (2019) *The Far Right Today*. Cambridge: Polity Press.

Mudde, C. and Rovira Kaltwasser, C. (2013) 'Exclusionary vs. Inclusionary Populism: Comparing Contemporary Europe and Latin America', *Government and Opposition* 48(2): 147–74.

Mudde, C. and Rovira Kaltwasser, C. (2017) *Populism: A Very Short Introduction*. Oxford: Oxford University Press.

Müller, J. (2016) *What is Populism?* Philadelphia, PA: University of Pennsylvania Press.

Panizza, F. (2005) 'Introduction', in F. Panizza (ed.), *Populism and the Mirror of Democracy*, 1–31. London: Verso.

Pytlas, B. (2015) *Radical Right Parties in Central and Eastern Europe: Mainstream Party Competition and Electoral Fortune*. Abingdon: Routledge.

Rooduijn, M. (2019) 'State of the Field: How to Study Populism and Adjacent Topics? A Plea for Both More and Less Focus', *European Journal of Political Research* 58(1): 362–72.

Rooduijn, M. (2020) 'Kiezer Steeds Meer Radicaal-rechts?' [Voter increasingly radical right?], *Stuk Rood Vlees*. http://stukroodvlees.nl/kiezer-steeds-meer-radicaal-rechts.

Rooduijn, M., Burgoon, B., van Elsas, E. and van de Werfhorst, H. (2017) 'Radical Distinction: Support for Radical Left and Radical Right Parties in Europe', *European Union Politics* 18(4): 536–59.

Rooduijn, M., van Kessel, S., Froio, C., Pirro, A., De Lange, S., Halikiopoulou, D., Lewis, P., Mudde, C. and Taggart, P. (2020) *The PopuList: An Overview of Populist, Far Right, Far Left and Eurosceptic Parties in Europe*. www.populist.org.

Stanley, B. (2008) 'The Thin Ideology of Populism', *Journal of Political Ideologies* 13(1): 95–110.

Stanley, B. (2017) 'Populism in Central and Eastern Europe', in C. Rovira Kaltwasser, P. Taggart, P. Ochoa Espejo and P. Ostiguy (eds.) *The Oxford Handbook of Populism*, 141–60. Oxford: Oxford University Press.

Surowiec, P. and Štětka, V. (2020) 'Introduction: Media and Illiberal Democracy in Central and Eastern Europe', *East European Politics* 1(36): 1–8. https://doi.org/10.1080/21599165.2019.1692822.

Taggart, P. (2000) *Populism*. Buckingham: Open University Press.

Urbinati, N. (2019) *Me The People: How Populism Transforms Democracy*. Cambridge, MA: Harvard University Press.

Vachudova, M. (2020) 'Ethnopopulism and Democratic Backsliding in Central Europe', *East European Politics* 36(3): 318–40.

van Kessel, S. (2015) *Populist Parties in Western Europe: Agents of Discontent?* Basingstoke: Palgrave Macmillan.

Van Hauwaert, S. and van Kessel, S. (2018) 'Beyond Protest and Discontent: A Cross-National Analysis of the Effect of Populist Attitudes and Issue Positions on Populist Party Support', *European Journal of Political Research* 57(1): 68–92.

Weyland, K. (2001) 'Clarifying a Contested Concept: Populism in the Study of Latin American Politics', *Comparative Politics* 34(1): 1–22.

# Chapter 12

Bache, I. (1999) 'The Extended Gatekeeper: Central Government and the Implementation of EC Regional Policy in the UK', *Journal of European Public Policy*, 6(1): 28–45.

Bartolini, S. (2005) *Restructuring Europe: Centre Formation, System Building and Political Structuring between the Nation-State and the European Union*. Oxford: Oxford University Press.

Batory, A. (2016) 'Defying the Commission: Creative Compliance and Respect for the Rule of Law in the EU', *Public Administration* 94: 685–99.

Börzel, T. A. and Risse, T. (2000) 'When Europe Hits Home: Europeanization and Domestic Change', European Integration online Papers 4 (15). https://ssrn.com/abstract=302768.

Haas, E. B. (1968) *The Uniting of Europe: Political, Social and Economic Forces, 1950–57*, 2nd edn. Stanford, CA: Stanford University Press.

Hooghe, L. and Marks, G. (2003) 'Unraveling the Central State, but How? Types of Multi-Level Governance', *The American Political Science Review*, 97(2): 233–43.

Hooghe, L. and Marks, G. (2008) 'A Postfunctionalist Theory of European Integration: From Permissive Consensus to Constraining', *British Journal of Political Science*, 39(1): 1–23.

Jupille J., Caporaso, J. A. and Checkel, J. T. (2003) 'Integrating Institutions: Rationalism, Constructivism, and the Study of the European Union', *Comparative Political Studies*, 36(1–2): 7–40.

Kelemen, R. D. (2007) 'Built to Last? The Durability of EU Federalism', in S. Meunier and K. R. McNamara (eds), *Making History: European Integration and Institutional Change at Fifty*, 51–66. Oxford: Oxford University Press.

Kostaki, I. (2017) 'Tusk on Catalan Independence: "For EU Nothing Changes. Spain Remains Our Only Interlocutor"', *New Europe*, 27 October. https://www.neweurope.eu/article/tusk-catalan-independence-eu-nothing-changes-spain-remains-interlocutor/.

Krastev, I. (2012) 'A Fraying Union', *Journal of Democracy* 23(4): 23–30.

Lindberg, L. N. and Scheingold, S. A. (1970) *Europe's Would-be Polity: Patterns of Change in the European Community*. Englewood Cliffs, NJ: Prentice Hall.

Lindstrom (2020) 'Aiding the State: Administrative Capacity and Creative Compliance with European State Aid Rules in New Member States', *Journal of European Public Policy*. doi:10.1080/13501763.2020.1791935.

Menon, A. and Wager, A. (2020) 'Taking Back Control: Sovereignty as Strategy in Brexit Politics', *Territory, Politics, Governance*, 8(2): 279–84.

Moravcsik, A. (1993) 'Preferences and Power in the European Community: A Liberal Intergovernmentalist Approach', *Journal of Common Market Studies* 31(4): 473–524.

Moravcsik, A. (2016) 'The Great Brexit Kabuki: A Masterclass in Political Theater', *Financial Times*, 8 April.

Moravcsik, A. (2017) 'One Year after the Brexit Vote, Britain's Relationship with the EU is Unlikely to Change Much. Here's Why', *Washington Post*, Monkey Cage, 26 June.

Niemann, A. and Ioannou, D. (2015) 'European Economic Integration in Times of Crisis: A Case of Neofunctionalism?', *Journal of European Public Policy* 22(2): 196–218.

Pierson, P. (1996) 'The Path to European Integration: A Historical Institutionalist Analysis', *Comparative Political Studies*, 29(2): 123–63.

Rosamond, B. (2019) 'Theorising the EU in Crisis: De-Europeanisation as Disintegration', *Global Discourse: An Interdisciplinary Journal of Current Affairs* 9(1): 31–44.

Schimmelfennig, F. (2018) 'European Integration (theory) in Times of Crisis. A Comparison of the Euro and Schengen Crises', *Journal of European Public Policy*, 25(7): 969–89.

Schimmelfennig, F., Leuffen, D. and Rittberger, B. (2015) 'The European Union as a System of Differentiated Integration: Interdependence, Politicization and Differentiation', *Journal of European Public Policy* 22(6): 764–82.

Schmidt, V. (2020) *Europe's Crisis of Legitimacy: Governing by Rules and Ruling by Numbers in the Eurozone*. Oxford: Oxford University Press.

Schmitter, P. (1971) 'A Revised Theory of Regional Integration', *International Organization* 24 (4): 836–68.

Schmitter, P. (2012) 'A Way Forward?' *Journal of Democracy* 23(4): 39–46.

Vollard, H. (2014) 'Explaining European Disintegration', *Journal of Common Market Studies* 52(5): 1142–59.

Webber, D. (2019) 'Trends in European Political (Dis)Integration: An Analysis of Postfunctionalist and Other Explanations', *Journal of European Public Policy* 26(8): 1134–52.

Webber, D. (2020) 'Why Brexit Has Not and Will Not Trigger EU Disintegration', The Conversation, 31 January. https://theconversation.com/why-brexit-has-not-and-will-not-trigger-eu-disintegration-130719.

Zielonka, J. (2014) *Is the EU Doomed?* Cambridge: Polity Press.

# Chapter 13

Anderson, M. (2002) 'Trust and Police Cooperation', in M. Anderson and J. Apap (eds), *Police and Justice Cooperation and the New European Borders*, 35–46. The Hague: Kluwer Law International.

Argomaniz, J., Bures, O. and Kaunert, C. (2015) 'A Decade of EU Counter-Terrorism and Intelligence: A Critical Assessment', *Intelligence and National Security*, 30(2–3): 191–206.

Barrett, G. (2018) 'Poland's Assault on the Rule of Law Echoes Problems in Other EU Member States', *The Irish Times*, 14 March. https://www.irishtimes.com/news/crime-and-law/poland-s-assault-on-the-rule-of-law-echoes-problems-in-other-eu-member-states-1.3425945.

Boer, M. D., Hillebrand, C. and Nölke, A. (2008) 'Legitimacy under Pressure: The European Web of Counter-terrorism Networks', *Journal of Common Market Studies*, 46 (1): 101–24.

Burguburu, J., Devalmy, Q., Guérin, M., van Rij, A. and Wilkinson, B. (2018) 'The UK-France Defence and Security Relationship: How to Improve Cooperation. Reports of the UK-France Task Force', *Montaigne Institute at Kings College London.* https://www.institutmontaigne.org/en/publications/uk-france-defence-and-security-relationship-how-improve-cooperation.

Carrapico, H. (2014) 'Analysing the European Union's Responses to Organized Crime through Different Securitization Lenses', *European Security* 23(4): 601–17.

Costi, A. (2019) 'Complementary Approaches? A Brief Comparison of EU and United States Counter-Terrorism Strategies since 2001', *Victoria University of Wellington Legal Research Papers* 9(5): 167–95.

Council of the European Union (2002) 'Framework Decision 2002/584/JHA of 13 June 2002, the European Arrest Warrant and Surrender Procedures between Member States', published in Official Journal L 190/2002, 1–20.

Council of the European Union (2003) *A Secure Union in a Better World: European Security Strategy.* Brussels: The Council of the European Union.

Council of the European Union (2005), 'EU Counter-Terrorism Strategy', Brussels: The Council of the European Union. https://data.consilium. europa.eu/doc/document/ST%2014469%202005%20REV%204/EN/pdf.

Council of the European Union (2017) 'Directive (EU) 2017/541 of the European Parliament and of the Council of 15 March 2017 on combating terrorism'.https://eur-lex.europa.eu/legal-content/EN/ TXT/?uri=CELEX%3A32017L0541.

Davies, L. and Limbada, Z. (2019) 'Education and Radicalisation Prevention: Different Ways Governments Can Support Schools and Teachers in Preventing/Countering Violent Extremism', 6 May, Ex Post Paper, *Radicalisation Awareness Network.* https://ec.europa.eu/home-affairs/ system/files_en?file=2019-08/ran_edu_different_ways_governments_can_ support_schools_teachers_052019_en.pdf.

Davis-Cross, M. (2007) 'An EU Homeland Security? Sovereignty vs. Supranational Order', *European Security* 16 (1): 79–97.

Eurojust (2020) 'Over EUR 2.8 Billion Worth of Drugs in Eurojust-Supported Cases in 2019'. http://www.eurojust.europa.eu/press/PressReleases/ Pages/2020/2020-01-20.aspx.

European Commission (2017) *A European Agenda on Security. State of Play: June 2017*, Brussels: the European Commission. https://ec.europa.eu/ home-affairs/sites/homeaffairs/files/what-we-do/policies/european-agenda-security/20170629_a_european_agenda_on_security_-_state_of_play_ june_2017_en.pdf.

European Commission (2019) *The Security Union: A Europe that Protects.* October. Brussels: The European Commission. https://ec.europa.eu/ commission/presscorner/detail/en/FS_19_6194.

European Court of Justice (ECJ) (2018) 'Press release no 113/18 Judgment in Case C-216/18 PPU. Minister for Justice and Equality vs LM (Deficiencies in the system of justice)', *Court of Justice for the European Union.* Luxembourg, 25 July.

European Public Prosecutor's Office (EPPO) (2022) 'Mission and Tasks', Brussels: European Public Prosecutor's Office. https://www.eppo.europa.eu/ en/mission-and-tasks.

EUROPOL (2017) *EU Serious and Organised Crime Threat Assessment (SOCTA) 2017.* The Hague: European Union Agency for Law Enforcement Cooperation.

EUROPOL (2020) *European Union Terrorism Situation and Trend Report 2020*. The Hague: European Union Agency for Law Enforcement Cooperation. https://www.europol.europa.eu/activities-services/main-reports/european-union-terrorism-situation-and-trend-report-te-sat-2020.

Fenwick, H. (2019) 'Critiquing Approaches to Countering Extremism via Certain Preventive Measures', Commission for Preventing Extremism, Gov. UK. https://www.gov.uk/government/publications/critiquing-approaches-to-countering-extremism-via-certain-preventive-measures.

*Financial Times* (2020) 'EU Counterterror Paper Lays Bare Bloc's Policy Divisions', 5 November. https://www.ft.com/content/57c9f719-b05b-474c-96c9-fd5e2c71e00f.

Fijnaut, C., ed. (1993) *The Internationalisation of Police Cooperation in Western Europe*. Deventer: Kluwer.

Fijnaut, C. and Paoli, L. (2004) 'Comparative Synthesis of Part III', in C. Fijnaut and L. Paoli (ed.), *Organised Crime in* Europe, 1035–42. Dordrecht: Springer.

Gay, C. (2006) *The European Arrest Warrant and its Application by the Member States*. European Issue 16. Foundation Robert Schuman Research and Studies Centre on Europe, 23 January.

Gruszczak, A. (2016) 'EU Criminal Intelligence Cooperation Challenges of Oversight and Accountability', *The Academic Association for Contemporary European Studies* (ACEAS) 46th Annual Conference. London, 5–7 September.

Guille, L. (2010) 'Police and Judicial Cooperation in Europe: Bilateral versus Multilateral Cooperation', in D. F. Lemieux (ed.), *International Police Cooperation: Emerging Issues, Theory and* Practices, 25–41. Abingdon: Willan Publishing.

Harper, J. (2016) 'Poland Joins Hungary in Planning Stringent Anti-Terrorism Laws in Wake of Brussels Attacks', *Deutsche Welle*, 23 March. https://www.dw.com/en/poland-joins-hungary-in-planning-stringent-anti-terrorism-laws-in-wake-of-brussels-attacks/a-19141781.

HM Government (2020) EU–UK Trade and Cooperation Agreement. 'Trade and Cooperation Agreement between the European Union and the European Atomic Energy Community, of the One Part, and the United Kingdom of Great Britain and Northern Ireland, of the Other Part', 24 December.

Jaffel, H. B. (2019) *Anglo-European Intelligence Cooperation: Britain in Europe, Europe in Britain*. London: Routledge.

Jansson, J. (2018) 'Building Resilience, Demolishing Accountability? The Role of Europol in Counter-Terrorism', *Policing and Society* 28 (4): 432–47.

Kaunert, C. and Léonard, S. (2019) 'The Collective Securitisation of Terrorism in the European Union', *West European Politics* 42(2): 261–77.

Kaunert, C., Léonard, S. and Wertman, O. (2020) 'EU Counter-Terrorism Cooperation with the Middle East and North Africa', in E. Cusumano and S. Hofmaier (eds), *Projecting Resilience Across the Mediterranean*, 87–102. London: Palgrave Macmillan.

Lavut, L. (2016) 'Building Partnerships Towards a Democratic Police Force in the Post-Revolutionary Tunisia Context', *Journal for Deradicalisation* 8.

Lefebvre, S. (2003) 'The Difficulties and Dilemmas of International Intelligence Cooperation', *International Journal of Intelligence and Counter Intelligence* 16 (4): 527–42.

Ljubas, Z. (2020) 'Malta Delays Start of European Prosecutors Office'. Organised Crime and Corruption Reporting Project. https://www.occrp. org/en/daily/12375-malta-delays-start-of-european-prosecutor-s-operation.

Monar, J. (2014) 'EU Internal Security Governance: The Case of Counter Terrorism', *European Security* 23(2): 195–209.

Mortera-Martinez, C. (2019a) 'Catch Me if You Can: The European Arrest Warrant and the End of Mutual Trust', *Centre for European Reform*.

Mortera-Martinez, C. (2019b) 'The EU's Security Union: A Bill of Health', *Centre for European Reform*.

Neumann, P. R. (2013) 'The Trouble with Radicalisation', *International Affairs* 89(4): 873–93.

Ou, A. (2016) 'Hearts and Minds: A Comparison of Counter-Radicalization Strategies in Britain and the United States', *Cornell International Affairs Review* 9 (2).

Rhinardt, M., Boin, A. and Ekengren, M. (2007) 'Managing Terrorism: Institutional Capacities and Counter-Terrorism Policy in the EU', in D Spence (ed.), *The European Union and Terrorism*, 88–104. London: John Harper.

Rusu, I. M. B. (2012) 'The European Arrest Warrant', *International Conference on European Integration Realities and Perspectives*, 7th Edition Danubius University, 18–19 May, 21–34.

Samaan, J. L. and Jacobs, A. (2020) 'Countering Jihadist Terrorism: A Comparative Analysis of French and German Experience', *Terrorism and Political Violence* 32(2): 401–15.

Said, B. T. and Fouad, H. (2018) 'Countering Islamist Radicalisation in Germany: A Guide to Germany's Growing Prevention Infrastructure', *ICCT Policy Brief*. The International Centre for Counter-Terrorism: The Hague.

Sheptycki, J. W. E. (2002) *In Search of Transnational Policing: Towards a Sociology*. Aldershot: Ashgate.

Stephens, W., Sieckelinck, S. and Boutellier, H. (2019) 'Preventing Violent Extremism: A Review of the Literature', *Studies in Conflict & Terrorism*, online first: 1–16.

Sweeney, S. and Winn, N. (2021) 'Do or Die? The UK, the EU, and Internal/ External Security Cooperation after Brexit', *European Political Science*, online first: 1–18.

UN General Assembly (2015) 'Plan of Action to Prevent Violent Extremism: Report of the Secretary-General, A/70/674', 24 December, para. 44.

Van Dongen, T. (2010) 'Mapping Counterterrorism: A Categorisation of Policies and the Promise of Empirically Based, Systematic Comparisons', *Critical Studies on Terrorism* 3(2): 227–41.

Vaughan-Williams, N. (2015) *Europe's Border Crisis: Biopolitical Security and Beyond*. Oxford: Oxford University Press.

Volpicelli, G. (2019) 'The Curious Tale of Julian, the Last King of Brussels', *Wired*, 28 October. https://www.wired.co.uk/article/the-last-king-of-brussels.

Wolfstadter, L. M. and Kreilinger, V. (2017) 'European Integration via Flexibility Tools: The Cases of EPPO and PESCO', Jacques Delors Institut Berlin. Policy paper 209, November.

# Chapter 14

Aggestam, L. and Hyde-Price, A. (2020) 'Learning to Lead? Germany and the Leadership Paradox in EU Foreign Policy', *German Politics* 29(1): 8–24.

Cronberg, T.(2017) 'No EU, No Iran Deal: The EU's Choice between Multilateralism and the Transatlantic Link', *The Nonproliferation Review* 24(3–4): 243–59.

Deen, B. and Kruijever, K. (2020) *COVID-19 and Defence: Clingendael Alert the Need for EU Funding Why EU Budget Negotiators Should Not Only Focus on financial firepower*. The Hague: Clingendael Institute. https:// www.clingendael.org/sites/default/files/2020-05/Alert_COVID-19_and_ Defence_need_for_EU_funding_May_2020.pdf.

Emmott, R., Guarascio, F. and Pennetier, M. (2019) 'France under Fire for "Historic Error" of Blocking Balkan EU Hopefuls', *Europe News, Reuters*, 18 October. https://www.reuters.com/article/us-eu-summit-balkans/ france-under-fire-for-historic-error-of-blocking-balkan-eu-hopefuls-idUSKBN1WX1CT.

Erlanger, S. (2020) 'European Defense and "Strategic Autonomy" Are Also Coronavirus Victims', *New York Times*, 23 May.

European Council (2017) *Council Decision Establishing Permanent Structured Cooperation (PESCO) and Determining the List of Participating Member States*. Brussels: European Council. https://www.consilium.europa.eu/ media/32000/st14866en17.pdf.

European Council (2020) 'Special Meeting of the European Council (17, 18, 19, 20 and 21 July 2020) – Conclusions'. Brussels: European Council. https://www.consilium.europa.eu/media/45109/210720-euco-final-conclusions-en.pdf.

Featherstone, K. and Radaelli, C. M., eds (2003) *The Politics of Europeanization*. New York, NY: Oxford University Press Inc.

Fiott, D. and Lindstrom, G., eds (2021) *Strategic Compass. New Bearings for EU Security and Defense?*, EUISS, Challiot Paper 171.

Hadfield, A., Manners, I. and Whitman, R. G. (2017) 'Introduction: Conceptualising the Foreign Policies of EU Member States', in A. Hadfield, I. Manners and R. G. Whitman (eds), *Foreign Policies of EU Member States Continuity and Europeanisation*, 1–19. London: Routledge.

Haugom, L. (2019) 'Turkish Foreign Policy under Erdogan: A Change in International Orientation?', *Comparative Strategy* 38 (3): 206–23.

International Crisis Group (ICG) (2021) 'A Course Correction for the Sahel Stabilisation Strategy', Africa Report No. 299, 1 February. https://d2071andvip0wj.cloudfront.net/299-sahel-stabilisation-strategy_0.pdf.

Kaliber A. and Kaliber, E. (2019) 'From De-Europeanisation to Anti-Western Populism: Turkish Foreign Policy in Flux', *The International Spectator* 54 (4): 1–16

Orenstein, M. A. and Kelemen, R. (2017) 'Trojan Horses in EU Foreign Policy', *Journal of Common Market Studies* 55(1): 87–102.

Pomorska, K. (2017) 'Foreign Policies of Eastern EU States', in A. Hadfield, I. Manners and R. G. Whitman (eds), *Foreign Policies of EU Member States Continuity and* Europeanisation, 48–62. London: Routledge.

Roberts, K. (2017) 'Understanding Putin: The Politics of Identity and Geopolitics in Russian Foreign Policy Discourse', *International Journal* 72(1): 28–55.

Schekhovtsov, A. (2021) 'Moscow Using Far-Right to Infiltrate European Parliament', *EUobserver*, 5 May. https://euobserver.com/investigations/151679.

Simon, L. (2017) 'France and Germany: The European Union's "Central" Member States', in A. Hadfield, I. Manners and R. G. Whitman (eds), *Foreign Policies of EU Member States Continuity and* Europeanisation, 63–79. London: Routledge.

Smith, M. (2018) 'The EU, the US and the Crisis of Contemporary Multilateralism', *Journal of European Integration* 40 (5): 539–53.

Tocci, N. (2011) 'European Strategic Autonomy: What It Is, Why We Need It, How to Achieve It'. Rome: Istituto Affari Internazionali (IAI). https://www.iai.it/sites/default/files/9788893681780.pdf.

Tonra, B. (2015) 'Europeanization', in K. E. Jorgensen, A. K. Aarstad, E. Drieskens, K. Laatikainen and B. Tonra (eds), *SAGE Handbook of European Foreign* Policy, 182–95. Thousand Oaks, CA: SAGE Publications.

Whitman, R. G. and Stewart, E. J. (2011) 'The Foreign Policies of Europe and its States', in E. Jones, P. M. Heywood, M. Rhodes and U. Sedelmeier (eds), *Developments in European Politics* 2, 262–73. London: Macmillan.

Whitman, R. G. and Tonra, B. (2017) 'Western EU Member States Foreign Policy Geo-orientations: UK, Ireland and the Benelux', in A. Hadfield, I. Manners and R. G. Whitman (eds), *Foreign Policies of EU Member States Continuity and* Europeanisation, 32–47. London: Routledge.

Wong, R. and Hill, C. (2011) 'Many Actors, One Path? The Meaning of Europeanization in the Context of Foreign Policy', in R. Wong and C. Hill (eds), *National and European Foreign Policies Towards Europeanization*, 209–32. New York, NY: Routledge.

# Conclusion

Anghel, V. (2020) 'Together or Apart? The European Union's East–West Divide', *Survival* 62(3): 179–202.

Bhambra, G. K. (2022) 'A Decolonial Project for Europe', *Journal of Common Market Studies*, online first. https://doi.org/10.1111/jcms.13310.

Cartwright, N. and Hardie, J. (2012) *Evidence-Based Policy: A Practical Guide to Doing it Better*. Oxford: Oxford University Press.

Cooper, R. (1968) *The Economics of Interdependence: Economic Policy in the Atlantic Community*. New York, NY: Columbia University Press.

Fligstein, N. (2009) *Euroclash: The EU, European Identity, and the Future of Europe*. Oxford: Oxford University Press.

Hooghe, L. and Marks, G. (2009) 'A Postfunctionalist Theory of European Integration: From Permissive Consensus to Constraining Dissensus', *British Journal of Political Science* 39(1): 1–23.

Jones, E. (2021) 'Next Generation EU: Solidarity, Opportunity, and Confidence', *European Policy Analysis 2021:10epa*. Stockholm: Swedish Institute for European Policy Studies (SIEPS), June.

Jones, E. and Menon, A. (2019) 'Europe: Between Dream and Reality?', *International Affairs* 95 (1): 161–80.

Levitsky, S. and Ziblatt, D. (2018) *How Democracies Die*. New York, NY: Crown.

Milward, A. S. (1999) *The European Rescue of the Nation State*, 2nd edn. London: Routledge.

Ostrom, E. (2005) *Understanding Institutional Diversity*. Princeton, NJ: Princeton University Press.

Thurow, L. C. (1980) *The Zero-Sum Society*. New York, NY: Penguin.

# Index